Rethinking the Prophetic Critique of Worship in Amos 5 for Contemporary Nigeria and the USA

To: Very Rev. Raúl Gómez, SJ ?

From: Rev. Fr. Michael Udoekpo

Many Blessings!

8/21/2019

Rethinking the Prophetic Critique of Worship in Amos 5 for Contemporary Nigeria and the USA

Michael Ufok Udoekpo

FOREWORD BY
David A. Bosworth

PICKWICK *Publications* · Eugene, Oregon

RETHINKING THE PROPHETIC CRITIQUE OF WORSHIP IN AMOS 5
FOR CONTEMPORARY NIGERIA AND THE USA

Pickwick Publications
An Imprint of Wipf and Stock Publishers
199 W. 8th Ave., Suite 3
Eugene, OR 97401

www.wipfandstock.com

PAPERBACK ISBN: 978-1-4982-9730-1
HARDCOVER ISBN: 978-1-4982-9732-5
EBOOK ISBN: 978-1-4982-9731-8

Cataloguing-in-Publication data:

Names: Udoekpo, Michael Ufok. | Bosworth, David A.

Title: Rethinking the prophetic critique of worship in Amos 5 for contemporary
Nigeria and the USA / Michael Ufok Udoekpo ; foreword by David A. Bosworth.

Description: Eugene, OR: Pickwick Publications, 2016 | Includes bibliographical
references and index.

Identifiers: ISBN 978-1-4982-9730-1 (paperback) | ISBN 978-1-4982-9732-5 (hard-
cover) | ISBN 978-1-4982-9731-8 (ebook)

Subjects: LCSH: Bible. Amos—Criticism, interpretation, etc. | Bible—Hermeneu-
tics.

Classification: BS1585.52 U36 2017 (print) | BS1181.2 (ebook)

Manufactured in the U.S.A.   12/06/16

This work is dedicated to my brother, Mr. Linus Elijah Udoekpo, and Colonel Donna Mary Roncarti, a friend, and to the Chibok Schoolgirls abducted in Northern Nigeria on April 14–15, 2014.

Contents

Foreword

Let justice roll down like waters and righteousness like an ever-flowing stream.

MARTIN LUTHER KING JR. repeatedly quoted and alluded to Amos 5:24 in ways calculated to move his audience (see chapter six of this book). This beautiful image of abundant justice is timeless because injustice seems ever-present.

As I write in the United States, worsening economic inequality is widely discussed and a major leak of documents details how the wealthiest people hide their money in offshore tax havens. Those most responsible for the economic collapse of 2008 have escaped consequences while their poorest victims suffer financial ruin. The religious and worship leaders who might have been expected to speak out against this injustice were busy cleaning up the mess created by pedophile priests. Some of them may too, have avoided punishment. The machinery of law enforcement applies punishments that vary significantly based on such considerations as class and race. The poor person who steals from a few faces stiff penalties and long incarceration potentially including solitary confinement (a form of torture) while the "white collar" criminal who steals from thousands may not even be prosecuted and, if charged, may face a light fine or brief stay in a minimum security prison or "Club-Fed."

We need not wonder what Amos would have said if he could see these present injustices. He speaks to them in Amos 5. He lived in a time of great economic inequality and denounced the wealthy for their exploitation of the poor (5:7–17). He informed the pious that their great expectations for "the day of the Lord" would be disappointed because their piety failed to incorporate justice (5:18–27). Amos promised national disaster as divine punishment for these sins. It eventually came because, to quote Dr. King, "the arc of the moral universe is long, but it bends toward justice."

Although it is tempting to apply Amos' words only to those at whom we are angry, they should also be used as a mirror. Injustice is not only "out there," but "in here," in our own selves and closest communities. Sometimes the chasm between who we are and who we wish to be is enormous. A prophet like Amos can remind us of this distance and call us to account. Part of our weakness is to forget our sin and imagine that we are good when we are not. The powerful elite whom Amos criticized, like elites everywhere, imagined that they earned their status because they were better than their neighbors. We all tend to think that our good fortune flows from our actions and our worthiness rather than grace. This self-confidence makes us cold and hard. A prophet like Amos can, if we listen, soften our hearts and foster gratitude, generosity, and justice.

Michael Ufok Udoekpo writes from the perspective of a biblical scholar with personal familiarity with both Nigeria and the United States. This book reflects his passion for applying the word of God to the two cultures that he knows best. He has long meditated on the message of Amos and its connection to these two worlds and he offers insights on both between the covers on one book. In one place, the reader may find a substantive exegetical-theological analysis of the book of Amos in its historical and literary context and a thoughtful and detailed discussion of its pastoral application to two contemporary cultures.

David A. Bosworth

School of Theology and Religious Studies
The Catholic University of America
April 14, 2016

Acknowledgments

THE APHORISM "IT TAKES a whole village to raise a child," is applicable to this book begun as a PhD research at Graduate Theological Foundation, Indiana, under the supervision of Professor Tim Allen, with the title: "Take Away from Me The Noise of Your Song" (Amos 5:23a): An Exegetical Re-Evaluation of the Theology of Worship in Amos 5, for Today." Thoroughly reworked, and as it stands, it reflects my passion for applying the Word of God (Amos 5:1–27) to two of the many cultures best familiar to me (Nigeria and the United States). In doing so, I received tremendous support from many institutions, libraries and people, some of which I would like to acknowledge here.

I am particularly grateful to God and to my Bishop, Most Rev. Camillus R. Umoh (Ikot Ekpene Diocese), his predecessor Most Rev. Camillus A. Etokudoh (Bishop of Port Harcourt) and Most Rev. John Ayah (Bishop of Uyo and Apostolic Administrator of Ogoja) for their fatherly encouragement in my studies and priestly apostolates beyond the shores of Africa, in Europe and in the United States. Here in the United States I am grateful to Most Rev. Jerome E. Listecki (Archbishop of Milwaukee), Most Rev. William Murphy (Bishop of Rockville Center, NY), Most Rev. Donald J. Hying (Bishop of Gary, Indiana), Most Rev. John F. Doerfler (Bishop of Marquette), Most Rev. Richard J. Sklba (Auxiliary Bishop- Emeritus, Milwaukee), Most Rev. Robert Brennan (Auxiliary Bishop, Rockville Center, NY), Msgr. Ross Shecterle (Rector SHSST) and Very Rev. John D. Hemsing (Rector, Saint Francis de Sales Seminary, Milwaukee). They have all in one way or the other facilitated my apostolate in the United States.

I am grateful to members of my family, especially my niece, Sr. Dr. Angela Iniobong Akpabio, HHCJ, all my brother priests, religious and friends of Calabar Ecclesiastical Province, Ikot Ekpene Diocese in particular. My gratitude also goes to the Provincials and priests of the Sacred Heart of Jesus of the North American Province, who owns the Sacred Heart

Seminary and School of Theology (SHSST), where I currently teach and research. I have also enjoyed tremendous support from my colleagues including Drs. Patrick Russell, John Gallam, Stephen Shippee, James Stroud, Charles Ludwick II, Revs. Javier Bustos, Scott Jones, Stephen Malkiewicz, OFM, George Mangiaracina, OCD, Deacon Steve Kramer, Mr. Brian Lee, Sr. Mary C. Carroll, SSSF and the entire administration and staff at SHSST, particularly the Dehon Library staff (Susanna, Kathy, Ann, and Jennifer). Professors Richard Lux of the Lux Center at SHSST and Bonnie Shafrin and Knut Holter of the Peter Lang series editor of Bible and Theology in Africa (BTA) are among several editors, colleagues, mentors, former professors and friends who constructively read parts of my manuscript with valuable suggestions. I am thankful to them, and to the editors of WIPF and Stock Publishers (Pickwick Publications) for undertaking the publication of this book.

My thanks also go to my friends, especially Very Rev. Dr. Anselm Camillus Etokakpan, Rev. Prof. Vincent Nyoyoko, Rev. Prof. John O. Umoh, Msgr. Cosmas M. Udomah, Very Rev. John O. Ukoh, Very Rev. Jan de Jong, SCJ (President-Rector Emeritus of SHSST), Revs. Paul Kelly, Jim Walters, Charles Brown, SCJS, Rev. Donald M. Baier, Msgr. Tom Spadaro, parishioners of the Church of the Good Shepherd, Holbrook, NY, and Prof. Dr. Michael Weigl of the University of Vienna for their unwavering support and immeasurable gestures of encouragement. Mr. Ed Collum, Fr. James Akpan, staff and the parishioners of Mother Cabrini in Coram, New York—particularly Mr. and Mrs. Werner and Doris Debis—have consistently supported and prayed for me.

To all my graduate and undergraduate students at SHSST whom I taught and shared the message of the Prophet Amos with for more than five years; I am thankful to you from whom I have learned so much! It also remains for me to thank another special friend and colleague, Dr. David Bosworth of the Catholic University of America, for generously contributing a valuable foreword to this book. Truly, "it takes a whole village to raise a child." To each and to all, my deepest gratitude.

Michael Ufok Udoekpo

Sacred Heart Seminary and
School of Theology
April 28, 2016

Abbreviations

AB	Anchor Bible
ABD	*Anchor Bible Dictionary* (D. N. Freedman et al., eds.)
AJT	*American Journal of Theology*
ATANT	Abhandlungen zur Theologie des Alten und Neuen Testaments
ATID	Das Alte Testament im Dialog
ATJ	*African Theological Journal*
ATR	*African Traditional Religion* (E. B. Idowu)
ATSAT	Arbeiten zu Text und Sprache im Alten Testament
BAGDW	W. Bauer, W. F. Arndt, and F. W. Gingrich (3rd ed.: and F. W. Danker), *Greek-English Lexicon of the New Testament and Other Early Christian Literature*
BASOR	*Bulletin of the American Schools of Oriental Research*
BCE	Before the Common Era
BDB	F. Brown, S. R. Driver, and C. A. Briggs, *A Hebrew and English Lexicon of the Old Testament.*
BDF	F. Blass, A Debrunner, and R. W. Funk, *A Greek Grammar of the New Testament and Other Early Christian Literature.*
BEI	*Biblia Hebraica Interlinieare*
BeO	*Bibbia e Oriente*
Bib	*Biblica*
BiKi	*Bibel und Kirke*
BN	*Biblische Notizen*
BSac	*Bibliotheca Sacra*

BTA	*Bible and Theology for Africa*
BTB	*Biblical Theology Bulletin*
BZAW	Beihefte zur Zeitschrift für die alttestamentliche Wissenschaft
BZNW	Beihefte zur Zeitschrift für die neutestamentliche Wissenschaft
CCC	Catechism of the Catholic Church
CAT	Commentaire de l'Ancien Testament
CBQ	*Catholic Biblical Quarterly*
CBQMS	Catholic Biblical Quarterly Monograph Series
CE	Common Era
CR	*Currents in Research*
DH	Deuteronomistic History
EDNT	*Exegetical Dictionary of the New Testament*
EG	Evangelii Gaudium
EM	Encyclopedia Migraith =Encyclopedia Biblica (Heb)
ExpTim	*Expository Times*
ETL	*Ephemerides Theologicae Lovanienses*
EvTh	*Evangelische Theologie*
GS	*Gaudium et Spes*
HCOT	Historical Commentary on the Old Testament
HeyJ	*Heythrop Journal*
HUCA	*Hebrew Union College Annual*
ICC	International Critical Commentary
IDB	G. A. Buttrick, ed., *The Interpreter's Dictionary of the Bible*
IJAC	*International Journal of African Catholicism*
ILB.PT	I Libri Biblici. Primo Testamento
Int	*Interpretation*
ISBE	G. W. Bromiley, ed., *International Standard Bible Encyclopedia*
ITC	International Theological Commentary

JBR	*Journal of Bible and Religion*
JBQ	*Jewish Bible Quarterly*
JETS	*Journal of the Evangelical Theological Society*
JRT	*Journal of Religious Thought*
JSJ	*Journal for the Study of Judaism in the Persian, Hellenistic, and Roman Periods*
JSOT	*Journal for the Study of the Old Testament*
JSOTSup	Journal for the Study of the Old Testament: Supplement Series
JSS	*Journal of Semitic Studies*
JTSA	*Journal of Theology for Southern Africa*
KAT	Kommentar zum Alten Testament
LXX	Septuagint
MT	Masoretic Text
NA	*Nostra Aetate*
NJBC	R. E. Brown et al., eds, *New Jerome Biblical Commentary.*
NSBT	New Studies in Biblical Theology
NT	New Testament
OBO	Orbis biblicus et Orientalis
ÖBS	Österreichische Biblische Studien
OCB	B. M. Metzger and M. D. Coogan, eds., *The Oxford Companion of the Bible.*
OJT	Ogbomosho Journal of Theology
OT	Old Testament
OTG	Old Testament Guides
OTL	Old Testament Library
OTS	Oudtestamentische Studiën
PBC	Pontifical Biblical Commission
ResQ	*Restoration Quarterly*
RevExp	*Review and Expositor*
RSR	*Recherches de science religieuse*

SBL	Society of Biblical Literature
SBLDS	Society of Biblical Literature Dissertation Series
SBLSP	*Society of Biblical Literature Seminar Papers*
SBLSymS	Society of Biblical Literature Symposium Series
SBS	Stuttgarter Bibelstudien
SBT	Studies in Biblical Theology
ST	*Studia Theologica*
SWJT	*Southwestern Journal of Theology*
TD	*Theology Digest*
TDNT	G. Kittel and G. Friedrich, eds., *Theological Dictionary of the New Testament*
ThLZ	*Theologische Literaturzeitung*
TLZ	*Theologische Zeitschrift*
TLOT	E. Jenni and C. Westermann, eds., *Theological Lexicon of the Old Testament*, 3 vols.
TWAT	*Theologisches Wörtebuch zum Alten Testament*
USTR	*Union Seminary Theolgical Review*
UR	*Unitatis Redintegratio*
VD	*Verbum Domini*
VT	*Vetus Testamentum*
VTSup	Vetus Testamentum Supplements
WMANT	Wissenschaftliche Monographien zum Alten und Neuen Testament
WUNT	Wissenschaftliche Untersuchungen zum Neuen Testament
ZAW	*Zeitschrift für die alttestamentliche Wissenschaft*
ZST	*Zeitschrift für systematische Theologie*

Introduction

THE PROPHET AMOS IS one of Israel's fountainhead prophets. He lived and prophesied in a paradoxical time, in the middle of the eighth century BCE. Of those prophets whose messages have been collected, preserved and transmitted from generation to generation in the prophetic books of the Hebrew Bible/Old Testament, Amos is considered the earliest to have prophesied. Amos' theology is socially outstanding and religiously elegant. In particular, Amos 5 focuses mostly on socio-political and economic justice, divine judgment and the ethics of worship. When closely examined, the entire book paints a picture of political stability and material prosperity in Israel of the eighth century BCE. Paradoxically, this prosperity was corruptly limited to an elite minority class of hypocritical worshippers to the neglect and abuse of the majority poor. This explains why many scholars, exegetes, pastors, spiritual leaders, students, theologians and human rights activists who champion the cause of the poor and promote the need for ethical worship of God are attracted to the book Amos. This work joins such ranks and offers a rethinking and thorough review of the theology of worship in Amos 5. It stresses Amos' raw messages of judgment and implicit hope that has been appropriated throughout history in various contexts.

In some of his sermons and speeches, including his legendary 1963 speech "I Have a Dream," civil rights activist, Martin Luther King Jr. for instance, appropriated the text of Amos 5 in order to address the worship hypocrisies and injustices of his time.[1] In addition to King's appropriation of the prophecy of Amos 5, many commentary volumes, books, essays, and theological texts have been enthusiastically generated on Amos in the past

---

1. For further details, see Ackerman, "Between Text and Sermon," 190–93.

fifty years.[2] Most of these studies concentrate overwhelmingly on areas of social justice rather than on matters of ethics of worship, which are addressed in this present work. Those studies that do address matters of worship do so broadly and limit their discussion to the context of the history of Israel's religion—and the prophetic critique of cult worship in the Hebrew Bible/OT.[3] Wellhausen's work which draws the line between the ethical religion of the pre-exilic prophets and rigid priestly cult of the postexilic period is no stranger in prophetic scholarship.[4] These broad studies, fall short in sufficiently applying their conclusions to the specific needs of today's contemporary society. This book takes us in a different but much needed direction. It builds on past and current scholarship on Amos 5 and rigorously attempts to reevaluate Amos' theology of worship in order to apply it to contemporary society, particularly the religious communities in Africa and especially, Nigeria, my native birth place, and the United States of America (USA), where I have spent the past decade studying, teaching and ministering the word of God, of which Amos 5 forms a part.[5]

2. For a broad bibliographical compendium of some of these past studies, see Roberts, "Recent Trends," 1–16; Craghan, "Prophets Amos," 242–61; Hasel, *Understanding the Book,* 121–66; Pigott, "Amos: An Annotated Bibliography," 29–35; Melugin, "Amos in Recent Research," 65–101; and Carroll R., *Amos—The Prophet,* 76–177.

3. Examples of earlier and notable studies that do not address the specific needs of today's contemporary religious communities in Africa and North America include: Wellhausen, *Prologomena*; Volz, "Die radikale Ablehnung der Kultreligion," 63–85; Würthwein, "Amos 5: 21–27," 143–52; Bentzen, "Ritual Background," 85–99; Kapelrud, "God As Destroyer," 33–38; Rowley, "Ritual," 338–60; Hentschke, *Die Stellung*; Buss, "Meaning of 'Cult,'" 317–25; Kapelrud, " Role of Cult," 44–56; Farr, "Language of Amos," 312–24; Kraus, *Worship in Israel*; Rowley, *Worship in Ancient Israel*; Sekine, "Problem der Kultpolemik," 605–9; Harrelson, *Fertility Cult*; Rector, "Israel's Rejected Worship," 161–75; Barstad, *Religious Polemics*; Albertz, *History of Israelite Religion*; Weiss, "Repudiation," 199–214; de Vaux, *Ancient Israel*, 426; Miller, *Religion of Ancient Israel*; Brueggemann, *Worship In Ancient Israel*; Klawans, *Purity,* 75–100; De Andrado, "Ḥesed and Sacrifice"47–67.

4. For extended discussion of Wellhausen and other scholars with broader approaches to prophetic critique of cult, see Klawans, *Purity,* 75; Lafferty, *Prophetic Critique*, 4–13 and De Andrado, "Ḥesed and Sacrifice,"49–50.

5. As an African theologian serving in the United States of America, I have decided to use my native birthplace, Nigeria (in West Africa) and the United States of America as a case study. Nigeria is the most populous country in Africa with the largest economy. The same could be said of the United States of America in North American Continents. However, focusing on these two entities as a case study does not limit the relevance of this study to only these two countries or continents, but it does allow me to make a first hand and concrete conclusions, thereby minimizing speculation and over-generalization.

Recent notable works on Amos 5 from the United States worth mentioning here include those of M. Daniel Carroll R. (2005), Jonathan Klawans (2006), Gerald A. Klingbeil and Martin G. Klingbeil (2007), Paul Westermeyer (2008), and Theresa Veronica Lafferty (2010, 2012). Carroll R. discusses the role of worship in the shaping of Christian identity. Using an interpretative anthropological approach, he proposes that Amos' cult criticism is an antidote to the tension prevalent in modern worship settings.[6] Klawans presents an impressive analysis of the modern study of prophetic cult critique and concludes that the opposition of the prophets to sacrifice reflects the social and economic messages of the prophets themselves. For him when it comes to sacrifice, ethics and rituals and inseparable.[7] Even though the prophets expressed their opposition to sacrifices and offerings, they had no intention of denying the validity of cultic worship, *per se*. Klawans sees the condemnation of Israel's sacrifices as a protest against ill-gotten goods. For him, "the (external) ritual is not rejected because of an (interior) ethical wrong. Rather, the prophets—or, at least, some of them—found sacrifice offensive because they believed that those who were offering gifts had themselves stolen them."[8] Furthermore, "the concern with property renders it impossible altogether to distinguish between a ritual violation and an ethical wrong. Sacrificing a stolen animal is, at one and the same time, both ethically and ritually wrong."[9] The Klingbeils, on the other hand, narrowly focus on the effects of Amos' cult polemics in society.[10] Westermeyer, with limited exegetical details, liturgically and pastorally examines the significance of the phrase "Take away from me the noise of your songs" (Amos 5:23a).[11] On the other hand, Lafferty's works seek to clarify prophetic criticism of the priority of cult during the time of Amos. She observes that the pre-exilic prophetic criticism of the cult "had in view neither an elimination of the cult nor merely a sympathetic care toward the widow, the orphan and the oppress . . . What is above all required by Yhwh is doing justice and righteousness."[12] Lafferty observes ritual-ethics divides. She argues that the life lived outside of the temple should reflect the same life

---

6. Carroll R., "Worship Wars?," 215–27.

7. Klawans, *Purity*, 87.

8. Ibid., 98.

9. Ibid.

10. Klingbeil and Klingbeil, "Prophetic Voice," 161–82.

11. Westermeyer, "Journey with Amos," 150–58.

12. Lafferty, *Prophetic Critique*, 84.

of reverence shown to God inside the temple. Not until the people received justice and righteous treat them as priorities, God would not accept cult and ritual practices offered hypocritically in the temple.[13] Yet, like earlier studies, she makes no effort to relate her conclusions to the faith contexts and contemporary worship communities of today.

On the other hand, there is commendable and recent Nigerian scholarship on Amos which focuses broadly on social issues rather than on matters of worship, in Amos 5, with specific theological conclusions for contemporary Nigeria.[14] Agboluaje's article for instance comments generally on the ministry of Amos and attempts to relate it to "the socio-economic situation in Nigeria."[15] Although Agboluaje cites the religious depravity in Nigeria his practical examples are not sufficiently drawn from Amos to relate to worship issues in Nigeria.[16] Iroegbu's book length study focuses extensively on the geo-political heritage of Nigeria. It aims to analyze the entire book of Amos. Though exegetically and textually impressive, Iroegbu's work is broadly addressed to issues of social injustice in Nigeria, and not on worship in the prophecy of Amos 5, which is the primary focus of this present work. In Iroegbu's words, "few would contest the need for Amos' blasting of Israel for great atrocities of social injustice be heard again in our world of today, in Africa and more so in Nigeria . . . there is much here that might serve to recover our Nigerian society from its social mess."[17] In their article, "Threats of Judgment in Amos and its Lessons for Nigeria," Folarin and Olanisebe concentrate overwhelmingly on the social implication of Amos for Nigeria, rather than on religious and worship dimensions. They stress the threats of judgment motifs found in the Book of Amos which functions as corrective measures, and do not extend that analysis to the theological realm of Amos 5 for today.[18]

13. Lafferty, *Prophetic Critique*, 84–88.

14. Notable Nigerians on Amos scholarship include: Ebo, "O that Jacob Would Survive"; Ebo, "Amos' Visions," 17–27; Ebo, "Re-ordering," 61–73; Agboluaje, "Ministry of Amos," 1–10; Iroegbu, "*Let Justice Roll Down Like Waters*"; Folarin and Olanisebe, "Threat of Judgement,"243–61.

15. Agboluaje, "Ministry of Amos," 6.

16. Ibid., 9.

17. Iroegbu, "*Let Justice Roll Down Like Waters*," 14.

18. Folarin and Olanisebe, "Threat of Judgement," 255–58.

Aims of this Study

The purpose of this present study is to exegetically examine and theological-ly re-evaluate for contemporary societies, especially Nigeria and the United States of America, the treasure of wisdom found in Amos 5. This involves studying block by block, the theological elements found in Amos 5, includ-ing its lamentation (vv. 1–3), its inherent motifs of hope for the remnant, its exhortation to seek the Lord, and the concepts of justice, righteousness (vv. 4–6; 14–15, 24), and judgment/the Day of the Lord (vv. 18–20) as they relate to the prophet's entire ethics of worship (vv. 21–27). This work seeks to examine the text in a manner that is unprecedented in the studies of Amos. It vigorously argues that for the prophet Amos, worship is not a matter of hypocritical pilgrimages, offerings, ceremonial songs, sacrifices, and empty rituals—especially by the elites of the community, who delight in neglecting the suffering of the poor and invest in the exploitation of their lowliness. This work seeks to lift up the lowly by stating with profound faith that authentic worship must find expression outside the temple by ethics of obedience to God, love of neighbors, the promotion of social justice of all dimensions, acts of kindness, and through righteousness in daily living.

In other words, this study seeks to demonstrate that in the prophecy of Amos, worship must find expressions in everyday life—and endeavor, as this so often easier said than done. This work strives to demonstrate how consistently Amos courageously and practically charges Israel for wrongly preferring external sanctuaries and their associated hypocritical rituals over the God they intended to honor (3:13–15; 4:4–5; 5:4–5). Amos sees that worship in Israel is becoming an end in itself instead of a means of worshiping God and charitably reaching out to one's neighbors. This means most importantly that, in Amos' view, Israel's worship and piety lacks justice and righteousness, risking God's judgment (5:18–20). This work uniquely argues that these deficiencies are displeasing to the Lord (5:21–24).

This study is also unique from previous work in that it is done within the overall context of the entire book of Amos, which is in turn part of the Twelve Minor Prophets, read as a whole in contemporary scholarship. Furthermore, unlike earlier works, this current enterprise is carried out with an awareness of the social and cultural characteristics of the person of Amos. This study constantly highlights the prophet's literary and linguistic skills, as well as his idiomatic ways of appropriating rich traditions in order to accomplish his theological purpose of calling his neighbors to the true worship of God.

This work also importantly aims to relate the theological findings of Amos 5 to the current daily life situations of contemporary societies, especially Nigeria and the United States of America, an approach defined by Justin Ukpong as "inculturation hermeneutics."[19] The choice of these two nations, Nigeria and the USA, if I may reiterate, does not make this work irrelevant to other cultures, nations and continents beyond the contemporary Africa and America. It rather allows me as a Nigerian-born African theologian, currently serving in the United States to draw concrete and first-hand examples from these two notable nations for the global readers of Amos, without unnecessary speculations.[20] Additional reasons for choosing these two nations are described in chapter 6. But it is helpful to acknowledge here that many scholars today support a more focused or contextual approach, including Walter Brueggemann and Robert J. Schreiter. For instance, in *The Prophetic Imagination*, Brueggemann observes that "what we understand about the Old Testament today must be somehow connected with the realities of the church today."[21] In his influential volume *New Catholicity*, Schreiter like Ukpong, also insists on the importance of contextualizing and appropriating biblical exegesis and theology. But he advises that "Theology must not be reduced to context in a crude contextualism, for then it is likely to lose its critical edge as it becomes simply a product of its surroundings."[22]

This study appropriates diverse exegetical and literary-theological resources addressing Amos 5, including ecclesiastical documents not found in some of the earlier exegetical research on Amos 5. By and large, this work adapts and bridges the gap between the historical faith of Amos' time (eighth century BCE) and our faith today, especially in Nigeria and in the

---

19. For details of this type of reading, see, Ukpong, "Inculturation Hermeneutics," 18.

20. Iroegbu ("Let Justice Roll Down Like Waters," 14–15) stresses the greatness of Nigeria geographically and demographically as follows: "Nigeria is a republic in West Africa, on the Gulf of Guinea, with an area of 923,773 sq.km or 356.699 sq. Miles. It is one of the largest countries and the most populous country in Africa . . . It is located within the tropics on the southern coast of western Africa, extending about 1,050 km (650 miles) from north to south hand 1,130 km (700 miles) east to west. It consist of a belt of tropical rain forest I the south, with semi-desert in the extreme north and highlands in the east. It is bordered by the republic of Niger and Lake Chad in the North, the Atlantic Ocean in the south, the Republics of Cameroon in the East and Benin Republic in the West. Nigeria has eight ecological zones, ranging from dry and intermediate savannah, through tropical rainforest to mangrove swamps and dry, sandy areas."

21. Brueggemann, *Prophetic Imagination*, 1.

22. Schreiter, *New Catholicity*, 1–27. See also the entire work of his student, Bevans, *Models of Contextual Theology*.

USA. This study also stresses the role of faith in interpreting Scripture. It recognizes the role of faith is vital as each culture and time seeks to address its current socio-economic, political, ethical, and religious challenges. According to Schreiter universal reflection often neglects to address issues that are the most pressing in a local context, such as the burden of poverty and oppression, the struggle to create a new identity after a colonial past (as in the case of Africa), or "the question of how to meet the challenge of modernization and the commodification of the economy in traditional culture and village life."[23]

In line with Schreiter's observation, over the past few years, Nigeria and the USA have not only witnessed unique challenges, including worship debates and calls for liturgical renewals, but also a proliferation of churches and pluralism of religion. Experiences felt in Africa (Nigeria) and in the USA today include advancements in technology, new fashions in dress, terrorism, religious extremism, wars, increases in violence, drug trafficking, materialism, Islamic militancy, Boko Haramism and abduction of schoolgirls in the Chibok town of northern Nigeria, Al-Qaida threats, and shootings at religious/public places (e.g., the Sikh Temple in Milwaukee, the movie theater in Aurora, and the parking lot in Tucson).[24]

In different parts of Africa (Nigeria) today, people are facing various religious, social, political, and economic challenges and would benefit from the soothing effect of the message of Amos 5. For instance, there is a proliferation of religions, including African Traditional Religion (ATR), Islam, and Christianity. This proliferation comes with unethical practices in some worship centers. There have been recorded cases of abuses, such as the distribution of expensive gifts and cash by public office holders to religious groups, without accountability—even when civil servants in their areas of jurisdiction have not been compensated for months and years. In the case of ATR, there are also strong inclinations to certain aspects of worship that contradict the tenets of Christian faith, justice, and righteousness expressed in the theology of Amos 5.

The socio-political situations of many African countries—Nigeria in particular—reflect the socio-political situation of Amos' time, when world empires like Assyria, Egypt, and Babylon were in conflict with one another. Israel took advantage of this tension to grow politically and economically

23. Schreiter, *New Catholicity*, 1.

24. Recently there have also been incidences of religious extremism in Australia, France, Brussels, Nigeria, and in other parts of the world.

strong. It was a time of political equilibrium, relative peace and economic prosperity. Unfortunately, Israel's prosperity led to religious hypocrisy, including economic and political injustice against the poor. The rich constructed for themselves more homes (3:15) and purchased for themselves personal comforts such as furniture and material goods (3:12; 4:1; 6:6). The poor were neglected, ignored, exploited, trampled upon, and exchanged "for a pair of sandals" (2:6–7; 5:10–12). Some of the poor were extorted at marketplaces and denied justice in courts of law by corrupt officials (8:5). The people of African nations, particularly Nigeria, can see their current struggles in the problems addressed by Amos. An unstable political leadership that leads to corruption in public places has become the order of the day in many African nations. There are unjust economic structure across Africa, their currencies have become devalued when compared to the U.S. dollars or Euros. This is in addition to many other challenges, such as child trafficking, tribal conflicts, exploitation and economic violence against the poor and the needy. These challenges require the healing effect of the message of Amos 5, which conveys judgment on one hand (5:18–20; 7:1–6; 7–9; 8:1–3) and hope on the other (vv. 4–6, 14–15, 21–2; 9:11–15).[25] Amos' message and its application for the religious, socio-political, and economic issues plaguing authentic worship in Africa, Nigeria in particular, will be fully developed in chapter six.

The people of the United States of America also face many socio-political, economic, and religious problems that beg for the message of Amos, including acute individualism, isolationism, and syncretism. Lamenting some of these contemporary issues, Raymond Brown notes, "the sense of community concern has disappeared from many contexts in contemporary life. The ruthless pursuit of personal satisfaction has left many of our contemporaries with little time for projects which may benefit others."[26] Selfishness and injustice have also become the order of the day.[27] David Wells speaks of unethical isolationism between the rich and the poor, even in public places of worship, and notes, "our computers are starting to talk to us while our neighbors are becoming more distant and anonymous."[28] In Brueggemann's view, the "contemporary American church is so largely

---

25. Amos' message at first reading appears dooming, lacking hope for salvation. This will be fully and rigorously debated and reconciled in the exegetical section of this study.

26. Brown, *Message of Nehemiah*, 26.

27. Ibid.

28. Wells, *God in the Wasteland*, 48.

enculturated to the American ethos of consumerism that it has little power to believe or to act . . . Our consciousness has been claimed by false fields of perception and idolatrous systems of language and rhetoric."[29] He goes on to argue that "the internal cause of such enculturation is our loss of identity through abandonment of the faith tradition," which is traded for a false sense of ideologies and political parties, Republican or Democratic.[30]

In much religious practice in the United States, the integrity of worship and ethics must be re-examined and separated from a false sense of security or exceptionalism, which was also common in Amos' time. Religious centers were flooded with worshipers—especially the elites—who attended festivals (5:21), made sacrifices (v. 22), and took part in external songs and entertainment with a sense of entitlement (v. 23) but without justice and love of neighbor. For Amos such hypocrisy has no place in God's presence. There is no place for election theology, or national ideology, without a sense of responsibility (2:10; 3:1–2; 5:14–15).

Besides mixing faith and national ideologies, the devotion to entertainment found in secular society is increasingly engulfing the spirit of prayer and worship in American worship centers. This is why Carroll R. warns that America, driven by entertainment and technology, is broken in so many ways, including persona trauma, abuse of guns and drugs, ignorance of other people's cultures and world geography, family dysfunction, and isolationism. He further argues that the Church must not neglect its primary mission of addressing poverty, hunger, racism, and wars, as well as personal brokenness.

The United States today is socio-economically blessed, as was Israel during the time of Amos. But many millions of people in the United States today lack access to housing, food, health, and education, as did so many of the poor during the time of Amos. In the United States, the recent economic crash also revealed widespread predatory lending that has led many students and families into unsurmountable debt. Those who utilize slave labor or cheap labor in underdeveloped countries are also regular worshipers in American churches. Loopholes in the U.S. tax system have placed the burden of paying more taxes on the shoulders of the poor rather than on the rich—a phenomenon that was common during the time of Amos. In addition, there are cases where market outlets are scarce in poor urban areas in the United States; this scarcity often makes poor residents victims

29. Brueggemann, *Prophetic Imagination*, 1.

30. Ibid.

of predatory pricing. In America, the poor—especially African American males—know too well that it can be difficult to find justice, without disputes and controversies, in the U.S. court system. A typical case in hand is the Ferguson report of 2015 from the U.S. Department of Justice.

Although these contemporary problems are separated by time from the context of the Israelite prophets—especially the original audiences of Amos' prophecies—their relevance cannot be denied. Amos' experiences of idolatry, injustice, harsh taxation, exploitation of the poor, and economic abuse of the underprivileged, along with luxurious homes for the elite, unethical, noisy worship with hypocrisy, and neglect of widows and migrants, are undeniably familiar to us today.

Relating ancient Old Testament texts like the prophecy of Amos to our times can be very challenging. These challenges are minimized when the principle of prophetic contemporaneity is applied and, more importantly, when the given biblical text (OT/NT) is approached not only as the Word of God, but as a single continuum.[31] In other words, Christians must read the Bible, of which Amos 5 is a part, as one revelation from "the same Holy Spirit Who is, because He is God, is timeless. He has insights into God's Being, His providence, and His expectations of man that cannot and should not be dated."[32] Thus, John A. Hardon observes:

> The calling of Abraham, the Exodus, the Decalogue, the Psalms, and the prophecies of Isaiah and Jeremiah are no less meaningful today than they were when the events took place or when the words were spoken or written. In fact, they should be more meaningful and pertinent now, provided we change our perspective. Although they were written then, they were meant for all times . . . After all, this is not merely the word of man, it is the Word of God.[33]

This passage undoubtedly echoes Vatican II's position that, "just as the life of the Church is strengthened through more frequent celebration of the Eucharistic mystery, similarly we may hope for a new stimulus for the life of the Spirit from a growing reverence for the Word of God, which 'lasts forever' (Isa 40:8; see 1 Pet 1:23–25)."[34] Echoes of this position reverberate in *Verbum Domini* (2010), which says;

31. See Honeycutt, "Amos and Contemporary Issues," 441–57.
32. Hardon, *Catholic Lifetime,* 12.
33. Ibid., 12–13.
34. Paul VI, *Dei Verbum,* no. 26.

The word of the Lord abides forever." This word is the Gospel which was preached to you" (1 Pet 1:25; cf. Isa 40:8). With this assertion from the First Letter of Saint Peter, which takes up the words of the Prophet Isaiah, we find ourselves before the mystery of God, who has made himself known through the gift of his word. This word, which abides forever, entered into time. God spoke his eternal Word humanly; his Word "became flesh" (Jn 1:14). This is the good news. This is the proclamation which has come down the centuries to us today.[35]

These passages support the assertion that the message of Amos 5 is capable of traveling centuries and penetrating barriers of culture and ideology to reach us in our time. It is adaptable. It is also a global pedagogical approach that can be used in Africa (Nigeria) and in America (USA) to address the ongoing contemporary worship and ethical issues. Thus, Amos' message "is capable of entering into and finding expression in various cultures and languages, yet that same word overcomes the limits of individual cultures to create fellowship between different peoples."[36] That is to say, when viewed as the Word of God, Amos 5 is enshrined as "a creative genius whose fidelity to the ancient covenant and whose concern for contemporary issues combined to reflect the manner in which both past and present must be creatively linked in order to ascertain the present relevance of divine revelations."[37]

Terms and Limitations of This Study

Two terms, "cult" and "worship," are used interchangeably throughout this study. These terms require some clarification. King notes that they "are basically the same, just as the worship of God and the service of God are synonymous terms."[38] In biblical theology, the term "worship" refers to both the event and the manner of worship. This aligns well with the ancient conception that the deity had needs that were ministered by his servants. Hence, the very idea of service is among those concepts that form the biblical meaning of worship and cult.[39] One of them is the expression "to bow

---

35. Benedict XVI, *Verbum Domini*, no. 1.

36. Ibid., 116.

37. Honeycutt, "Amos and Contemporary Issues," 441.

38. King, *Archaeological Commentary*, 88.

39. Ibid.

down/worship" (השתחוה).[40] Other terms include "to serve" or "to work" (עבד) and "to minister" (שרת), which imply service to God in a liturgical or cultic sense.[41]

Amy-Jill Levine traces the etymology of the term "cult" to the Latin root "*cultus*," meaning "adoration" or "care," as one would care for a shrine. According to her, this term "indicates formal forms of worship: sacred space such as temples and shrines; rituals such as sacrifices, dietary restrictions, and ablutions; and religious professionals such as priests and temple singers."[42] *Cultus*, therefore, is the public expression of religion. It "signifies communally recognized orthopraxy rather than idiosyncratic or individualistic religious activity."[43]

The essence of Levine's views can be traced to the work of Roland de Vaux, who also defines "cult" as "those acts by which communities or individuals give outward expression to their religious life, by which they seek and achieve contact with God."[44] Similarly, Marva J. Dawn suggests that the term "worship" comes from the Old English roots "*weorth*" ("honor," "worthiness") and "*scipe*" ("to create"). Dawn argues that we cannot "create" God's honor "because it is inherently God's, but we do devise ways to honor God that bespeak his worthiness."[45] Dawn sees worship as a way through which we worship God.

Behind Levine, de Vaux, and Dawn's conceptual analyses is the notion of Sacred Liturgy and its trajectories: public worship, mystical body of Christ, sacrifice, priests, temple, Eucharist, praise, thanksgiving to God, and other sacred elements, which are expressed particularly in the Vatican II's Constitution on the Sacred Liturgy.[46] This document defines liturgy as "the summit toward which the activity of the church is directed; it is also the source from which all its power flows ... all who are made children

---

40. See Lambdin (*Biblical Hebrew*, 254–55); and Pratico and Pelt (*Basics of Biblical Hebrew* 400–401), where it is noted that this verb was formerly taken as *Hithpalel* form of root שחה but is generally accepted today as a *Histaphel* with the root חוה ("to bow down, worship") and occurs about 173 times in the Hebrew Bible.

41. King, *Archaeological Commentary*, 88.

42. See Knight and Levine, *Meaning of the Bible*, 165.

43. Ibid.

44. De Vaux, *Ancient Israel*, 271.

45. Dawn, *Reaching out without Dumbing Down*, 76–77. See also Allen and Borror (*Worship*, 16) and Peterson (*Engaging with God*, 20) for additional definition of "worship."

46. See Vatican II, *Sacrosanctum Concilium*, 1–10; and Udoekpo, "Liturgy," 83–104.

of God by faith and Baptism should come together to praise God."[47] Even though this study is more of an exegetical-theological work than a liturgical work, these forms of worship and their relevance are fully highlighted in chapter six, which relates Amos 5 to contemporary societies, particularly Nigeria and the USA.

This work is exegetically and theologically limited in scope to the text of Amos 5. This limited approach is necessary since the complexity of the nature of worship in the entire Old Testament is beyond the focus of a work devoted specifically to Amos' critique of the unethical cult and its relevance for today's life in Nigeria and in the USA, for legitimate reasons already stated, to include the fact that the author is an African scholar-theologian ministering in the USA. However, the relationship between the narrative of worship in Amos 5 and the remainder of the book of Amos and other cultic passages and themes in the prophetic tradition, especially the Twelve Minor Prophets, will be outlined. This measure is necessary because modern scholarship on the themes of worship, justice, righteousness, and judgment in the writings of the biblical prophets is increasingly focused on interpreting the entire Twelve Minor Prophets as a literary and thematic whole. A holistic reading of the Twelve Minor Prophets does not completely limit the significance of individual books, but rather (among several advantages) provides a canonical perspective and supplements theological insight on the tradition of the ethics of worship that might be missed by narrowing the investigation to Amos 5. Several literary elements link Amos 5 to the composite unity of the Twelve, such as *inclusio*, repetition of words, catchwords, framing devices, motifs, and theological themes. The relationship is most apparent in the shared notion of the Day of the Lord. Greater attention will be devoted to the theme of the Day of the Lord in chapter three.

Approaches Adopted in This Book

There is a scholarly consensus among biblical exegetes today regarding the pluralism of methods and approaches to biblical interpretation.[48] That is to say, there has been a widespread acknowledgement of a hermeneutical

---

47. Cf. *Sacrosanctum Concilium*, no. 10.

48. Echoes of these approaches and methodological opinions are found in Brown and Schneiders, "Hermeneutics," 1146–65; Fitzmyer, "*Interpretations*"; McKenzie and Haynes, *To Each Its Own Meaning*; Schneiders, *Revelatory Text*; Countryman, *Interpreting the Truth*; and Night, *Methods of Biblical Interpretation*.

shift in methods and approaches to biblical studies as a whole. Fernando Segovia writes, "the world of biblical criticism today is very different from that of the mid-1970s . . . the field has undergone a fundamental and radical shift."[49] Teresa Okure calls this shift "a revival of interest" in biblical scholarship that is mainly inspired by the changing situation in mission lands, where previously silent and passive recipients of mission have now become its active agents, either in their own countries or in other lands.[50] Okure's emphasis is on the necessity of making biblical passages relevant to the reader's faith context, which this study intends to underline, especially in the final chapter.

Contextualizing or appropriating an ancient text like Amos 5 requires sufficient knowledge of the historical background of such texts. It requires a familiarity with not only what stands behind such texts, but also what is in those texts, as well as what lies before or in front of the texts.[51] To accomplish this, the present study uses various methods of historical-critical methods, complimentarily with literary criticism and "faith hermeneutics."[52] By faith hermeneutics, we mean "the harmony of faith and reason," exegesis and theology, biblical and systematic.[53] Irrespective of the biblical text, it is a "scientific" reading with an "explanatory power" from the heart of the Church in an ecclesial spirit.[54] Therefore, faith hermeneutics, as suggested by Ratzinger, has a twofold unifying power: (1) the power to hold fast the

49. Segovia and Tolbert, *Readings from This Place*, 1.

50. Okure, *Johannine Approach*, xv.

51. See Schneiders (*Revelatory Text*, 97–174) for in-depth explanation of the world behind the text (history, imagination), world of the text (witness and narrative language), and the world before the text (meaning, appropriation, adaptation of the revealed text).

52. See Brettle, Enns, and Harrington (*Bible and the Believer*, 3–20, 8–125) for extended analysis and defense of historical-critical methods.

53. Hahn, *Covenant and Communion*, 41–62.

54. Cf. Ratzinger (*Behold the Pierced One*, 42–62) where Pope Benedict XVI explains that interpretation of Scripture today should not be restricted to historical method. It should be done from the standpoint of science that does not interfere with the integrity of the text. He stresses, "From a purely scientific point of view, the legitimacy of an interpretation depends on its power to explain things . . . the less it needs to interfere with the sources, the more it respects the corpus as given and is able to show it to be intelligible from within, by its own logic, the more opposite such an interpretation is. Conversely, the more it interferes with the sources, the more it feels obliged to excise and throw doubt on things found there, the more alien to the subject it is. To that extent, its explanatory power is also its ability to maintain inner unity of the corpus in question. It involves the ability to unify, to achieve a synthesis, which is the reverse of superficial harmonization . . . only faith hermeneutic is sufficient to measure up to these criteria."

entire testimony of the sources, comprehend their nuances and pluriformity, and (2) the power to transcend their differences of cultures, divisions, times, peoples, civilizations, and values.[55]

This approach is vital to an attempt to re-examine Amos 5 for specific geographic and faith contexts since there are values and cultures that are not upheld in the United States of America, just as there are some North American values that are not given prime place in Africa, particularly, Nigeira, or other parts of the world. Faith hermeneutics helps shed light on how Amos 5 could be interpreted within specific cultural milieu. Pope Benedict XVI further highlights the significance of this approach when he states, "Faith traditions formed the living context for the literary activity of the authors of sacred Scripture . . . In like manner, the interpretation of sacred Scripture requires full participation on the part of exegetes in the life and faith of the believing community of their own time."[56]

Broadly speaking, a combination of these methods (diachronic, synchronic, and theological exegesis) has the advantage of not only illuminating the theological meaning of every aspect (structure, literary, linguistic, canonical, and thematic features) of Amos 5, but it also enables a balanced reading, which mediates the needs of contemporary Africans and Americans.[57]

Given the premise of this introduction then, this study methodologically proceeds in six concise chapters followed by a summary reflection and a general conclusion. Chapter one addresses in a preliminary fashion the socio-historical background of the person, occupation, book, and message of the prophet Amos. The discussion takes into consideration the historical backdrop of the cult/worship traditions in ancient Israel. Chapter two focuses critically on the text of Amos 5. Chapter three discusses the relationship between Amos (particularly Amos 5) and the other books of the twelve Minor Prophets. Chapter four concentrates on literary criticism,

55 See ibid., 45; and Hahn (*Covenant and Communion*, 45–46) where Pope Benedict XVI's interpretative method is further explained as "reverent listening, a seeking after the living voice of God who in his gracious love speaks to man in the human words of the biblical texts . . . Reading Scripture is a dialogue in faith with God who speaks to us from the living experience of his people, the Church . . . hermeneutic of faith begins in the heart of the Church, where the task of understanding and interpreting Scripture is part of the church's larger response to the divine Word that has been spoken to it."

56. Pope Benedict XVI, *Verbum Domini,* 29, 46.

57. Okoye (*Scripture in the Church,* esp. 69–92) explains further the principles of biblical exegesis and the advantages and disadvantages of both diachronic and synchronic methods are extensively examined.

analyzes the structure of Amos, and delimits the text of Amos 5 within the overall book of Amos. Chapter five exegetes the passage and examines it theologically. The final chapter aligns the theological message of Amos 5 with contemporary religious communities, using Nigeria and the USA as case studies. The study concludes with a general conclusion and synthesis of the entire six-chapter volume.

In the synthesis, the goal and the limits of the project are reiterated. It remains an exegetical and theological re-examination of Amos' theology of worship. Its fundamental purpose is to make an honest attempt to adapt and bridge the gap between the historical faith of the time of Amos and today. In Amos' theology, Israel must seek the Lord in the right place (i.e., Judah) and in the right manner in order to evade the judgment intended to bring the remnant back to God.

Amos teaches us that worship should not be restricted to hypocritical offerings, ceremonial songs (המון שרים), sacrifices, and empty rituals. God rejects such worship, as implied in the saying, "Take away from me the noise of your song" (5:23a). In Amos 5, songs of worship and adoration must find expression in the practical ethics of obedience to God, love of neighbors, social justice (משפט), acts of kindness (חסד) and righteousness (צדקה) in the daily events of life.

1

Amos' Background, His Book, and His Theological Message

General Historical Context

ALTHOUGH IT IS AN ancient text, the prophecy of Amos is the timeless Word of God that is ever relevant to believers today.[1] It "speaks to our age with tremendous challenge."[2] Perhaps the more reason numerous texts, some of which have been cited in the introductory section, have been generated on Amos. These texts are intended to address today's socio-economic, religious, and political problems.[3] In fact, no prophetic book seems to have a bibliography comparable in size to that on Amos.[4]

This chapter offers a general review of the historical context of the prophet Amos. It reviews the different aspects of the person of Amos, including his native town, profession prior to his prophetic calling, and the cultic/worship traditions upon which he stood. It also explores and reflects on the formation history of the text of Amos. That is, it investigates how this massive text was put together and notes relevant debates surrounding its editorial processes. Amos' theology is broadly and foundationally outlined toward the end of this chapter.

---

1. Paul VI (*Dei Verbum*, no. 26; cf. Isa 40:8; 1 Pet 23:25); Benedict XVI (*Verbum Domini*, no. 1); Leclerc (*Prophets*, 129) further testify to the enduring relevance of the Word of God of which Amos is a part.

2. Agboluaje, "Ministry of Amos," 1.

3 The situations (social, political, religious, and economic) that Amos' theology can address today have been cited already in various Nigerian and American scholarship on Amos, and are currently being discussed by global nations including the Vatican. See Pope Francis, *Evangelii Gaudium*, 176–258.

4. Peterson, "Book of the Twelve," 107.

The groundwork established in this chapter is essential to the exegetical and theological arguments of the remainder of the study. Our cultural patterns, origins, and context, among other things, influence our thoughts, preaching, writings, values, and reflections. The same would have been true for Amos, particularly with regard to his message of ethical worship (Amos 5), which remains the centerpiece of this study.

Kapelrud, a renowned student of Amos, argues that the best place to begin when studying Amos—especially when searching for his origins—is the initial verse of the book,[5] the superscription: "The words of Amos, a shepherd from Tekoa, which he received in vision concerning Israel, in the days of Uzziah, king of Judah, and in the days of Jeroboam, son of Joash, king of Israel, two years before the earthquakes" (1:1).[6] This brief third-person superscription introduces to us the prophet Amos: his person, his socio-political, cultural, and religious settings, his native town, and his original profession before his calling as a prophet.

The Name "Amos"

The prophet bears a unique Hebrew name, Amos (עָמוֹס), whose meaning is not completely known. The *BDB* notes that the root meaning of the name can be traced to the verb עָמַס/עמש, which has two meanings: "load" and "carry."[7] Old Testament passages outside of Amos use the verb עָמַס/עמש in the sense of carrying a load or putting a load on a donkey or on someone (Gen 44:13; Isa 46:1; Neh 13:15; Zech 12:3). This had led scholars like Finley to suggest that the prophet's name (עָמוֹס) is probably the shortened form of עֲמַסְיָה, which was familiar to the Judeans (2 Chr 17:16).[8] If this is the case, the literal meaning of the prophet's name, according to Finley, is "The LORD loads" or "The LORD carries the load of the people." Finley

---

5. Kapelrud, *Central Idea*, 5.

6. The un-pointed Hebrew in this study is drawn from the *Biblia Hebraica Stuttgartensia* (*BHS*), which contains the Masoretic edition of the Hebrew Old Testament that is widely regarded as a reliable extant Hebrew Old Testament textual witness. Otherwise, all my English quotations are drawn from *The Catholic Study Bible: New American Bible*. The fonts are the ones made available by the Society of Biblical Literature (SBL).

7. See Brown, Driver, and Briggs (*BDB)* and Holladay (*Concise Hebrew and Aramaic Lexicon,* 276) for further details.

8. Finley, *Joel, Amos, Obadiah*, 106.

argues that this name is theologically relevant for those who interpret the text of Amos with faith.[9]

Amos' Native Place

In addition to providing Amos' unique Hebrew name, the superscription also mentions the native place of this prophet, Tekoa. This place is a known biblical town in Judah, estimated to be about eleven to twelve miles south of Jerusalem (Josh 15:59; 2 Sam 14:9; 23:26; 1 Chr 11:28; 2 Chr 11:5–6). Strijdom observes that "on the way to En-Gedi, a settlement next to the road carries the name, מעלה עמוס ('ascent of Amos')."[10] In fact, the reference to Tekoa has caught the attention of many researchers on Amos.[11] Some argue for tracing Amos to Tekoa while others are just interested in the topography of the village of Tekoa. For instance, Hasel meticulously notes that the elevation of Tekoa is about 2,800 feet (850 meters), which is higher than either Bethlehem or Jerusalem, perhaps very dry, rocky and uninhabitable to the east of the Dead Sea.[12] Siegfried Wagner argues that Amos' hometown was Judean Tekoa.[13] While Klaus Koch prefers to link Amos with the Galilean Tekoa, since it "is attested in post-biblical times."[14]

Commenting on Amos' birthplace, Stanley N. Rosenbaum argues that Amos came from the northern kingdom of Israel but became a rebel after unsuccessfully attempting to overthrow the northern government. To substantiate his arguments, Rosenbaum points to agricultural references and linguistic issues. For instance, he notes that the sycamore tree that Amos tended (7:14–15) does not grow in Tekoa, partly due to the high elevation of the town. Rosenbaum also observes that Amaziah accused Amos of treasonable offense for conspiring (קשר) against Jeroboam (7:10). He argues

---

9. Ibid.; McKenzie, *Dictionary of the Bible*, 27–28; Stamm, "Der Name des Propheten," 137–42; Udoekpo, *Re-thinking the Day of YHWH*, 119.

10. Steijdom, "What Tekoa did to Amos," 273–93; Iroegbu, "*Let Justice Roll Down like Waters*," 238–39; Hasel, *Amos*, 50, have extensive comments on characteristic features of Tekoa.

11. Cf. Kapelrud, Central *Ideas in Amos*, 5.

12. Hasel, *Amos*, 49.

13. Wagner, "Überlegungen zur Frage," 653–70.

14. Koch (*Prophets,* 70) argues particularly that Amos preached as an insider, not as an onlooker, but "after his expulsion from Bethel, Amos actually did cross over to Judah (7:12)." See also Hasel, *Amos*, 50, for features and a description of this town in "postbiblical (Talmudic) times."

unconvincingly that, in this dramatic episode, Amos spoke a northern elite dialect when he was told to "flee" (ברח) to the land of Judah (7:12), just as he understood that he was being banished from his native place, to which he had become a threat.[15] Rosenbaum's argument is weak since it is unclear whether the priest of Bethel, Amaziah, expected Amos to flee to his home or to leave the north (7:10–17).[16]

Philip J. King is also of skeptical of Rosenbaum's views. King observes that "the biblical sycamore tree grows only in the lowlands and coastal plains, protected from the frost. . . . [I]ts fruits are smaller and inferior in quality to the common fig, and has always been an important item of food for the poor."[17] If this is true, then northern Tekoa in Upper Galilee hardly qualifies as a better candidate than Judean Tekoa as the hometown of Amos.[18]

Although this study leans toward viewing the south as the birthplace of Amos, the theological effectiveness of Amos' prophetic message is ultimately not affected by whether he came from the southern kingdom of Judah or the northern kingdom of Israel. However, Amos' movement from the south to the north portrays Amos as a prophet on a mission in a cultural environment slightly different from his own, who abandoned his first profession in the south to preach in the north. It also raises the legitimate question of whether the prophet Amos can serve as a model for today's missionaries, challenged to abandoned themselves for others in mission lands. Or in the words of Iroegbu, from a modern perspective, some might consider Amos as one of the earliest foreign missionaries.[19]

Amos' Profession Prior to His Prophetic Mission

Amos' original profession unquestionably forms a part of the historical context of his prophetic message. The superscription calls Amos the "shepherd" (נקד, nōqēd) from Tekoa (1:1).[20] Later in the book, when the priest Amaziah

---

15. Rosenbaum, *Amos of Israel,* 30–100. Also for a good summary of Rosenbaum's position, see Hasel, *Amos,* 50–52.

16. Hasel, *Amos,* 53–54.

17. King, *Amos, Hosea, Micah,* 116–17.

18. Hasel, *Amos,* 52,

19. Iroegbu, *"Let Justice Roll Down Like Waters,"* 239.

20. נקד (nōqēd) is commonly translated as "shepherd," "sheep-breeder," "sheep-raiser," "sheep dealer," or "tender."

instructed Amos never to prophesy again in Bethel (7:10–17), Amos sarcastically responded: לא־נביא אנכי ולא בן־נביא אנכי כי־בקקר אנכי ובולס שקמים, ("I was not a prophet, nor have I belonged to a company of prophets/son of the prophet; I was a shepherd and a dresser of sycamores" (7:14b).[21] As to the expression לא־נביא אנכי ("I was no prophet). many scholars generally agree to its meaning, namely, a prophetic group.[22] It also implies that he was not a paid palace prophet, but God's mouthpiece, called and commissioned by God (Amos 7:15).

Besides the expression "I was not a prophet" (לא־נביא אנכי) other significant terms and expressions in Amos' response are: "shepherd" (נקר, nōqēd); "a cattle breeder/herdsman" (בוקר) and "dresser/gatherer of sycamore tree" (בולס). Amos' response has fueled scholarly curiosity and debates regarding his profession prior to his mission.[23] As in the case of Tekoa, his native birthplace, some scholars have dedicated an entire monograph to examining Amos' profession before his prophetic mission, with details beyond the scope of this work.[24]

However, James Luther Mays argues that Amos "followed an agricultural life, but he is not to be thought a simple, uncultured rustic. 'Sheep breeder' probably means an owner in charge of other shepherds, a substantial and respected man of his community."[25] Mays bases his argument on the style and quality of Amos' speeches, including his idioms, riddles, proverbs, pronouncements, judgments, woe cries, exhortations, lamentations, hymns, and doxologies (Amos 5). Amos was a skillful speaker and was knowledgeable of the cultural, historical, religious, economic, and socio-political situations and oral arts of his time.[26] Hasel similarly argues that if Amos was not a member of the upper class, he at least belonged to the professional middle class in Judah or Israel.[27] That is to say, he belonged to the "haves," where נקד (nōqēd), a large-scale sheep breeder, would have

---

21. Amos meant to say he was not a professional or paid prophet, but a vocational prophet called by God.

22. See Iroegbu, "*Let Justice Roll Down Like Waters,*" 250–51.

23 Hasel (*Amos*, 29–32) has extensive scholarly debates and conclusions on the professions of Amos before his prophetic calling.

24. Steiner (*Stockmen from Tekoa*) is a classic example.

25. Mays, *Amos,* 3.

26. Ibid., 4.

27. Hasel, *Amos,* 36.

been categorized.[28] Iroegbu describes Amos as "a progressive businessman who managed probably shepherds (נקד) and grew figs (Amos 7:14) before he was called by God for a vocation that was short-lived, Amos was interested in the dynamics of Israel's national economic system."[29]

Kapelrud, who also comments on Amos' profession prior to his prophetic duties, observes that the term נקד (nōqēd), which is used to describe Amos, is used only once in the book of Amos (hapax legomena) and twice in the entire Old Testament (dis legomena). Outside the book of Amos, the word appears in 2 Kings 3:4, which states that Mesha, king of Moab, was a נקד (nōqēd) who paid thousands of rams to the king of Israel as tribute.[30] We do not know if the use in 2 Kings has any influence on or relationship to the usages in the text of Amos. An interesting distinction drawn between the two occurrences is found in Francis I. Andersen and David Noel Freedman's comment that "if Amos was in any way like the king of Moab, he would have been wealthy and influential. Amos in 7:14–15 gives a different impression."[31]

There are extra-biblical parallels to the biblical term נקד (nōqēd) in Arabic, Mesopotamian, Sumerian, Moabite, and Ugaritic cultures with specific reference to an ordinary shepherd or a wealthy herdsman.[32] This has deepened speculation that Amos was a high-ranking professional, officer, chief priest, or cult prophet in the Jerusalem temple who perhaps also owned flocks in the Tekoa region. Murtonen views such speculations as tenuous and unfounded in the text, where Amos himself says he was not in the company of professional prophets (7:14).[33]

In spite of these divergent views, most scholars would agree that Amos was a respectable member of Judean society. He was also an outspoken individual who knew how to conduct business and manage his large-scale herds.[34] He was not a professional prophet. Although he was known as a נקד

---

28. Ibid., 36, also notes that "the root nqd was used in Akkadian, Arabic, and Syriac for both sheep and shepherd."

29. Iroegbu, "Let Justice Roll Down Like Waters," 234.

30. Kapelrud, Central Ideas, 5–6.

31. Andersen and Freedman, Amos, 188.

32. See Hasel (Amos, 36); Soggin (Prophet Amos, 24); Andersen and Freedman (Amos, 187); and Kapelrud (Central Ideas in Amos, 6) for additional comments on נקד (nōqēd).

33. Cf. Murtonen, "The Prophet Amos," 293–96; Andersen and Freedman, Amos, 188; and Paul, Amos, 33–35, for this debate.

34 Craigie, "Amos the noqed," 29–32.

(*nōqēd*), Amos had no problem being synonymously recognized as a בוקר (*bôqēr*), "a cattle breeder or herdsman," and a בולס שקמים (*bôlēs shiqmîm*), "dresser or gatherer of sycamore trees" (7:14b). In other words, although the majority opinion is that Amos was an experienced farmer prior to his prophetic calling, the prophet must have had some connection with herds and sycamores in an educated manner (1:1; 7:10–14). He was also generally familiar with the socio-political, religious, and worship traditions of his people.

Amos' Worship/Cultic Traditions

Amos was familiar with the cultural traditions and religious customs of his audience. This familiarity is reflected in his prophecies, which mark an alternative and distinct turning point in the history of biblical worship, as evident throughout the text. His notion of proper worship is based on ancient Israel's worship traditions, which are composed of cultic events, worship, and service to God. It was traditionally believed that the deity had needs that his servants met,[35] as communicated in language such as "bow down/worship" (השתחוה), "serve/work" (עבד), and "minister"(שרת). These concepts communicate external acts and gestures "by which communities or individuals give outward expression to their religious life, by which they seek and achieve contact with God."[36]

Israel's cult/worship, therefore, consists of the community's faithful management of the signs and actions by which God interacts with the individual or the community.[37] A detailed historical development of this divine-human interaction in ancient Israel transcends the scope of this study.[38] Typically, that would take us back to the primitive patristic period, through the polytheistic era of the exodus, to the time of the founding of the monotheistic temple and the subsequent emergence of its critique by the eighth-century prophets—particularly Amos, who announces judgment on Israel.

A summary of such divine-human interaction in ancient Israel suffices here. During the time of Abraham, Isaac, and Jacob, worship in the

---

35. See King (*Amos, Hosea, Micah,* 88) where "cult" and "worship" are read interchangeably "just as the worship of God and the service of God are synonymous terms."

36. De Vaux, *Ancient Israel,* 11.

37. Brueggemann, *Worship in Ancient Israel,* 2.

38. Ibid.

form of prayer and sacrifice was simple. At this time, worship was oriented around the individual and the family. Its focus was not on the priesthood or extended communitarian elements that are often associated with worship today.[39] The worship practices of ancient Israelites were influenced by the Israelites' neighbors, particularly the Canaanites.[40] For instance, Abraham worshiped God at Shechem (Gen 12:6–7), and Jacob also erected an altar there when returning from a long sojourn with his uncle, Laban (Gen 33:18–20; Jos 24:32). Besides Shechem, other places of worship associated with Israel's patriarchs include Bethel (Gen 28:10–22), Mamre (Gen 13:18), and Beersheba (Gen 26:23–25).[41]

After the patriarchal period, the worship practices in Israel underwent some changes, including the development of the priesthood and cooperative acts of worship such as the Passover (Exod 12), the ritual Decalogue (Exod 34), and sacrifices (1 Sam 7:9–10).[42] After their exodus from Egypt, the Israelites had a portable sanctuary for worship. Moses also consulted God from this portable sanctuary (Exod 33:7, 11; Num 12:8). The ark of the covenant (Exod 26:33; 40:21; Num 9:15; Deut 10:5–8; Josh 7:6; Judg 20:27; 1 Sam 3:3; 43–11; 5:5–7:1; 2 Sam 6; 1 Kgs 6:19; 8:1–9) was the center of ancient Israel's worship from their time of wandering in the desert until the destruction of the temple (586/7 BCE).[43] In the eighth century BCE, sanctuaries were located at Gilgal (Josh 4:19; 7:6; 1 Sam 7:16; cf. Hos 4:15; Amos 4:4), Shiloh (Josh 18:1; 21:2; 22:9; 1 Sam 3; Judg 21:19–21), Mizpah (Judg 20:1–8), Ophrah (Judg 6), Dan (Judg 17–18), and Jerusalem, where Solomon eventually built a well-furnished temple for the Lord (2 Sam 6; 24:16–25; 1 Chr 21:15–22:12).[44]

This well-furnished temple gave the Israelites renewed hope. It was a house of prayer and place of worship, where God and his glory dwelled (1 Kgs 8:1–13). It was also a sacred place where the Israelites could truly seek God and worship him (2 Chr 6:18–21). This temple was later abused, stripped of its furniture, and finally destroyed by the Babylonian armies

39. Rowley, *Worship in Ancient Israel*, 1–36.

40. Brueggemann (*Worship in Ancient Israel*, 3) further argues that "Israel participated in and appropriated from the worship practices of its environment that were very old and well established, for the propensity to worship was in that culture long antecedent to the emergence of Israel."

41. Castelot, "Religious Institutions," 710–11.

42. Ibid., 37–70.

43. Ibid., 711.

44. Ibid., 712–14,

(1 Sam 4). Deuteronomistic theologians have interpreted this destruction against the backdrop of the sins and abuses committed by those who were supposed to make good use of the temple for offerings, sacrifices, and ethical services to the Lord and the community (2 Kgs 25).[45]

In his text *Religion of Ancient Israel,* Patrick Miller gives a list of the common features or characteristics of the ancient Israelite cult. His list includes such features as exclusive worship of God, oracular prophecy, and sanctuaries used for devotion, prayer, festivity, songs, and sacrifices.[46] The ancient Israelite cult is also characterized by its set times for praising the Lord, as well as moral responsibility to care for the welfare of others in the community.[47]

Unfortunately, during the time of Amos, these core features of true worship to God—particularly its correspondent ethics of obedience to God's will, justice, and righteousness—were neglected, and the shrines were abused. In Iroegbu's words, "all was not well in the religious realm. Social disintegration went hand in hand with religious decay."[48] It is such religious decay and negligence that Amos 5, the focus of this study, challenges in light of Amos' eighth-century BCE socio-historical context.

Amos' Sociopolitical/Economic Contexts

In addition to the theological insight gained from exploring the background of Amos' name, his native place, his profession prior to prophesying, and his worship traditions, a brief review of the socio-political and economic realities of his time is imperative. The book places Amos' prophecy in the northern kingdom of Israel in the eighth century BCE, during the reigns of Uzziah of Judah (786–733 BCE) and the Jeroboam II (789–747 BCE) of

---

45. See Rowley, *Worship in Ancient Israel,* 71–110; Gerstenberger, *Theology of the Old Testament,* 111–16.

46. Some of these sacrifices and feasts already discussed in de Vaux, *Ancient Israel,* 415–23, 507–17 include: "Ritual Sacrifices" such as (a) Holocausts, (b) communion sacrifices, (c) expiatory sacrifices, (d) vegetable offerings, and (e) showbread; and "Later Feasts" such as (a) the day of atonement, (b) the feast of the Hanukkah, and (c) the feast of Purim. For additional studies on festivities and ritual sacrifices in ancient Israel, see Castelot, "Religious Institutions," 718–25; Brueggemann, *Worship in Ancient Israel,* 25–62.

47. Miller, *Religion of Ancient Israel,* 48–51; Brueggemann, *Worship in Ancient Israel,* 6.

48. Iroegbu, *"Let Justice Roll Down Like Waters,"* 237.

Samaria. This period was characterized by a unique socio-economic and political reality.[49] Shalom M. Paul describes this period as the "Silver Age" of Israel's history, when Israel reached the summit of its material power and economic prosperity. It was also the apogee of territorial expansion, comparable only to the "Golden Age" under David and Solomon.[50]

During this "Silver Age," Israel's old nemesis, Aram, was distracted to the north by the threat of Assyria, leaving Israel free to flex her political muscle in the region.[51] It was a period of unprecedented peace and political equilibrium.[52] Jeroboam II and Uzziah reigned side by side without conflict for more than forty years.[53] The territories of Israel and Judah were expanded to the east, west, and the south at the expense of other regions, including Hamath and Damascus (2 Kgs 14:23–29; 2 Chr 26:6–8). This expansion brought the northern and southern kingdoms huge economic gains.[54]

While Israel and Judah experienced political and economic growth, Assyria and Syria experienced declines both in their military and commercial interests.[55] Trade and commerce flourished to the advantage of Israel and Judah. They became major trade routes and "natural land bridges."[56] The Egyptians traveling north for business had to pass through Israel and Judah, as did the Syrians and Assyrians traveling south.[57] Due to their strategic location for business and trade, Israel and Judah were also able to charge tolls from investors and travelers.

Ironically, the result of this economic boom was a marked abuse of worship and, as Ellis states, "social stratification, with wealth resting in the hands of a few powerful Israelites, leaving a large population of impoverished peasants."[58] Premnath judges that "the entire trade enterprise was

---

49. See Mays, "Words" 263, Smart, "Amos," 118; Wolff, *Joel and Amos,* 89; Koch, *Prophets,* 36–39; Leclerc, *Prophets,* 123–24; Andersen and Freedman, *Amos,* 18–23; Jeremias, *Amos,* 1–2; Finley, *Joel, Amos and Obadiah,* 107–9; Branick, *Understanding the Prophets,* 40–41 for elaborate entries on this socio-historical, economic, and political background, but with slight variation in dating.

50. Paul, *Amos,* 1.

51. Ellis, "Amos Economics," 463.

52. Udoekpo, *Re-thinking the Day of YHWH,* 200.

53. Moore, "Book of Amos," 31.

54. Premnath, "Amos and Hosea," 125.

55. Ibid.,31; Heschel, *Prophets,* 33.

56. Moore, "Amos," 31.

57. Ibid.

58. Ellis, "Amos Economics," 456.

geared towards procuring items of interest and demand (military items, horses, chariots, luxurious and fine linens, jewelry, perfume and spices) for the elites."[59] Those in Judah and Israel with political connections also gained wealth through the acquisition of surplus food and grain and by exploiting the poor for labor.[60] These elites seized the opportunity for idle banqueting. They wastefully designed summer and winter homes for their families and furnished them with ivory (3:15). They trampled the heads of the poor into dust and would trade them for a pair of sandals (2:6–7; 8:6).

Amos did not take these injustices kindly. He sarcastically mocked the wives of these elite perpetrators as the "cows of Bashan" (פרות הבשׁן).[61] These women supported their husbands in ignoring "the needy" (אביונים), "the poor" (דלים), "those who resign to God's will" (ענוים), and "the righteous" (8:4; 5:12; 4:1; 2:7, צדק).[62] With their support, Israel was unnecessarily stratified into two classes: the upper/lower class, which could also be called the wealthy/poor, the sick/healthy, or the haves/have-nots. Amos witnessed these ironies and called out the perpetrators as follows: "Alas for those who lie in beds of ivory, and lounge on their couches, and eat lambs from the flock, and calves from the stall, who sing idle songs to the sound of the harp and like David improvise on instruments of music, who drink wine from bowls, and anoint themselves with the finest oils, but are not grieved over the ruin of Joseph" (6:4–6).

Corruption became the order of the day on the watch of those whom Amos addressed (6:4–6). Merchants used false weights in business transactions (8:5–6), and judges received bribes (5:12).[63] Israel's moral decay was accompanied by hypocritical displays of religious fervor. The nation was

59. Premnath, "Amos and Hosea," 127.

60. Carroll R., Amos—The Prophet & His Oracles, 23.

61. For a recent study of the "Cows of Bashan," see Irwin, "Amos 4:1 and the Cows of Bashan," 231–46. Three interpretations of the "Cows of Bashan" are presented: (1) his own position is that it refers to the elite women of Samaria who were perpetrators of injustice because of the high demand they made of their masters or "lords"; (2) "the mixture of masculine and feminine forms in the verse has led many interpreters, beginning from the Targum, to understand 'cows' to refer to the elite citizens of Samaria, male and female who conspire with their rulers (לאדניהם) ('to their lords') to plunder the poor"; and (3) "a third view has understood פרות הבשׁן ('Cows of Bashan') to refer to all of the inhabitants of the city of Samaria and לאדניהם ('to their lords') to the deities venerated by them."

62. See Koch, Prophets: Assyrian Period, 48–49, for extensive discussion of these classes of people.

63. Moore, "Amos," 32.

religiously bankrupt. Citizens—including the "cows of Bashan"—flocked and rolled to shrines in Bethel, Gigal, and Dan with their offerings and sacrifices (4:1–13; 21–23).[64] Additionally, Israel's worship centers were filled with loud songs chanted faithlessly by worshipers whose hearts lacked love and charity toward their neighbors. Their mechanical worship had little effect on the practical life of the average Israelite in the marketplace. Such forms of worship were not acceptable to God.

The prophecy of Amos 5 is incessantly addressed to "these nations of ironies," which were characterized by paradoxes of new wealth and poverty, peace and war, austerity and prosperity, stability and instability, and high attendance at the temple but spiritual drought in the marketplaces. Since the book of Amos as a whole communicates these interesting ironies using different forms of speeches and genres, scholarly interest over the years has focused on the form/literary composition of this massive theological text, with special effort to highlight the ethical demands for true worship.[65]

The Composition/Literary History of the Book of Amos

The composition and literary history of the text of Amos, though complex, continues to receive scholarly attention.[66] To fully appreciate the theology of Amos, scholars examine not just the person, native place, original profession, and the socio-political setting in the life of Amos, but also the traditional developments, genre, materials, and the redactional history of the book of Amos. Knowledge of the book's history and literary genre sheds significant light on the meaning of the message of Amos 5. Are there poems, hymns, idioms, exhortations, lamentations, woe cries, riddles, or proverbs in this passage (Amos 5)? If so, what are their traditions and their effects on the theology of the text? Finley notes that scholars want to know how the message of Amos 5 evolved—whether from a sermon, oral prophecy, or book—in relationship to the other eight chapters.[67]

64. See Motyer, *Message of Amos,* 105–08 for details on the shrines at Bethel (vv. 6–13), Beersheba (vv. 14–20), and Gilgal (vv. 21–27).

65. Moore, "Amos," 31.

66. Hasel (*Amos,* 91–99); Melugin ("Amos in Recent Research," 65–101) all have additional details and impressive comments on the composition and literary approaches of Amos.

67. Finley, *Joel, Amos, Obadiah,* 110.

As mentioned earlier, the book of Amos has been widely admired not just for its social and ethical messages (which are of particular interest to theologians and human-rights activists), but also due to the eloquence of its language and style.[68] Stylistically, chapters 1–2 constitute a series of judgment oracles against nations (Aram, Philistia, Tyre, Edom, Ammon, Moab, and Judah) that culminates in the denunciation of Israel (2:6–9). Chapters 3–6, from which we locate our particular chapter of concentration (Amos 5), consist of words, exhortations, songs and doxologies, and woes and sayings. These are followed by chapters on visions (7–9:6) and the conclusion (9:7–15).[69]

A few commentators argue that the vast majority of the book's oracles date to the eighth century; others find redactions, additions, glosses, expansions, emendations, and innovations in the text that they often attribute to the post-exilic period.[70] Some of these views deserve brief comments here.

In his classic commentary, Mays argues that, besides the introduction (1:1), the hynmic poetry (1:2; 4:13; 5:8f; 9:5f; 8:8), and wisdom saying (5:13), Amos is composed of three distinct materials: "(1) sayings spoken by a prophet in carrying out his commission; (2) first-person narratives told by the prophet; and (3) a third-person narrative about the prophet." Wolff, on the other hand, suggests six levels of formational materials:[71] (1) "the words of Amos of Tekoa" (3–6); (2) "the literary fixation of the cycles" (7:1–8; 8:1–2; 9:1–4) and the oracles against the nations (1:3–2:16, excluding the Tyre, Edom, and Judah oracles); (3) "the old school of Amos," who reworked the text after Amos' death (7:10–17; 8:4–14; 9:7–10; 5:13–15; 6:2 and 7:13); (4) the text of the time of Josiah (ca. 640–609 BCE; 4:13; 5:8–9; 9:5–6; 3:14; 5:6); (5) the Deuteronomistic redaction, which added the oracles of Tyre, Edom, and Judah (2:10–12; 5:25; 3:1b; 8:11–12) as well as the biographical information (1:1); and (6) post-exilic material (9:11–15).[72] It

68 Birch, *Hosea, Joel and Amos,* 168.

69. For recent study and re-ordering of the redactional materials dealing with Amos' vision, see Ebo, "Reordering," "Vision," 61–72, where he particularly argued for the originality of his effort highlighting the redactional materials of the original message of Amos by the deuteronomists who were out to give an explanation to the fall of Samaria in 721/722 BC. Ebo writes, "I am not aware of any attempt by anyone to rearrange these visions."

70. See Andersen and Freedman, *Amos,* 141–44; Paul, *Amos,* 6; Wolff, *Joel and Amos,* 106–13; Jeremias, *Amos,* 5–9, for some of these debatable views.

71 Wolff, *Joel and Amos,* 107–13.

72. Mays (*Amos,* 12) preset these materials as: (a) a large block of sayings (1:3—6:14),

includes the expression "like David, they devise their own accompaniment" (6:5).[73] Mays and Wolff appear to have taken for granted that the book of Amos constitutes a collection of independent short narratives discernable through form criticism. In their conclusion, the current text of Amos is post-exilic, spanning from Amos himself through various stages of transmission and historical tradition-redaction.[74]

A number of scholars have proposed alternative models of redaction history.[75] For instance, Robert B. Coote comments that, in its present form, the book of Amos was written by more than one author at more than one time. For him, like the rest of the prophetic books, it is the final work of a series of recompositions of the original words of the named prophet. Coote further interprets Mays' model as suggesting that between the time of Amos and the final edition of the book, there were other editions of Amos' words that may have been composed by several different authors.[76]

Soggin outlines eight stages of formation history (from a–h) of the book of Amos. He follows Wolff closely and concludes that the wisdom materials found in Amos are not only attributable to its redactors, but to the influence of the Israelites' wisdom tradition.[77] Wolff's school of thought has attracted several objections. For instance, Wilhelm Rudolph argues on the contrary that the concept of the unification of "genuine" material in Amos received a number of secondary glosses during the course of transmission.[78]

Roy F. Melugin also argues that it is difficult to navigate the six levels proposed by Wolff and his supporters. Melugin basically concludes that, "indeed, anyone who studies the formation of the Book of Amos must ask to what extent such a reconstruction is even possible."[79] Finley lists three objections to Wolff's model: (1) It lessens the authority of the OT books as

---

(b) four blocks of vision reports (7:1–3, 4–6, 7–9; 8:4–14), and (c) a third-person narrative about Amos set between the third and fourth vision report (7:10–17). In 8:4–14 the saying resumes, then there is a fifth vision (9:1–6) and the final sequence of sayings (9:7–15).

73 For additional details on Wolff's six levels, see Hasel, *Amos*, 92–93.

74. Cf. Melugin, "Amos in Recent Research," 65.

75. Nogalski, *Literary Precursors*, 76.

76. Coote, *Amos Among the Prophets*, 2–3. See also Doorly (*Prophet of Justice*, 1–17) for "how some scholars have divided the Book of Amos."

77. Soggin, *Amos*, 16–18; Schmidt, "Die deuteronomistische Redaktion des Amosbuches," 168–93.

78. Rudolph, *Joel-Amos-Obadja-Jona*, 100–103.

79. Melugin, "Formation of Amos," 375.

attested in the NT; (2) the material we find in the biblical books does not support the claim that the phrase "the words of Amos" (1:1) is different from the rest of the book, and there is no explicit example in the book of Amos of opinions of later ages; and (3) there is no objective evidence to support the six-layer analysis Wolff proposed. In Melugin's view, using logical or grammatical shifts and seeming contradictions in the text to discredit its unity is not sufficient.[80]

These objections gave birth to synchronic arguments for the literary composition and formation of the book of Amos. A typical example is the massive work of Klaus Koch and his colleagues, who promote the synchronic approach over the diachronic approach. Koch and his colleagues argue that the book of Amos is more a composition than a collection.[81] Adril van der Wal, who summarizes Koch's approach to Amos,[82] notes that Koch pays attention to three literary points in Amos. The first literary point Koch examines are the reoccurrences of "hear this word" (שמעו הדבר) formulas (3:1, 13; 4:1; 5:1; 8:4) in the book of Amos that, particularly the extensive ones (3:1; 5:1), uniquely mark the beginning of a new section in Amos' prophecy.[83] Koch also identifies doxologies that mark the limits of these sections. A doxology in Amos serves as an introduction (1:2); longer doxologies (4:13; 9:5–6) close the main section of the book, and a shorter one (5:8) closes part of a main section. Based on the "hear this word" (שמעו הדבר) formulae and the long doxologies, Koch proposes the following structure for the book of Amos: judgment to nations (1–2); woes against Israel as divine admonition (3–4); woes against his own people as prophetic funeral laments (5:1–9:6); and an appendix (9:7–15).[84] Koch also draws attention to the addressee—namely, "Israelites" (בני ישראל) in chapters 3–4 and "house of Israel" (בית ישראל) in 5:1—9:6.[85]

James Limburg points out that the "number seven appears to play a significant role both in the structure of the book of Amos and in the making up of the certain of the sayings."[86] In his view, the material of Amos' prophecy is divided into seven units and an additional unit by "divine

---

80. Finley, *Joel, Amos, Obadiah*, 111–12.

81. Koch und Mitarbeiter, *Amos*, 9.

82. Van der Wal, "Structure of Amos," 107–13; Garrett, "Structure of Amos," 275–76.

83. Van der Wal, "Amos," 107.

84. Ibid., 108.

85. Ibid.

86. Limburg, "Sevenfold Structures," 217–22.

speech formulas"—or in other words, "those stereotyped expressions that introduce or conclude sayings identifying them as words of the Lord."[87] He classifies three groups of these formulas: (1) אמר (ʾāmar) formulas, which occur about twenty-seven times in slightly different forms[88]; (2) נאם (neʾum) formulas, which occur about twenty-one times;[89] and (3) דבר (dibber) formulas.[90] Besides the first unit, which introduces the prophet and identifies his message (1:1–2), the rest of the sequence is 1:3—2:16; 3:1–15; 4:1–13; 5:1—6:14; 7:1—8:3; 8:4—9:15, indicating forty-nine (or seven times seven) speech formulas.[91]

John H. Hayes also supports the synchronic view in arguing that Amos' prophecy consists of a large rhetorical unit rather than multiple small, isolated units and multiple layers, as proposed by Wolff and Mays. In Hayes' view, the book of Amos must be understood through a close reading of the text in light of its historical setting, which can be reconstructed from available sources, since the prophet was interested in his specific historic situation rather than general moral and political issues.[92]

Hayes concludes that it is not evident in Amos that the prophet drew upon any specific OT laws. For him, it is "easier to assume that Amos wrote his own words, whether before or after delivering them or, more likely, that they were written down by someone in the audience, than it is to believe in the existence of a circle of disciples or an old school of Amos for which there is no evidence whatever."[93]

Andersen and Freedman maintain that most of the material in the book of Amos likely came from the prophet himself or from editors or a

---

87. Ibid., 217.

88. Examples from Amos of the occurrence of varied forms of the אמר (ʾāmar) formulas are: כה אמר יהוה, "thus says the Lord" (1:3, 6, 9, 11, 13, 2:1, 4,6; 3:12; 5:4, 16); אמר יהוה, "says the Lord"(1:5, 15; 2:4; 5:17, 27; 7:3); אמר אדני יהוה, "the Lord God said" (1:8; 7:6); למאר, "saying" (3:1); כה אמר אדני יהוה, "thus says the Lord GOD" (3:11; 5:3); ויאמר יהוה, "and the Lord said" (7:8; 8:2); ויאמר יהוה אלי, "and the Lord said to me" (7:15); אמר יהוה אלהיך, "said I, the LORD your God" (9:15).

89. Varied forms of נאם (neʾum) formulas are: נאם יהוה, "says the LORD" (2:11, 16; 3:10, 15; 4:3, 6, 8, 9, 10, 11; 9:7, 8, 12, 13); נאם אדני יהוה, "says the Lord God" (4:5; 8:3, 9, 11); נאם אדני יהוה אלהי הצבאות, "says the Lord GOD, God of hosts" (3:13; 6:8,14); נאם אדני יהוה אלהי צבאות, "say I, the LORD the God of hosts" (6:8); נאם אדני יהוה אלהי הצבאות, "say I, the Lord, the God of hosts" (6:14).

90. See Amos 3:1 (cf. 3:8).

91. Limburg, "Sevenfold Structures," 218.

92. Hayes, Amos, 38–39.

93. Ibid. See also Melugin, "Amos in Recent Research," 66–67.

college of disciples who were close to him personally (as alluded to in the beginning of this section). In their words, "insofar as we can speak about the Book of Amos, we can recognize one master hand. If not Amos himself, then at least an editor unified the text who must have been very close to his teacher and whose contribution was to arrange and integrate the prophecies that Amos himself produced."[94] Andersen and Freedman are cautious not to conclude based on signs of redaction, glosses, and updating that the entire text of Amos is postexilic, since any attempt to reconstruct the entire process is nothing but speculation and hypothesis.[95] They argue that the number of contradictory messages discernible in Amos (e.g., its announcements of doom [1—4:13] juxtaposed with a message of hope [9:7–15]) are a result of the four-phase evolution of Amos' career. In their view, phase one is represented by two visions of locust and fire (7:1–6). These visions presuppose YHWH's judgment on Israel and Judah in spite of the prophet's intercession that kept the possibility of repentance alive, as shown in the statement "yet you returned not to me" (cf. 4:6–11). The exhortation to seek the Lord and live (Amos 5) presents another opportunity for Israel to restore her relationship with God.[96] Phase two is marked by another pair of visions (7:7–9; 8:1–2) with the message that punishment has become unavoidable. God will not spare them again; the die has been cast. According to Andersen and Freedman, phase three is composed of the fifth vision (9:1–4), which addresses what the appropriate punishment for the corrupt leaders should be. In this case, the nation's destruction and exile are insufficient for the leaders, who would be pursued and executed while in exile as punishment for their sins. Phase four focuses on the restoration and reversal of fortune for the remnant (9:11–15).[97]

Nevertheless, Andersen and Freedman agree that there is a difference between the oral speeches of Amos and the reformulation of those speeches into a book. Additionally, apart from their proposed four-phase career evolution, Andersen and Freedman structure the contents of the book of Amos into four parts: (1) the "Book of Doom" (1:1—4:13), which consists of oracles against the nation (1:2–8), oracles against the whole of Israel (2:9—3:8), a message for Israel and Samaria (3:9—4:3), and a message for all of Israel (4:4–13); (2) the "Book of Woes" (5:1—6:14), which contains

94. Andersen and Freedman, *Amos*, 5.
95. Ibid., 4, 75–76.
96. Ibid., 78.
97. Ibid., 80.

exhortations for Israel and Judah (5:1–17), remarks on the Day of the Lord (5:18–20), questions of justice (5:21–24), the threat of exile (vv. 25–27), and woes and warnings (6:1–14); (3) the "Book of Visions" (7:1—9:6); and (4) the "Epilogue" (9:7–15).[98]

Douglas Stuart proposes a threefold structure for Amos (with the addition of an introductory superscription [1:1]): (1) oracles (1:2—6:14), (2) visions (7:1—8:3), and (3) oracles (8:4—9:15).[99] Gary V. Smith and a few other scholars likewise see a tripartite structure for Amos consisting of: (1) the nation's judgment (1:1—2:14), (2) verification of divine judgment on Samaria (3:1—6:14), and (3) visions and exhortations (7:1—9:15).[100]

Finley sees the artistic structure of the entire book in the light of three major outlines: (1) Amos and his message (1–2), (2) words of warning and woes (3–6), and (3) visions of judgment and salvation (7–9).[101] He comments on the language and literary style of Amos' prophecy, which for the most part has been poetically rendered in modern translation. He notes that Amos "uses mostly a balanced line of three thought units per half-line (3+3, as in 1:2), as well as the uneven rhythm sometimes known as 'qinah' (3+2, as in 5:2) after the Hebrew term for 'lament.'"[102] He further points out that Amos also occasionally employs parallelism of thoughts (1:2; 5:24) and agricultural and nature imagery. For instance, in Amos we find the symbolism of a flowing river, locust, withered vegetation, plant blight, hills dripping with sweet vines, birds caught in traps, and a roaring lion.[103]

Amos' representation of various geographical areas supports our earlier assertion that the prophet was fully familiar with his environment and culture. He was neither a rustic famer nor a timid orator. In a given episode of his prophecy, Amos effectively posits a rhetorical question (3:3–8; 7:10–15). He adapts imperative expressions (3:9) and irony (4:5) successfully and with a great sense of humor (5:19–20). Other linguistic features utilized by Amos to his rhetorical advantage are: personification (5:2–3),

---

98. Ibid., 23–72.

99. Douglas Stuart, *Hosea–Jonah*, 287.

100. See Smith, *Amos*, 7–9; Hasel, *Understanding the Book of Amos*, 98, for an impressive list of these other scholars.

101. Finley, *Joel, Amos and Obadiah*, 115–16.

102. Ibid., 113.

103. Ibid.

climactic tension (1:3—2:6), hyperbole (5:21–23), repetitive techniques, a courtroom-type scene, as well as hymns and exhortations (4–5:8–9; 9:5–6).[104]

Before we conclude this chapter, two other commentators are worth mentioning. First, Shalom M. Paul believes the book of Amos is "a composite of independent collections with well-organized literary and stylistic structures arranged according to common literary genres."[105] He notes that the book has a superscription as well as an introductory motto (1:1–2). This is followed by six oracles against foreign nations, Judah, and Israel (1:3—2:16). Next is the messenger formula section (3:1—5:17), the woe oracle (הוי) section (5:18–27; 6:1–7), and the section on visions (7:1–3, 4–5, 7–9; 8:1–3; 9:1–4). These are followed by a biographical narrative (7:10–16) and a collection of independent and interspersed judgmental oracles (8:4–14; 9:7–10). According to Paul, the final unit (9:11–15) comes from Amos himself. Paul's entire division is based on his conviction that almost all of the arguments for later interpolations and redactions—including a Deuteronomistic one—are based on fragile foundations and inconclusive evidence. He thinks that "when each case is examined and analyzed on its own, without preconceived conjectures and unsupported hypotheses, the book in its entirety (with one or two minor exceptions) can be reclaimed for its rightful author, the prophet Amos."[106]

Jörg Jeremias, on the other hand, argues that the book of Amos was not transmitted to preserve past historical interests, but was artistically written down and constantly updated for its time and culture. Thus, it "underwent its constitutive formation after the fall of Jerusalem during the exile-early, or during the postexilic period. Even . . . during the age of Jeremiah."[107] Jeremias concludes that Amos' centuries of exilic formation and post-exilic growth highlight the high esteem given to the book in biblical scholarship, which today's exegetes and literary critics cannot afford to ignore.[108]

Two broad conclusions can be drawn from the foregoing analysis of the text of Amos' complex history of formation. The first conclusion concerns the methodological issue alluded to in the introductory section of this study: whether the study of Amos 5 should be approached synchronically or diachronically. In what precedes, it is evident that the text of Amos

---

104. Ibid., 113–114; Super, "Figures of Comparison," 67–80.

105. Paul, *Amos*, 6.

106. Ibid., 6–7.

107. Jeremias, *Amos*, 5.

108. Ibid., 7–8

(including Amos 5) was spoken, written, edited, and redacted at various points in its long formation history. It is an ancient text that was written and updated according to the criteria of ancient conventions and culture. Modern analytical techniques, rhetorical techniques, or literary or historical approaches alone cannot sufficiently offer the clearest meaning of the text of Amos 5 without faith and the ecclesial community. In fact, it is to this end that Pope Benedict XVI exhorts that "the study of the word of God, both handed down and written, be constantly carried out in a profoundly ecclesial spirit, and that academic formation take due account of the pertinent interventions of the magisterium."[109]

Jean-Louis Ska rightly suggests that the "synchronic study itself should lead scholars to examine the historical contexts of the text." For him, with faith, there is nothing to be gained by "provoking a war of methods or of fighting to defend one form of analysis over another."[110] Ska's suggestion is congruent with our approach, which combines both diachronic and synchronic methods complimented with the "hermeneutics of faith." In other words, Amos is best read as a unified work with the knowledge of its overall background in dialogue with both what lies behind the text and what is in the text as handed on to us, so as to bring out the clearest and most balanced theological meaning of his critique of worship (Amos 5).

The second conclusion concerns the question of discerning the benefits to our study of investigating the formation history of Amos. The advantages of exploring the historical background of Amos (person, hometown, profession prior to prophesying, worship traditions known to him, and his socio-political realities) for this work cannot be overstated. These investigations form a solid foundation to the exegetical section. What precedes in terms of the complex compositional/literary history, style, genres of exhortation, hymn, lamentation, riddles, proverbs, woe-cry, pronouncements, and the traditions behind each element will be amplified to shed light on the theological messages of Amos.

Outline of the Theological Message of Amos

The goal of this chapter has been to explore the historical background of Amos, including his person, book, and theological message. We have already explored Amos' person and book; Amos' theological message is the

109. Benedict XVI, *Verbum Domini*, no. 10.

110. Ska, *Reading the Pentateuch*, 164.

focus of this last section, where we will provide a brief outline of the theology of Amos.

Birch admirably summarizes Amos' theological message into six interrelated themes: (1) the end of Israel, (2) the sovereignty of God, (3) the appeal for justice, (4) the hypocrisy of worship, (5) the inevitability of judgment, and (6) the promise of blessing.[111] Each of these themes can be retrieved in different locations from our discussion thus far and amplified more in the discussion yet to come. In the following paragraphs I will offer brief comments on some of these theological themes to help lay the broader theological foundation for the topic of worship, which is the focus of this volume.

God's Name and His Sovereignty

The first theme upon which we will comment is that of God and his sovereignty. Like those in ancient Israel who lived during and after his time, Amos uses יהוה ("LORD") several times when expressing his idea of God.[112] As noted by Kapelrud, ancient Israel perceived God as a national God (2 Kgs 5:17; 9–10; 1 Sam 26:19),[113] an idea Amos seems to portray in the beginning and the end of his preaching against foreign nations, saying "the LORD roars from Zion" (1:2), as well as in his expressions of hope for Judah (9:11–15).[114] Kapelrud thinks these expressions were used as a rhetorical tool in connection with the verb דרש ("seek") with the goal of reminding Israel that God must be sought for life, in the temple of Jerusalem rather than at Bethel (5:4–6, 14–15, 24). Yet, in Amos' theology God cannot be localized in Israel and Judah only (2:1).[115] This is further noted by Birch

---

111. Birch, *Hosea, Joel and Amos*, 169–72.

112. Mitchell, "Idea of God," 33. Cf. Amos 1:2, 3, 5, 6, 9, 11, 13, 15; 2:1, 3, 4 (x2), 6, 11, 16; 3:1, 6, 10, 12, 15; 4:3, 6, 8, 9, 10, 11; 5:4, 6, 8, 17, 18 (x2), 20; 6:10, 11; 7:3 (x2), 6, 8, 15 (x2), 17; 8:2, 7, 11, 12; 9:6, 7, 8, 12, 13, 15.

113. Kapelrud (*Central Ideas,* 33), a famous student of Amos, observes that although "the idea painted in these narratives (2 Kings and 1 Samuel) shows him as a national God . . . we shall also have to face the methodical question, about the historical value of narratives written after the time of Amos." Caution, he says, is necessary in using some of these materials.

114. Kapelrud, *Central Ideas,* 46.

115. Ibid.

who observes that for the prophet Amos, "Israel had no exclusive claim to God's grace."[116] He is the sovereign of creation and nations.

As the sovereign of all creation, God chose Israel in the first place (i.e., he is the God of election). However, his authority and judgment reach far beyond the borders of Israel and Judah, and even to Sheol and heaven (4:13; 5:8–9; 9:2–7).[117] In other words, Amos' God intervenes in human history (2:9–10; 5:25) by liberating and wishing to save Israel (4:6–11; 9:11–15). He is great, omnipresent, and omnipotent.[118] Thus, he deserves proper worship.

Election Comes with a Responsibility

The second theme upon which we will comment is that of election and the responsibility that accompanies it. This theme is fully developed in chapter 5, in the exegetical section (5:18–20) of this work. Here we will simply stress that in Amos, God alone is the one Israel must constantly seek and truly worship, since election (2:10; 3:1–2) has a responsibility (3:2; 5:14–15). God opposes sins and judges Israel (8:2; 9:1). Unless Israel repents, punishment on the Day of the Lord is inevitable. Amos is emphatic that although various crises have served to remind Israel of God's judgment, Israel has refused to turn back to God and to practice justice and righteousness (4:6–12). The consequence of this refusal is exile and God's wrath and judgment.

God of Justice and Righteousness

The third theme upon which we will comment is the fact that God is a God of justice who seeks righteousness. The prophet Amos carefully develops Israel's lack of loyalty to the covenant. As noted by Birch, Amos' most frequent charge against Israel is that the wealthy and the powerful have exploited the poor and the weak (2:6–8; 4:1–3). They have also denied them access to the courts and bribed judges so that the complaints of the oppressed cannot be brought (5:10–13).[119] These powerful and privileged citizens also engaged in false and deceitful merchandizing (8:4–6). Amos

116. Birch, *Hosea, Joel and Amos*, 169.

117. Ibid., 27.

118. Mitchell, "Idea of God," 36–37.

119. Birch, *Hosea, Joel and Amos*, 170.

does not accept these practices. Rather, he upholds and tenaciously and passionately preaches the important principles of the nature of true worship as well as Israel's relationship with God. These principles are justice and righteousness, which the wealthy—particularly those who conduct pilgrimages to worship centers—have ignored (5:7, 15, 24; 6:12).

God's Outward Display of Worship

The fourth theme upon which we will comment is the theme of hypocritical worship, which is central in this study. Israel's God is served by worship without ethics. Amos' devoted prophecy centers on this topic. In his theology, the prophet exposes Israel's outward display of worship, which falls short of compensating for her lack of compassion, justice, love, neighborliness, and humanitarian spirit—the demands of the covenant ethos. Amos' God cannot be satisfied by sacrifices and pilgrimages to shrines without justice, righteousness, and moral accountability.[120] Amos believes that God punishes sins, external tributes, vain sacrifices, and misguided trust in pilgrimages (2:6–7; 4:4; 5:7–13; 7:7 8:4–7). God also rejects recalcitrant nations and judges them on the Day of the Lord (5:18–20).[121]

Hope for Salvation

Finally, in Amos there is the theme of hope for salvation, which will also be fully developed in the course of this study. Here we will briefly note that, due to lack of justice, righteousness, fear of the Lord, fidelity to the covenant, and ethical worship in Israel, Amos' message initially appears to be predominantly that of judgment and doom. But a second reading leads one to agree with Birch that "with almost no prior hint of divine mercy or grace, the book of Amos ends with promises of future restoration and blessings (9:11–15)."[122] In other words, although the message of judgment reverberates loudly in Amos, death is not God's final word, but life. Ebo draws the same hopeful conclusion in his 1985 study on Amos 9:11–15. He argues "(i) that the remnant motif is indigenous to Amos, (ii) that the

---

120. See Jeremias, *Amos*, 2–3 for additional discussion on the message of Amos.

121. Udoekpo (*Re-thinking the Day of YHWH*, 201–4) also has an extensive discussion on the Day of the LORD prophecy of Amos.

122. Birch, *Hosea, Joel and Amos*, 171.

visions manifest selective judgment, (iii) that Amos' exhortations have a corollary function indispensable beyond the judgement, and (iv) that the undiluted hope oracle in all probability goes back to Amos himself."[123]

Speaking of Amos' message of hope Ebo in his "Re-ordering Amos' Visions" writes, "such a kindly prophet would not, in my thinking, be in any hurry to proclaim a message of unrelieved doom. Amos would, therefore, have spent quite some time in a heart searching struggle with the one sending him on a mission."[124] In other words, there is a message of salvation in Amos: God forgives and shows mercy to Israel. He also restores and saves the remnant, all the descendants of David—that is, the fallen "booth of David" (9:11)—as demonstrated in the salvific concluding tone of the book (5:4; 9:11–15).[125]

Summary of Chapter 1

The goal of chapter one has been to demonstrate that Amos' understanding of God can hardly be separated from his background. His theology of worship is also interrelated to many other themes and theological trajectories that run throughout his prophecy, including election/responsibility, the sovereignty of God, justice and righteousness, judgment, worship of the true and one God alone, seeking God for life, and God's mercy and hope for salvation. This chapter also aimed at demonstrating that the prophet Amos (likely along with other prophets) had a profession prior to being called to challenge unethical worship in Israel. He lived in a particular land with rivers, hills, cities, and villages, like Tekoa. In other words, this study extends the reach of work by others discussed in this chapter to various contexts (geographical, historical, socio-cultural, economic, political, literary, and religious) that informed Amos' theological message, contexts which will be more fully developed in the chapters that follow.

123. See Ebo, "O that Jacob would survived," as cited in Holter, *Old Testament Research*, 29.

124. Ebo, "Re-ordering," 66.

125 Mays (*Amos*, 6–12) also confers an impressive detailed theological message of Amos.

2

Textual Critical Analysis
of Amos 5:1–27

Introduction

THIS CHAPTER FOCUSES CRITICALLY on the Masoretic Text of Amos 5 and on other texts, printed in variant versions.[1] It functions within the general purview of textual criticism.[2] In this context, the primary task of textual criticism is to clear away errors that may have crept into the Hebrew text of Amos 5 during its many years of transmission.[3] Granting that there are already many existing English translations of the book of Amos, the translation adopted in this study is not only provisional but helps shed light on how best to actualize and appropriate the meaning of Amos 5 for contemporary readers.[4]

Our basic textual point of departure is the Masoretic Text (MT) of Amos found in the Hebrew text of the Old Testament, the *Biblia Hebraica Stuttgartensia* (*BHS*), which is a revised edition of Rudolf Kittel's *Biblia Hebraica* (*BHK*).[5] Historically, both texts (*BHK* and *BHS*) were developed

---

1. For example, in the Septuaginta, the Peshitta, the Vulgata, and the Targum. My English quotations are taken from the NRSV.

2. Soulen and Soulen (*Biblical Criticism*, 189–92) has a detailed listing of the functions of textual criticism.

3. For comments on textual criticism, its detailed meaning, nature, and advantages, see Harrington, *Interpreting the Old Testament*, 97–106.

4. Harrington (*Interpreting the Old Testament*, 109–20) again presents recent English Translations while Binz (*Introduction to the Bible*, 15–23) gives the formal equivalence (word-for-word) and dynamic equivalence (meaning-for-meaning) translations of the Bible. Both approaches are adopted in this study.

5. Cf. Würthwein, *Text of the Old Testament*, 10.

from the *Leningrad Codex* (B19A), an eleventh-century CE manuscript of the Saltykov-Schedrin Public Library of St. Petersburg, Russia.[6]

Although there are some obscure portions of the text (e.g., Amos 5:25–27), the MT is the most reliable witness of the Hebrew OT. Anderson and Freedman are among those scholars who attest to its reliability. They attest that "for the most part . . . we find no serious alternative to the Masoretic Text. . . . [T]he study of the MT as it stands is a straightforward and intrinsically legitimate activity."[7]

Translation and Textual Critical Commentary on Amos 5

This section translates and comments on Amos 5. It is divided into three parts: (vv. 1–17, 18–20, and 21–27). The translation and commentary on verses 1–17 is further broken up into verses and smaller units (vv. 1–5, 6, 7, 8, 9, and 10–17) with the goal of being more accessible to readers. The numbering of the verses is provisional and does not necessarily follow the punctuation in the Hebrew Masoretic Text.

Translation and Textual Critical Commentary on vv. 1–17

As previously intimated, the point of departure for our commentary on this unit (5:1–17) is the MT of the book of Amos. The commentary focuses mainly on obscure concepts and terms that require clarification or reconciliation, especially when compared with other ancient versions such as the *Septuaginta* (LXX), *Peshitta* (Sry), *Vulgata* (Vg) or the Targum (Tg), and with the translations adapted in this study.

Verses 1–5 form the second to the largest block of our division of verses 1–17. Verses 1–5 read;

שמעו הוה אשר אנכי נשא עליכם v. 1a. Hear this word which I say to you,

קינה בית ישראל v. 1b. As a lamentation, O House of Israel

---

6. Ibid., 10–11.

7. Anderson and Freedman, *Amos*, 139–40.

נפלה לא־תוסיף קום בתולת ישראל	v. 2a. Fallen to rise no more, O virgin Israel
נטשה על־אדמתה	v. 2b. Forsaken on her land
אין מקימה	v. 2c With no one to raise her up
כי כה אמר אדני יהוה	v. 3a. For my Lord GOD has spoken
העיר היצאת אלף	v. 3b. The city that goes out with a thousand
תשאיר מאה	v. 3c. Shall have only a hundred left
והיוצאת מאה	v. 3d. And another marches out with a hundred
תשאיר עשרה כבית ישראל	v. 3e. Shall be left with only ten of Israel's house
כי כה אמר אדני יהוה ישראל	v. 4a. For thus says the LORD to the house of Israel
דרשוני והיו	v. 4b. Seek me,
ואל־תדרשו בית־אל	v. 5a. And do not seek Bethel
והגלגל לא תבאו ובאר שבע לא תעברו	v. 5b. Do not come to Gilgal nor to Beersheba
כי הגלגל גלה יגלה	v. 5c. For Gilgal shall go to exile
ובית־אל יהוה לאון	v. 5d. And Bethel shall become nothingness

Following this translation, the MT version of Amos 5:1a simply states, "Hear this word which I say to you" (שמעו את־הדבר הוה אשר אנכי נשא עליכם). In the LXX, κυριου ("of the Lord") is added to this initial statement to read, "Hear this word of the Lord." According to J. Alberto Soggin, this is done "wrongly, because it is the prophet who pronounces the discourse."[8] In spite of this objection, the addition can still be read positively since the essence of the prophet's pronouncement or lamentation is aimed to persuade his audience to worship the Lord alone or "seek YHWH" and "reject the sanctuaries

8. Soggin, *Prophet Amos*, 81.

in Beth El, Gilgal, and Beer Sheba."[9] In spite of their freedom and creativity, the prophets are nevertheless God's messengers and mouthpieces.

The expression בית ישראל ("O house of Israel") in verse 1b of the MT has parallels in verses 2a, 3e, and 4a. It is strongly debatable if this expression refers to the same groups in verse 2a, בתולת ישראל ("virgin Israel"), verse 3e, לבית ישראל ("of the house of Israel"), and in verse 4a. In the LXX it is attested as οικος Ισραηλ ("the house of Israel," v. 1b), παρθενος του Ισραηλ ("virgin of Israel," v.2a), τω οικω Ισραηλ ("to the house of Israel," v.3e), and τον οικον Ισραηλ ("the house of Israel," v. 4a).[10] In each of these cases, Israel is evidently the subject of lament. The "city that goes out" (העיר היצאת) in verse 3b is the same city "that marches out" (והיוצאת) in verse 3d. Again, the MT expression אדני יהוה ("my Lord YHWH/God") is attested as κυριος in the LXX and *Dominus Deus* in the *Vulgata* (Vg). These divine epithets, particularly as attested in the MT, serve to remind Amos' audience of the nature of the God they are called to worship: He is YHWH, whose dwelling place is in Jerusalem.[11]

Translation and Textual Analysis of v. 6

In verse 6 we read:

דרשו את־יהוה וחיו	v. 6a. Seek the LORD that you may live
פן־יצלח כאש בית יוסף	v. 6b. Lest, like fire he comes upon Joseph's house
ואכלה ואין־מכבה לבית־אל	v. 6c. And consumes Bethel with none to put it off

---

There are noticeable obscurities in verse 6, which some texts seek to emend. One such obscurity that has generated debate among scholars is the expression in verse 6b, פן־יצלח כאש ("lest it comes, rushes up/will burn like fire"). According to Soggin, the verb xlc ("to burn," *ṣālaḥ*) is normally used to indicate success, and its usage here is thus out of place. This has generated

---

9 Sweeney, "Amos," 232.

10. In the *Vulgata* (*Vg*) we have *domus Israhel* (v. 1b), *virgo Israhel* (v. 2a), *domo Israhel* (v. 3e) and *Dominus domui Israhel* (v. 4a).

11. Niehaus, "Amos," 418.

a number of emendations.[12] One such emendation is suggested in the MT apparatus and represented in aorist subjunctive third person singular as μη αναλαμψη ("so that it does not flame up") in the LXX.

In Hans Walter Wolff's view, the backdrop of the following MT reading ("lest like fire, he comes upon the house of Joseph"), פֶּן־יִצְלַח כָּאֵשׁ בֵּית יוֹסֵף, was none other than the general context of the message of the prophet Amos. That is, it is a warning with reference to those who were slow in worshiping God alone in the central shrine of Jerusalem.[13] Similar contextual attestations are found in the Targum, Peshitta, and particularly in the *Vulgata* (*ne forte conburatur ut ignis domus Ioseph*).

This fire that comes upon the house of Joseph (v. 6b) is also said to (לְבֵית־אֵל) "consume Bethel with none to put it off" (v. 6c). Also of interest is לְבֵית־אֵל (literally, "to the house of El"), which is the MT's prepositional phrase. The LXX renders this phrase as τω οικω Ισραηλ ("for the house of Israel"), partially due to the fact that "Bethel" in verse 6c of the MT is taken with a relational dative *lamed* preposition ל ("to," "with," "for") as לְבֵית־יִשְׂרָאֵל ("for the house of Israel"). This house of Israel, the chosen house of God, is called to repent from practicing idolatry. The house of Israel is invited to reject the northern sanctuaries as well as their leadership. In other words, Israel is God's bride, and she must return to worshiping the Lord in Judah.[14]

Translation and Textual Analysis of v. 7

In verse 7 we read:

הַהֹפְכִים לְלַעֲנָה מִשְׁפָּט	v. 7a. Woe, to you who turn justice to wormwood
וּצְדָקָה לָאָרֶץ הִנִּיחוּ	v. 7b. and put righteousness to the ground

---

Like the preceding text, verse 7 has its own textual difficulties. For example, the initial participle-*qal* הַהֹפְכִים (*hahopekîm*) in the MT ("'woe' to you who turn") seems not to have an explicit subject. As indicated in the

12. Soggin, *Prophet Amos*, 85.

13. Wolff, *Joel and Amos*, 228.

14. For some of these scholars see ibid.; Soggin, *Prophet Amos*, 85.

MT's apparatus, this is usually remedied by adding the "woe" (הוי), which is a genre of literary invective or an article of peril and lament (cf. 5:18; 6:1).[15] Others have argued that the particle (הו/י) could have been lost in verse 7a by *haplography*—that is, the scribes who copied or worked with these ancient manuscripts omitted the article accidentally. This affirms Wolff's position that "woe" (הוי) originally preceded the text, as attested in the MT (v. 7a).[16]

Besides the debates surrounding the "woe" (הוי) particle, further ambiguity is found in verse 7a with regard to the noun "wormwood"(ללענה) *Artermisia absinthium*. Some other places in the Hebrew Bible use the term: לענה ("bitter plant," "bitterness"), sometimes in a metaphorical sense (cf. Jer 9:14; Lam 3:15, 19; Prov 5:4; Amos 6:12). However, the LXX reads the entire verse 7 as κυριος ο ποιων εις υψος κριμα και διαιοσυνην εις γην εθηκεν ("it is he, the Lord, who is doing judgment from on high and who placed righteousness on earth"). Clearly the LXX not only makes God the subject of the phrase ("author of justice"), but it translates: ללענה as εις υψος ("into the high," "upward").[17]

As suggested in the MT apparatus, the LXX was probably influenced by the Hebrew *Vorlage*, למעלה ("upside down"). This *Vorlage* is also found in the book of Judges, which describes a loaf of barley bread whirling through the Midianite tent, causing the tent to turn upside down: ויהפכהו למעאלה ונפל האהל (Judg 7:13).[18] For the LXX of the text of Amos, it is truly the Lord who performs justice and righteousness (v. 7b). This, then, will be similar to the conclusions of the theology of the doxologies (vv. 8–9), which present the Lord as the maker of the universe (cf. Amos 9:5–6). Therefore, if we go by the poetic language of the MT, the ethical context and the metaphorical sense of the text (v. 7) must be taken into consideration.

In other places in the book of Amos (6:12), a very similar expression is found, whereby לענה ("wormwood") is in parallel to ראש ("poisonous plant"). But as insisted less poetically in other places (5:24), it is human beings who "poisonously" and unethically trample upon justice. They are the ones who unethically turn justice upside down, violating the *Torah*. In

15. For detailed commentary on the הוי ("woe") literary genre, see Udoekpo, *Rethinking the Day of YHWH*, 203.

16. Wolff, *Joel and Amos*, 229.

17. Cf. Soggin, *Prophet Amos*, 89.

18. Some of the vocalized texts throughout this study are taken from the *Bible Works 7: Software for Biblical Exegesis & Research,* mainly for clear illustrations. English quotations other than my translations are consistently from the NRSV.

doing so, they refuse to practice righteousness and abandon the worship of YHWH alone in the proper sanctuary of Jerusalem (v. 7b).[19]

Translation and Textual Analysis of v. 8

In verse 8 we read:

עשׂה כימה וכסיל	v. 8a. He who made Pleiades and Orion
והפך לבקר צלמות	v. 8b. And turns dark shadow into morning
ויום לילה החשׁך	v. 8c. And darkens day into night
הקסרא למי־הים	v. 8d. And summons the waters of the seas
וישׁפכם על־פני הארץ	v. 8e. And pours it upon the surface of the earth
יהוה שׁמו	v. 8f. And his name is LORD

The nature and authenticity of this verse are subjects of textual critical debate. Wolff, for instance, thinks "this isolated three-stress colon is apparently either secondary, or we must suppose that an originally parallel colon has been lost."[20] A close grammatical study of the above translation reveals that it is filled with participial phrases such as עשׂה ("he who made," v. 8c), והפך ("and the one who turns," v. 8b), and הקורא ("and the one who summons," v. 8d). It also seems to lack a beginning or an antecedent, at least literarily.[21]

Significantly, in verse 8f, the MT concludes with יהוה שׁמו ("and his name is LORD"). To this conclusion, several other medieval manuscripts add צבאות ("Hosts"). In particular, the LXX reads: ο θεος ο παντοκρατωρ ονομα αυτω ("God Almighty is his name"). Perhaps the LXX's addition is in harmony with the expression יהוה אלהי־צבאות שׁמו ("the LORD, the God

19. Niehaus, "Amos," 418.

20. Wolff, *Joel and Amos*, 229

21. Cf. Soggin, *Prophet Amos*, 90.

Almighty is his name"), which is found in Amos 4:13. In my view, the overall theological purpose of verse 8 is to highlight God's role as the creator of the universe. It also affirms God as the true source of justice and peace.

Translation and Textual Analysis of v. 9

In verse 9 we read:

המבליג שד על־עז   v. 9a. He brings destruction upon
the stronghold

ושד על־מבצר יבוא   v. 9b. And ruins upon the fortress

The text of verse 9, critically speaking, begins interestingly with the masculine singular of a *hiphil* participle המבליג ("he who causes/brings/flashes/ flares up"). There is a general consensus among scholars that the Hebrew root of this participle, בלג, means "to gleam," "to smile," or "to become cheerful/glad" (cf. Ps 39:14; Job 9:27; 10:20).[22] But this root meaning does not seem to fit into the overall theological context of Amos' message. As noted in the MT apparatus, this explains the emendation we find in the LXX as ο διαιρων ("he who distributes," "he who divides/apportions"), which is the present active participle and masculine singular of διαιρεω ("divide," "destroy," "distribute," or "apportion"). There is also a probability that the LXX's emendation is based on reading the Hebrew root word בלג as פליג ("separate" or "divide").

In other words, the entirety of verse 9: מפליג שד על־עז ושד על־מבצר יבוא, in the Hebrew MT could be read instead as "he who makes destruction separates the strongholds and brings ruins upon the fortress." This is why the entire verse is fully attested as ο διαιρων συντριμμον επ ισχυν και ταλαιπωριαν επι οχυρωμα επι οχυρωμα επαγων in the LXX. Even comparing these two readings (MT and LXX), the Hebrew *vorlage* יבוא (*qal*) or יביא in *hiphil* ("he brings," "causes to bring," or "will bring") translates the Greek επαγων ("who brings upon"). Soggin thinks this is a "makeshift solution."[23] Wolff, on the other hand, thinks "the repetition of שד ('violence,' 'ruin'), in the MT, violates the law of variation within *parallelismus membrorum* which is otherwise sustained throughout the hymnic pieces (4:13; 5:8;

22. Wolff, *Joel and Amos*, 230; Soggin, *Prophet Amos*, 90; Niehaus, "Amos," 419.

23. Soggin, *Prophet Amos*, 90.

9:5–6)."[24] In an attempt to resolve the ambiguities surrounding this text, many scholars still prefer to replace שד with שבר ("ruin," "breach") and pair it with יביא in *hiphil* ("to carry," "bring").[25] The theological import of this text, despite these ambiguities, will be fully highlighted in the exegetical section of this study.

Translation and Textual Analysis of vv. 10–17

This is the largest block of translation within the first subunit (vv. 1–17). Verses 10–17 read:

שׂנאו בשׁער מוכיח	v. 10a. They hate the one who reproves at the gate
ודבר תמים יתעבו	v. 10b. and abhor the one who speaks the truth
לכן יען בושסכם על־דל	v. 11a. Indeed, because you have trampled the poor
ומשׂאת־בר תקחו ממגו	v. 11b. and take from them levies of grain
בתי גזית בניתם	v. 11c. even though you have built houses of stone
ולא־תשׁבו בם	v. 11d. you shall not live in them
כרמי־חמד נטעתם	v. 11e. you have planted delightful vineyards
ולא תשׁתו את־יינם	v. 11f. but you shall not drink their wine
כי ידעתי רבים פשׁעיכם	v. 12a. For I know how many are your crimes
ועצמים חטאתיכם	v. 12b. and how countless your sins
צררי צדיק לקחי כפר	v. 12c. oppressing the righteous, you take bribes

24. Wolff, *Joel and Amos*, 230.

25. For a list of these scholars, see Soggin, *Prophet Amos*, 90–91.

ואביונים בשער הטו	v. 12d. subverting the needy at the gate
לכן המשכיל בעת ההיא ידם	v. 13a. Indeed the prudent man is silent at this time
כי עת רעה היא	v. 13b. for it is an evil time
דרשו־תוב ואל־רע למען תחין	v. 14a. Seek good, not evil so as to live
וייהי־כן אלהי־צבאות אתכם	v. 14b. the LORD, God of Hosts will be with you
כאשר אמרתם	v. 14c. according as you desire/claim!
שנאו־רע ואהבו טוב	v. 15a. Hate evil, love good,
והציגו בשע משפט	v. 15b. and let justice prevail
אולי יחנן יהוה אלהי־צבאות	v. 15c. perhaps, the LORD, God of Hosts pities
שארית יוסף	v. 15d. the remnants of Joseph
לכן כה־אמר יהוה אלהי צבסות אדני	v. 16a. Indeed, thus says the LORD, God of Hosts
בכל־רחבות מספד	v. 16b. in every street there shall be lamenting
ובכל־חוצות יאמרו הוי	v. 16c. in every field they shall cry Alas, woe!
וקראו אכר אל־אבל	v.16d. and shall call the plowman to mourning
ומספד אל־יודעי נהי	v. 16e. and skilled wailers to lament
ובכל־כרמים מספד	v. 17a. In all vineyards there shall be laments
כי־אעבר בקרבך אמר ישוה	v. 17b. when I cross through your midst, says the LORD.

In the above translation, verse 10 begins with the third person invective against those who persecute the just judges—a theme we saw earlier in verse 7. In verse 11, the MT attests בושסכם ("you have trampled"), but בוסכם ("your trampling") is also suggested in the same MT apparatus. Commenting on this, Niehaus writes, "בּוֹשֲׁסְכֶם is a *hapax legomenon* and probably a by-form of בוס (to trample), with an interchange of שׂ and ס, a frequent switch in the Old Testament."[26] Others have suggested that בוס be interpreted in connection with the Akkadian *šabāsū* ("requiring contributions in kind in terms of rent or taxes"). This practice was also familiar to Julius Wellhausen.[27]

Another ambiguous expression in this pericope (vv. 10–17) worthy of textual critical attention is ומשאת־בר ("an exaction or levy of grains"). First of all, the root of משאת ("exaction") is נשא ("lift"). Various English translations have been offered for this term, including "burden," "uplifting," "tax," or "exaction." The LXX prefers καὶ δῶρα ἐκλεκτα ("selecting gift"), perhaps with the sense of corruption and exploitation of the poor class, which is the subject of the entire passage.

Verse 12 also has textual challenges concerning the feminine plural noun, חַטּאתיכֶם; ("your crimes/sins") with the masculine predicate of וַעֲצמים ("and countless, numerous/mighty"). This is why, and as indicated in the MT apparatus, some scholars would prefer חתּאֵיכֶם; having *aleph* pointed with a *sere* instead of a defective *holem*, while *tau* is dropped.[28] The LXX retains the feminine expression to read: καὶ ισχυραι αι αμαρτιαι υμων ("and how strong your sins"). According to Soggin, inconsistencies of this type between the subject and the noun predicate are frequent, especially if the latter precedes the former. Above all, emendation of this sort, he thinks, may not be necessary.[29] In verses 14–15, the reading of יהוה אלהי־צבאות ("the LORD God of Hosts") is an addition (cf. 4:13), which is translated in the LXX as κυριος ο θεος παντοκρατωρ ("the Lord God the Almighty").

In the MT, verse 16a reads יהוה אלהי צבסות אדני ("the LORD God of Hosts"). This is rendered as ο θεος παντοκρατωρ in the LXX. Following the suggestion of the MT apparatus, a closer look indicates that אדני ("lord") is absent both in the LXX and in the Peshitta (Syr). Wolff attributes this absence to an "intermediary stage between the style of Amos, which was probably quite terse, and the liturgical breadth of the final redaction."[30] Fur-

---

26. Niehaus, "Amos," 420.

27. Soggin, *Prophet Amos*, 89.

28. Wolff, *Joel and Amos*, 230.

29. Soggin, *Prophet Amos*, 90.

30. Wolff, *Joel and Amos*, 231.

thermore, in verse 16b the original reading of the expression ומספד אל־יודעי ("and skilled wailers to lament") could be read as אל־ומספד ("and to lament"), which is in keeping with the preceding parallel colon in verse 16d. The transposition of אל, Wolff suggests, can be interpreted as an error by those who copied the text, since the LXX also simply reads και κοπετον και εις ειδοτας θρηνον ("and mourning and those knowing how to lament").[31]

In verse 17a, the MT reads ובכל־כרמים מספד ("and in all vineyards there shall be lamenting"), while the LXX attests και εν πασαις οδοις κοπετος ("and in all ways there shall be lamentation"). This idiomatic meaning harkens back to Exodus 12:2, where the Lord passes through the land of Pharaoh with his sword of judgment.[32] This brings us to another important section of the text that focuses on the prophetic woes of judgment and on the cultic leadership in Israel, with emphasis on the Day of the Lord (Amos 5:18–20).

Translation and Textual Analysis of vv. 18–20

This judgment unit reads:

הוי המתאוים את־יום יהוה	v. 18a. Misfortunes! For you who desire the day of the Lord
למה־זה לכם יום יהוה	v. 18b. what is this day of the Lord for you?
הוא־חשך ולא־אור	v. 18c. this (day) shall be darkness, not light
כאשר ינוס איש מפני הארי	v.19a. It is as a man who escapes from the lion
ופגעו הדב	v. 19b. but he is attacked by a bear
ובא הבית	v. 19c. then coming home
וסמך ידו על־הקיר	v. 19d. and leans his hand on the wall
ונשכו הנחש	v. 19e. but he is bitten by a snake

---

31. Ibid., 231.
32. Niehaus, "Amos," 425–26.

הלא־חשך יום יהוה ולא־אור   v. 20a. Is not the day of the Lord
darkness and not light?

ואפל ולא־נגה לו   v. 20b. (and) Gloomy and no
brightness to it?

This section has two major verses that can be analyzed. The initial verse of Amos 5:18a begins with הוי ("woe/misfortune"). This has attracted many scholarly comments, particularly with reference to the MT phrase הוא־חשך ("this shall be darkness") in verse 18c. The LXX renders this phrase και αυτη εστιν σκοτος ("and this is darkness").[33] In Wolff's observation, the LXX reading αυτη ("this") does not understand the MT זה ("this") of verse 18b as an intensification of the interrogative למה ("what"). Rather, it simply understands it as a demonstrative pronoun.[34] Regardless of this ambiguity, verse 18 as a whole anticipates verse 20.[35]

Verse 19 continues with the imagery of dangers, "as a man escapes from the lion he is attacked by a bear" (v. 19b). For the phrase in verse 19c ובא הבית ("and coming home/ to the house"), the LXX attests εις τον οικον αυτου ("into his house/home"). Here, הבית ("the house") is read as ביתו (οικον αυτου, "his house"), with reference to the man who had just returned home (v. 19a).

Moreover, it is worth noting that in the LXX's version of the entire verse 20, reference is made to the Day of the Lord of verse 18c. It reads as follows: ουχι σκοτος η ημερα του κυριου και ου φως και γνοφος ουκ εχων φεγγος αυτη ("Is the Day of the Lord darkness and not light, gloomy and no brightness in it?"). In the LXX, attributes of the Day of the Lord, "darkness, light, gloomy and brightness," are clearly understood as nouns. But we have the *waw-conjunction* ו ("and") on ואפל ("gloomy"). As to the concluding לו ("to it") of verse 20b, Wolff explains that it satisfactorily indicates that we are dealing with an independent nominal sentence.[36] This nominal sentence introduces us to the next and last section of this textual commentary (vv. 21–27), with emphasis on ethical worship and rejection of acts of injustice.

---

33. Detailed comments on Amos 5:1–20 will be developed in the exegetical section.

34. Wolff, *Joel and Amos*, 253.

35. Soggin, *Prophet Amos*, 94.

36. Wolff, *Joel and Amos*, 254.

Translation and Textual Analysis of vv. 21–27

This final prophetic units reads:

שנאתי מאסתי חגיכם	v. 21a. I hate, and I refuse your festival gathering
ולא אריח בצרתיכם	v. 21b. and I take no delight in your assemblies
כי אם תעלו לי עלות	v. 22a. Even if you offer me burnt offering
ומנחתיכם לא ארצה	v. 22b. and your gift offering, I will not be pleased
ושלם מריאיכם לא אביט	v. 22c. your peace offering from your fatling, I will not look
הסר מעלי המון שריך	v. 23a. Take away from me the noise of your song
וזמרת נבליך לא אשמע	v. 23b. I will not listen to the melody of your instrument
ויגל כמים משפט	v. 24a. But let justice roll along like water
וצדקה כנחל איתן	v. 24b. and righteousness like an ever-flowing wadi/stream
הזבחים ומנחה הגשתם לי	v. 25a. Sacrifices and offering did you bring to me
במדבר	v. 25b. in the wilderness
ארבעים שנה בית ישראל	v. 25c. forty years, O house of Israel
נשאתם את סכות מלככם	v. 26a. You shall take up Sakkut your king
ואת כיון צלמיכם כוכב אלהיכם	v. 26b. and Kaiwan your images, your star god
אשר עשיתם לכם	v. 26c. which you have made for yourselves

והגליתי אתכם מהלאה   v. 27a. Then I will take you towards there (exile)

לדמשק אמר יהוה   v. 27b. into Damascus, says YHWH

אלהי צבאות שמו   v. 27c. the God of Hosts is his name.

The last two major sections of Amos 5 began with the messenger formula, "hear these words" (v. 1a), and the prophetic warning, "woe/misfortune," (v. 18a), respectively. Verse 21 builds on this but uses a verbal compilation of the Lord's rejection of bad worship. This compilation forms a hendiadys: שנאתי מאסתי ("I hate and I refuse/reject").[37]

This is followed by the colon, כי אם תעלו לי עלות ("even if you offer me burnt offering"), which many scholars see as disturbing the strict parallelism of verses 21–24.[38]

Textual Analysis of v. 22

The MT apparatus suggests that some words or phrases must have been omitted after עלות ("burnt offerings") in verse 22a. According to Wolff, the pattern of the sentence is also broken by its change of subject from first person singular in verses 21–22a to the second person plural in verse 22b. Apart from this change of subject and persons, there is also the noticeable absence of a pronominal suffix on עלות ("burnt offerings"), which is a feminine plural. Additionally, the MT suggests that ושלם ("and the peace offering/sacrifice") was probably intended by the scribes as a construct, ושלמי ("and the sacrifice of peace/well-being").[39]

Textual Analysis of vv. 23–24

Verses 23–24 have several textual and syntactical problems. The text of verse 23a, for instance, says הסר מעלי המון שריך ("take away from me the noise of

37. See Soulen and Soulen (*Biblical Criticism*, 72) where a hendiadys is actually explained with the Greek meaning, "one through two [words]." It is the name for "a form of syntactic coordination in which two or more terms are joined by the use of 'and' (*kai*), rather than by subordinating one term to another." However, in the case of the MT text of Amos 21a, the "and" (ו) is actually absent. My translation has added the "and."

38. Cf. Soggin, *Prophet Amos*, 97; Wolff, *Joel and Amos*, 259.

39. Wolff, *Joel and Amos*, 259.

your song"). In this sentence, הסר ("take away") is in the singular, as is שריך ("your song" with a singular suffix), in contrast to the plural expressions in verses 21–22. Even נבליך ("your instrument/jar") is surprisingly presented in the singular (v. 23b). These could have been pluralized as הסירו ("take away," pl.), שיריכם ("your songs"), and נבליכם ("your jars/instruments"). According to Wolff, "the transition to the singular along with the transition to an imperative construction is to be explained on the basis of dependence of the new formal element upon another genre."[40] In spite of these grammatical changes, verse 24 is considered a theological conclusion to verses 21–23. It makes a transition from the rejection of worship without ethics to contrasting some positive statements in verses 25–27, which many scholars regard as secondary.[41] This will be fully discussed later in this study.

TEXTUAL ANALYSIS OF VV. 25–27

This subunit (vv. 25–57) begins in verse 25a with an interrogative particle ה ("did"), which serves as a rhetorical tool with regard to the presentation of sacrifices and offerings (הזבחים ומנחה) to the Lord. But the occurrence of מנחה ("offering") in the feminine singular after the masculine plural form מנחריכם ("your offerings") in the MT of verse 22b is fascinating. As noted in the MT apparatus, some manuscripts omit the singular, while others retain it. In the original or unrevised form of the LXX, "the wilderness" (במדבר, εν τη ερημω), for instance, is probably not attested.[42] If it is attested, it is a conjecture or a later addition.[43]

Another textual element in this section worth commenting on is the expression "the house of Israel" (v. 25c). In Theodotion's Greek Translation of the Old Testament (θ'), λεγει κυριος ("thus says the Lord") is added to the ending.[44] Perhaps this continues the messenger or divine oracle formula נאם יהוה ("thus says the LORD"), which is common in the book of Amos.[45]

40. Ibid.

41. Soggin, *Prophet Amos*, 97.

42. See also the LXX textual apparatus.

43. Soggin (*Prophet Amos*, 98); Wolff (*Joel and Amos*, 260) have extensive arguments on this subject.

44. Andersen and Freedman, *Amos*, 469.

45. Wolff (*Joel and Amos*, 143) notes that this formula occurs about twenty-one times in Amos. It occurs thirteen times in the conclusion of an oracle (2:11; 16; 3:15; 4:3, 5, 6, 7, 8, 9, 10, 11; 9:7, 8, 12), three times in a medial position (3:10; 6:14; 8:3), and five times with other formulas (3:13; 6:8; 8:9, 11; 9:13).

Verse 26a is another difficult text that should not go unnoticed. First of all, it has וּנְשָׂאתֶם ("you shall take up") at the beginning of the sentence. The MT apparatus suggests pointing this term as ונשסתם. ("and you shall take up"), which is represented in the LXX as καὶ ἀνελάβετε ("and you take up"). Secondly, "Sikkuth" and "Kiyyun" are vocalized and pronounced differently in various texts. For example, in the LXX, סכות מלכבם is translated as τὴν σκηνὴν τοῦ Μολοχ ("the tent of Molech"). The implication is that סֻּכַּת u (sukkat) is taken to mean "hut," "tent," or "booth." Some have viewed it with reference to an Akkadian deity, which raises the question of whether the proper vocalization is סכּוּת (sakkuth) or the MT's סכּוּ i (sikkuth), with the intention of reminding readers of שִׁקוּץ. ("detested thing").[46]

Jeffrey Niehaus alternatively argues that סכּוּת (sakkuth) rather than the MT's סכּוּ (sikkuth) is wrongly presented in the LXX as σκηνὴν ("tent," "hut," or "booth"), and by the *Vulgata* as *tabernaculum*. He stresses that Sakkuth was the name of a Syrian god of war, Adar. Another misrepresentation, in Niehaus' view, is that the LXX renders מלכבם ("your king") as Moloc ("Molech"). Niehaus suggests that Sakkuth is called a king because Sakkuth basically means, "king of decision"—that is, "chief arbiter" of war.[47]

A few difficulties are associated with verse 26b. These have to do especially with כיון (kêwān) or כיון (kiyyôn). A number of scholars suggest that the LXX's Ραιφαν appears to be an inner Greek corruption of the Hebrew (cf. Ραιφαν in Acts 7:43). In Assyrian, Syriac, and Arabic, this is called *ka-ai-va-nu* (Saturn's name), *ke'wan*, and *kaiwan*, respectively.[48]

In addition, צלמיכם ("your images") is used with reference to several idols found in the Old Testament. For example, in the book of Numbers we read, "You shall drive out all the inhabitants of the land from before you, destroy all their figured stones, destroy all their cast images (כָּל־צַלְמֵי מַסֵּכֹתָם), and demolish all their high places" (Num 33:52 NRSV). Later, in 2 Kings, we read, "Then all the people of the land went to the house of Baal, and tore it down; his altars and his images (וְאֶת־צְלָמָיו) they broke in pieces" (2 Kgs 11:18; cf. Ezek 7:20). In light of these OT references, Niehaus argues that since the word "images" is in the plural, the referent is to both Sakuth and Kaiwan, which human beings have unfortunately made for their worship.[49]

---

46. Wolff, *Joel and Amos*, 260.

47. Niehaus, "Amos," 433.

48. Wolff, *Joel and Amos*, 260; Niehaus, "Amos," 434.

49. Niehaus, "Amos," 434.

Finally, in verse 27c of the MT we read: אלהי צבאות שמו ("The God of Hosts is his name"). The LXX characteristically renders this phrase as ο θεος ο παντοκρατωρ ονομα αυτω ("God the Almighty is his name"). The MT apparatus suggests this short messenger formula is an addition grafted to meet the pattern found elsewhere in the text of Amos (1:5, 8, 15; 2:3; 5:17).

Summary of Chapter 2

As intimated earlier, this chapter has focused critically on the text of Amos that is printed in ancient and variant versions. Our textual criticism of Amos 5, among other things, aimed at clearing errors in the manuscript tradition in an effort to reach the most pristine text possible. Therefore, in what precedes we have assembled the variant readings of the text of Amos 5, especially the parts that tend to present some obscurities. Our attention was specifically directed toward those texts that did not flow well due to unintentional changes or deliberate emendations made in an attempt to correct or harmonize the text.

Those obscurities that we addressed have led scholars to present various theories and readings of the text of Amos. The correctness of the readings depended on how much authority we assigned to the inventory of readings that stand some chance of being original, from the Hebrew, Greek, and other ancient versions, and to the sense behind them. In biblical exegesis of this nature, both excessive literalism, fundamentalism, and undue liberality in translation are usually forms of extremism that can distort the true meaning of a given text—in this case, the theology of worship in Amos. This study has sought to avoid those extremes but has adhered, where necessary, to the "formal equivalence" (word-for-word) and "dynamic equivalence" (meaning-for meaning) forms of translation.[50] With these translation, the literary style, idiomatic and metaphorical traditions, the theology behind the worship critique in Amos 5 will be applied to our contemporary society. Before advancing to the analysis of its structure (chap. 4) and the exegesis of Amos 5 (chap. 5) we will consider its relationship to the other eleven Minor Prophets.

---

50. Binz (*Introduction to the Bible,* 19–23) has interesting comments on "formal" and "dynamic" equivalence(s) as earlier noted.

3

The Study of the Place of the Book of Amos in the Twelve Minor Prophets

Introduction

READING THE TWELVE MINOR Prophets as a composite unit is increasingly getting attention among scholars. Such scholars have noticed signs of editorial activities, literary techniques (e.g., *inclusio*, repetition, catchwords, framing devices, motifs), and shared themes (e.g., worship, the Day of the Lord, justice, and righteousness) among the Minor Prophets. This chapter concentrates on this unity approach. It attempts to emphasize the relationship of Amos 5 with the other books of the Minor Prophets, particularly as uniquely seen through their shared notion of the Day of the Lord and its implications for the ethical worship of the Lord with justice and righteousness.

The Twelve Minor Prophets and the Place of Amos in It

Over the past few decades, scholars have debated whether the Twelve should be studied as a literary whole or as twelve individual books. James D. Nogalski and Marvin A. Sweeney observed that the champions of nineteenth- and twentieth-century scholarship tended to read the Twelve diachronically as individual books, with emphasis on their individual historical backgrounds. As time passed, and with the advent of redaction criticism—which sought to assess the final form of biblical texts and discover their compositional history—newer forms of literary criticism, including synchronic reading, emerged. Nogalski and Sweeney insist that contemporary scholarship concentrates on reading the Twelve as a single, unified biblical text with shared themes.[1] There are many reasons for this unified reading, which offers enormous advantages.

Advantages of a Holistic Reading of the Twelve

Those who champion the holistic reading of Amos and the Minor Prophets do not deny the value of the Twelve as individual books with unique historical backdrops and theological messages. Rather, they argue that a unified reading provides, among other benefits, a canonical and deeper theological perspective on the texts. For our study, it also supplements theological and pastoral insights on the tradition of the ethics of worship that might be missed by narrowing this investigation to a diachronic reading of Amos 5.

Additional Reasons for a Holistic Reading

Scholars who argue for a unified reading posit various reasons and supporting arguments for doing so, ranging from citing how Amos and the rest of the Twelve differ from the Major Prophets or commenting on their positions in the canon. As mentioned earlier, scholars have also noticed signs of editorial activities, such as *inclusio*, repetition, framing devices, motifs, catchwords, and shared themes within the Twelve.

On this note, Nogalski and Sweeney have recently argued that in Jewish and Christian Bibles, the Twelve (of which Amos is a part) functions as a collection of individual books. For example, in the MT, Hosea, Joel, Amos, Obadiah, Jonah, Micah, Nahum, Habakkuk, Zephaniah, Haggai, Zechariah, and Malachi commonly begin with a superscription—a kind of narrative introduction. Moreover, they stand distinct from the Major Prophets such as Isaiah, Jeremiah, Ezekiel, and Daniel.

Secondly, various traditions considered the Twelve as a whole, including the Jewish/Aramaic traditions, Christian/Greek traditions, the Deuterocanonical Ben Sira 49:10, and the Talmudic traditions.[2] So also did Jerome and the first-century CE Jewish historian Flavius Josephus. This belief is particularly evident in Jerome's introductory section of the Latin

---

1. For some of these studies See, Nogalski and Sweeney, "Preface," vii–ix; Udoekpo, *Re-thinking the Day of YHWH*, 230–34; Ko, "Ordering of the Twelve," 315–32.

2. The Twelve is popularly known as *těrê ăśār* in the Aramaic tradition and *'oi dōdekaprophētai* or *ton dōdekaprophēton* in Christian/Greek Traditions.

Vulgate, where he declares with his theological pen, *unum librum esse dou-decim Prophetarum* ("the Twelve Prophets are one book").[3]

Observations regarding Amos' position in the Twelve have also been used as support for this unified approach. Amos holds the third position in the MT's ordering of the Twelve (Hosea, Joel, Amos, Obadiah, Jonah, Micah, Nahum, Habakkuk, Zephaniah, Haggai, Zechariah, and Malachi), and second in the LXX ordering (Hosea, Amos, Micah, Joel, Obadiah, Jonah, Nahum, Habakkuk, Zephaniah, Haggai, Zechariah, and Malachi).

Regardless of Amos' position in the MT and LXX, scholars such as Ehud Ben Zvi have argued that the Twelve, including Amos, were preserved as a whole since antiquity. However, Ben Zvi is not sure whether these books were meant to be read as a coherent unit. In his view, the Twelve are distinct from one another but have a shared discourse and a common linguistic heritage, as well as shared literary and ideological/theological features. These features include textually-inscribed requests to the readership of these prophetic books to understand each book and prophetic personage as distinct from others.[4]

Other scholars have noticed signs of editorial, historical, and theological activities that support the coherent reading of the Twelve as a unit. Nogalski for instance, identifies several types of intertextual features that bind Amos with the rest of the Twelve, including quotations, allusions, catchwords, motifs, and framing devices.[5] A quotation includes the use of already existing phrases, sentences, or paragraphs taken from another source. For example, Obadiah 1–5 tends to quote Amos 9:1–15, while Joel 4:16 modifies Amos 1:2: "The LORD roars from Zion and utters his words from Jerusalem; the pastures of the shepherd wither, and the top of Carmel dries up."[6]

I would like to comment further on the relationship between Amos 9 and Obadiah in light of Nogalski's illustration.[7] Nogalski notices that a substantial number of changes in the prophecy of Obadiah are best classified as structural alterations on the basis of Amos 9:1ff. These changes do not alter the substance of the parallel passage so much as they adapt the framework of the booklet in order to synchronize more closely to Amos

3. Nogalski and Sweeney, "Preface," viii–ix.

4. Zvi, "Twelve Prophetic Books or 'The Twelve,'" 125–56.

5. Nogalski, "Intertextuality," 104–24.

6. Ibid., 103–8.

7 Nogalski, *Redactional Processes*, 61–71.

9:1ff. These changes, he observes, announce judgment upon Edom in terms that parallel the judgment upon Israel in Amos 9:1ff. Obadiah strengthens the description since the promise of Amos (vv. 11–15) is in opposition to the judgment against Israel (vv. vv.1–4), while Edom receives no such reprieve in Obadiah.[8]

The connection between Obadiah and Amos can be seen even in the superscription. The introductory element in Obadiah 1 (the "vision" [חזון]of Obadiah) rhymes with that of Amos 9:1ff. Moreover, the phrase "I will bring you down" commonly appears in both Amos 9 and Obadiah. Nogalski also believes that Obadiah 5 functions as a thematic summary of Amos 9:7–10, which is characterized by the themes of destruction and a remnant.[9] Obadiah 5 also contains two rhetorical questions that begin with the particle הלוא ("if," "surely"), which is also found in Amos 9:7. Nogalski further notes that the formula הלוא ביום ההוא נאם־יהוה ("surely, on that day, thus says the LORD") in Obadiah 8 also appears in Amos 9:7; 11.[10] Additionally, the theological perspective of Obadiah 16, 17–21 also appears in the insertion of Amos 5: 12a. And the theological motif shared by both texts portrays the restoration of the Davidic kingdom for those who seek to worship the Lord in justice and righteousness—a theme that dominates Amos 5.

There are also allusions among the Twelve, but with some subjectivism in terms of the use of concepts and phrases. For example, the root רעש ("shake," "quake") occurs about ten times in the Twelve, either in the context of the Lord's judgment (Joel 2:10; 4:16; Amos 1:1; 9:1; Nah 1:5; 3:2; Hag 2:6, 7, 21; Zech 14:5) or in the context of the earthquake in the time of Uzziah (Amos 1:1; Zech 14:5).[11] We further discover the beauty of the unity of the Twelve by examining catchwords (*Stichwörter*), which usually appear at the beginning and concluding passages of the Twelve. For example, there is a link between Joel 4:18 and Amos 9:13 in portraying the fertility of the land after the restoration of the faithful remnant. Joel's text reads, "In that day the mountains shall drip sweet wine, the hills shall flow with milk, and all the stream beds of Judah shall flow with water; a fountain shall come forth from the house of the LORD and water the Wadi Shittim." Amos follows closely in reading, "the time is surely coming, says the LORD, when the

---

8. Nogalski, *Redactional Processes,* 64.

9. Ibid., 66.

10. Ibid., 67.

11. Nogalski, "Intertextuality," 108–11.

one who plows shall overtake the one who reaps, and the trader of grapes the one who sows the seed; the mountains shall drip sweet wine, and all the hills shall flow with it." The unity in the seams of these two texts cannot be overlooked.[12] Ko, who follows Nogalski's study on catchwords, observes that Nogalski emphasizes the link between Amos 9:12, where the name "Edom" is mentioned, and a similar reference in Joel 4:19. This catchword is repeated in Obadiah 1 (see previous paragraphs).

Similarly, Jonah 4:2 and Micah 7:18 conclude with a partial link to the forgiving or compassionate nature of God in Exodus 34:6–7 (cf. Nah 1:2–3), while the command "but the LORD is in the holy temple, let all the earth keep silence before him!" is repeated in Zephaniah 1:7.[13] Terms like "inhabitants" (Hos 14:8; Joel 1:2), "vine" (Hos 14:8; Joel 1:7, 12), "wine" (Hos 14:8; Joel 1:5), and "grain" (Hos 14:8; Joel 1:10) are shared in Hosea and Joel, which strengthen agricultural ties between Hosea, Joel, and the rest of the Twelve.[14]

Apart from the intertextual features of quotations, allusions, and catchwords, several other motifs and themes link the book of Amos with the other books of the Twelve. A good example is the motif of judgment. In Joel, the metaphor of locusts provides the imagery of divine judgment, which can also come in the form of fire, drought, and enemy attack (Joel 1–2). Similar metaphors appear in other passages of the Twelve (Amos 4:9; Nah 3:16; Hab 1:9; Mal 3:10).[15] Besides the motif of judgment, themes such as theodicy, restoration of fortunes, and the Day of the Lord give coherence to and serve as common links between Amos and the rest of the Twelve.

Another scholar David L. Petersen not only argues for the existence of the Twelve based on scribal practice, size, and chronological order, but he also affirms Nogalski's views on catchwords and the presence of the common theme of the Day of the LORD (יום יהוה) in the Twelve. In Petersen's view, just as Isaiah focuses on Zion, Jeremiah on the rhetoric of laments, and Ezekiel on the glory of the Lord, the Twelve as a whole focuses on

---

12. Cf. Ko, "Ordering of the Twelve," 317.

13. Ibid.

14. Nogalski ("Intertextuality," 113–16) argues that agricultural motifs such as grain, wine, oil, wool, linen, vines, figs, olives, and food appear extensively in the Twelve (cf. Hos 2; 14; Joel 1:2—2:17; 4:19; Amos 4:6–11; 9:13–14; Hab 3:17; Hag 1:6, 10–11; 2:15–19; Zech 8:12; Mal 3:8–11). Similar argument in made in Nogalski, "Joel as a 'Literary Anchor,'" 91–109.

15. Nogalski, "Intertextuality," 117–18.

the Day of the Lord (יום יהוה).[16] This theme, he insists, is first explicitly introduced in Amos 5:18–20 and was later adapted in the remaining books of the Twelve (Hos, 9:5; Joel 3:4; Obad 15; Mic 2:4; Hab 3:16; Zeph 1:7–16; Hag 2:23; Zech 14:1; Mal 4:1), with the exception of Jonah and Nahum, where it is found implicitly (e.g., Nah 1:7).[17]

Rolf Rendtorff has advanced similar arguments regarding the unifying motif of the Day of the Lord (יום יהוה) in the Twelve, of which Amos forms a significant part. Rendtorff argues that the expression "a day of battle" in Amos 1:14 does not differ dramatically from the theological notion of the Day of the Lord (יום יהוה) expressed in Amos 5:18–20.[18] In light of all these commonalities, Aaron Schart asserts that no other prophetic book than the Twelve contains as many passages about this day. In his view, the Day of the Lord passages are at the same time central to the overall structure.[19]

An additional literary feature that binds Amos to the rest of the Twelve is what Nogalski broadly calls "framing devices." According to him, the most popular framing devices within the Twelve are superscriptions, genre, structural parallels, juxtaposition of catchwords, and canonical allusions. Superscriptions play a pivotal role in the macrostructure of the Twelve, especially in Hosea, Amos, Micah, Zephaniah, and Haggai, where they have chronological indicators.[20] In other words, similar introductory titles are found in these books, including Amos. With this commonality one gets the sense of the unity of the Twelve and that which it intends to communicate—namely, the common history of prophecy.[21]

Regarding the repetition of genre, Nogalski gives the example of the appearance of the "vision" of Obadiah 1–5 with the pattern of Amos 9:1–4, which was discussed above.[22] Structural parallels that attest to the unity of the Twelve are found in Amos 9, Obadiah, Nahum 3, and Habakkuk 1.[23] The Hosea–Joel connection mentioned earlier serves as a good example of catchword devices (cf. Zeph 3:18–19; Hag 1:2). Lastly, Nogalski observes

---

16 Petersen, "Book of the Twelve?," 3–10.

17. Ibid., 9.

18. Rendtorff, "Theological Unity," 75–87.

19 Schart, "Reconstructing," 40–41; Udoekpo, *Re-thinking the Day of YHWH*, 232.

20. Nogalski, "Intertextuality," 118–19.

21. Jones, *Formation of the Twelve*, 129–69; Schart, *Entstehung des Zwölfprophetenbuchs*, 290.

22. Ibid, 120; Nogalski, *Redactional Processes*, 61–65.

23. Nogalski, "Intertextuality," 122.

that canonical framing allusions are evident in Malachi 3:22, which clearly alludes to Joshua 1:2, 7.[24]

Paul R. House writes of Amos' unifying role within the Twelve. His argument stems mainly from the history of Israel. For House, the theological content of this history parallels the tripartite formula of sin, punishment, and restoration that characterizes the Twelve. In this case, the books of Hosea, Joel, Amos, Obadiah, Jonah, and Micah focus on sin, while Nahum, Habakkuk, and Zephaniah (the late pre-exilic prophets) cover the theme of punishment or judgment of those sins. The third division, composed of Haggai, Zechariah, and Malachi, emphasizes the theme of the restoration of the fortunes of Israel.[25]

The book of Amos occupies an important place in the Twelve. While it is important to read the books of the Twelve individually, the common themes, motifs, and editorial activities in the Twelve encourage the appreciation of the Twelve as a unity. As noted in Sweeney's comments earlier in this section, this new holistic approach to the Twelve as a literary unity is not designed to replace the consideration of the texts that comprise the Twelve as individual books. Rather, this new way of reading the Twelve presents a refreshing and renewed way of embracing a non-fragmented interpretation of the prophetic messages, supported by the discussed intertextual evidences in the Twelve.[26]

In my judgment, Nogalski in particular has done a very good job of describing the "dovetailing genre from Hosea to Joel and Amos," which I do not consider necessary to repeat here.[27] It is worth noting that Joel 4:1–21, especially verse 16 in the MT (ויהוה מציון ישאג), transitorily presents a profound eschatological message in Amos 1:2: "The Lord will roar from Zion" (יהוה מציון ישאג) in Judah.

The backdrop of these premises is the fact that Israel's prophets as a whole, especially the Twelve, embarked on explaining the historical experience of the fall of the northern and southern kingdoms (in 722 BCE and 587 BCE, respectively). The prophets approached this mission in light of Israel's covenant relationship with YHWH, calling for obedience, faithfulness, and the worship of YHWH alone in a centralized place at Zion (Exod

---

24 Ibid., 123–24.

25. House, *The Unity of the Twelve*, 63–109.

26. Sweeney, "Sequence and Interpretation in the Book of the Twelve," 49–50.

27. See Nogalski, "Joel as 'Literary Anchor,'" 94–99.

20:22–23:33; Deut 12; 2 Sam 7).[28] In other words, the prophets, including Amos, view Israel's history as a dynamic covenant relationship between YHWH and Israel—an antecedent theme dear to the hearts of Deuteronomistic historians (Deut–2 Kgs).[29] By challenging Israel's unfaithfulness and infidelities (Hos 4:1–3), the crimes of the priests (vv. 4–10), the crimes of the leaders (Hos 5:1–2), and insincere conversion (Hos 5:8–6:7), Hosea, Joel, and Amos set the stage for the rest of the prophetic messages. They also warn of the impending divine judgment without repentance (Hos 14:2–9).[30]

This theme of divine judgment found in Hosea is central to Joel's metaphor of the locusts (Joel 1–2) as well as Amos' theology of the Day of the Lord (Amos 5:18–20). In Amos, this divine judgment is proclaimed against evil doers (1:1–2:16; 3:8), oppressors of the poor (3:9–4:3; 8:4–10), abusers of religion, worship centers, and covenant breakers. They are the ones who are invited not only to be aware of the Day of the Lord, but to seek the Lord (5:1–27).

Amos 5, the Twelve, and the Day of the Lord

The strong relationship Amos 5 has with the other books of the Minor Prophets is uniquely evident in the notion of the Day of the Lord, which Amos shares with the other books of the Twelve. The Day of the Lord is an "umbrella" theological concept that integrates themes found in the other books of the Minor Prophets, such as justice, righteousness, mercy, repentance, exhortations to "seek the Lord" alone, judgment, eschatology, and hope of salvation, into a coherent and unified scenario. For instance, the exhortation to "seek the LORD" in Amos (5:4–6,14–25, 24) is found in different forms and places throughout the other books of the Minor Prophets (e.g., Hos 2:2–4; 4:15; 6:6; 10:12; 12:7; 14:2–4; Mic 6:6–8; Zeph 2:1–3). Often these different forms of occurrences of "seek the LORD" are aimed at dashing the false hope of those who rely on empty worship (Amos 5:21–27) or have broken the covenant relationship long established by God with Israel.

Hunter has studied the exhortation "seek the LORD" in Hosea as well as in Amos.[31] He notes that there is a general consensus among scholars

---

28. Chisholm, "Theology of the Minor Prophets," 399.

29. Ko, "Ordering of the Twelve," 331.

30. Wcela, *Prophets*, 31–41.

31. Hunter, *Seek the Lord*, 120–75.

that through these exhortations (Hos 2:2–4; 4:15; 6:6; 10:12; 12:7; 14:2–4), Hosea, like Amos, went beyond merely announcing judgment upon the covenant breakers in Israel.[32] For Hosea, the coming judgment was a necessary means through which God's people, Israel, would receive salvation.[33] Hunter concludes that, in as much as Hosea's intention was not to provide a last minute escape from the impending judgment, his prophecy (like that of Amos) underlines the conditions for salvation.[34] In the case of Amos, "instead of placing a condition on the judgment, these exhortations serve to place a condition on salvation, producing a kind of backhanded way of affirming the certainty of judgment."[35]

James Nogalski has also linked Amos 5 with the prophet Hosea through the concept of the Day of the Lord. He argues that Hosea's presentation of God's metaphorical role as the husband to Israel (Hos 1–2) parallels the role played by the personification of Lady Zion in other prophetic texts (Isa 60; Jer 30:12–17; Ezek 22), including some of the Twelve (Mic 7:8–13; Zeph 3:14–19).[36] Nogalski further notes that the "Day" evident in Amos 5 appears about eight times in different places in the prophecy of Hosea (2:2, 5, 15, 17[2x], 18, 20, 23), but it is used only four times (vv. 2, 18, 20, 23) with reference to the time of God's future intervention.[37]

Kenneth H. Cuffey stresses that the prophecy of Micah conveys in theophanic form a similar judgment formula with the implication of repentance. In his work "Remnant, Redactor, and Biblical Theologian," Cuffey argues that in the past, critical scholars took delight in dissecting prophetic texts, as if there was a discontinuity in the theology of the material. He is pleased that the text has recently been examined as whole. Cuffey examines the coherence in the Minor Prophets, pointing to the judgment, remnant, and restoration indicators in the text, of which Amos 5 forms a part (cf. Amos 5:15d).[38]

---

32. Stinespring ("Hosea, Prophet of Doom," 220–27) argues that Hosea, like Amos, is a prophet of doom. For addition information see Hunter, *Seek the Lord*, 123.

33. For additional insight into the theology of Hosea, see Eichrodt, "'The Holy One in your Midst'" 259–73; Wolff, "Guilt and Salvation," 274–85; Ward, "Message of the Prophet Hosea," 387–407; Wcela, *Prophets*, 29–33; McComiskey, "Hosea," 1–237; Birch, *Hosea, Joel and Amos*, 7–121.

34. Hunter, *Seek the Lord*, 175.

35. See ibid., 122.

36. Nogalski, "The Day (s) of YHWH," 623.

37. Ibid., 623.

38. Cuffey, "Remnant," 185–208. The "remnant of Joseph" in Amos 5:15d will be

The prophecy of Joel, one of the Twelve, is also thematically related to Amos 5, as demonstrated by Rolf Rendtorff. He argues that when it comes to the use of the Day of the Lord in Amos 5, readers are aware of the context of this expression (which is closely related to Joel 4[3]), which highlights God's punishment on Israel's enemies as well as those Israelites who broke the covenant laws (Joel 2:2). Just as Amos 5:7–12 serves as both a critique of Israel's injustices and an invitation, particularly to the remnant, to seek the Lord (vv. 14–15), Joel 2:12–14 invites the people to return to the Lord after the locust plague (vv. 1–27). In other words, for Rendtorff, the Day of the Lord in Joel, just like in Amos 5, can be experienced under the circumstances of threat, doom, judgment, repentance, and restoration.[39]

A similar theme of the Day of the Lord is found Habakkuk. The difference is that in Habakkuk, the judgment is focused on Edom or Esau, Judah's enemy; Obadiah, Jonah, and Nahum also have different addressees.[40] In Nahum, even though the Day of the Lord refers to judgment and punishment of the Ninevites, its goal (like in Amos 5) is repentance and forgiveness by God, who is full of mercy and kindness (Nah 1:3; Joel 2:13).

Zephaniah is another prophet closely related to Amos 5 with a shared umbrella theme of the Day of the Lord. Zephaniah preached shortly before the Babylonian exile. For him, the Day of the Lord was a Day of Judgment, covenant renewal, repentance, and reassurance of God's love. This concept is more pronounced in Zephaniah than in Amos 5. In Zephaniah the judgment is specific (Zeph 1:4–10) as well as universal (Zeph 1: 18, 3:18–20). It is both a day of judgment (vv. 14–18) and a day of hope for the restoration of the fortunes of the poor, the humble of the land, and the repentant remnant.[41] Zephaniah is also closely related to Amos 5 in terms of its very specific imperatival elements of "seek the LORD" (Zeph 2:1–3). In my previous work "The Theological Functions of 'Seek Lord' (*bāqqaš ʾădōnāy*) in Zephaniah 2:1–3, for Contemporary Society," I examined, among other things, the addressee and the theological functions of the exhortation "seek the LORD" in Zephaniah. The article concluded that, like Amos 5, "Zephaniah 2:1–3 functions not only to exhort Judah and inspire every nation to repentance, it ethically invites everyone to seek the Lord, humility, justice

---

further discussed in chapter 4.

39. Rendtorff, "Book of the Twelve," 75–87.

40. Rendtorff, "Alas for the Day!," 192–93; Rendtorff, "Book of the Twelve," 80–82.

41. See Udoekpo, *Re-thinking the Day of YHWH*, 28, 109–94, which discusses this notion in Zephaniah in detail.

and righteousness . . . And it is related to the notion of the Day of the Lord (Zeph 2:1–3), central in the entire book of Zephaniah, and prominent in the rest of the prophetic traditions."[42]

Since restoration and fulfilment are related to the Day of the Lord, judgment is implicit in the post-exilic prophetic books of Haggai, Zechariah, and Malachi, where the theme of rebuilding the temple is obvious.[43] In fact, perhaps due to this concept's role in binding Amos 5 with the rest of the Twelve, and its relationship with biblical eschatology (or the handling of the question of the eschatological nature of Amos 5), this concept has won a place in the minds of scholars. There is consensus among scholars that the Day of the Lord is one of "the most intriguing theological concepts in the Hebrew Bible."[44] Many in the past have engaged in a detailed investigation of this concept, some of which I would love to briefly outline.[45]

Research History on the Day of the Lord

A summary outline of scholarly views and research on the origin and meaning of the concept of the Day of the Lord is a crucial concept in the Twelve Minor Prophet. This concept has played a pivotal role in connecting Amos 5 with the other books of the Twelve. Paying attention to this concept sheds light on how Amos fought the injustices and unethical worship of his time by reworking the standard idiom of his tradition and adapting it to his own purposes. With these idioms—particularly the Day of the Lord—Amos reminded Israel of the consequences of oppressing the poor and hypocritically worshiping God in Bethel, Gilgal, and Beersheba with a false sense of security. Observing the concept of the Day of the Lord in Amos also helps us address, at least broadly, the eschatological nature of Amos 5.

John Merlin Powis Smith, one of the earliest researchers on the meaning and origin of this concept, believes the Day of the Lord was a familiar

---

42. Udoekpo, "'Seek the Lord' (*bāqqaš 'ădōnāy*)," 77–91, where I have discussed this at length, noting the relationship between Zephaniah and Amos 5.

43. See Udoekpo, *Re-thinking the Day of YHWH*, 226–30, for additional insight.

44. Barstad, *Religious Polemics,* 89; Nogalski, "'The Day(s) of YHWH,'" 617–42, Udoekpo, *Re-thinking the Day of YHWH*, 197–234; Chester, *Future Hope*, 15–21, for a comprehensive study of the Day of the Lord in traditions other than Amos.

45 See Černý, *Day of Yahweh,*; Barstad, *Religious Polemics,* 89–97; Udokepo, *Re-thinking the Day of YHWH*, 43–80; Chester, *Future Hope and Reality,* 11–14, for a detailed and selected survey of the history of current research on the Day of the Lord with impressive bibliography.

RETHINKING THE PROPHETIC CRITIQUE OF WORSHIP IN AMOS 5

concept to the Israelites before the time of classical prophets such as Amos. The Day of the Lord was a time or desired period when great glory and successes would be inaugurated for Israel, a chosen nation with divine favors.[46]

Hugo Gressmann confirms Smith's position but traces the eschatological Day of the Lord in Amos 5:18–20 to ancient methodological elements. Gressmann believes that, just as Palestinian eschatological concepts originated from ancient oriental myths, biblical eschatology was influenced by ancient Near Eastern culture.[47] In regard to the OT/Hebrew Bible, Gressmann believes the genesis of eschatology is found in Amos 5:18–20.[48] The common criticism often leveled against Smith and Gressmann is whether we can strictly speak of biblical eschatology prior to the exile, since "eschatology proper" arose in the exile.[49]

Sigmund Mowinckel sees the Day of the Lord as a day of the Lord's manifestation in the cult of the New Year festival, that is, in the annual cultic festival of Yahweh's enthronement. It is a day when the Lord, as a king, comes and works salvation for his people, Israel.[50] Simply put, the "matrix of eschatology is in the cult."[51] Mowinckel arrived at his conclusions while reading the Psalms (e.g., Pss 24; 47:8; 93:1; 96:8; 97:1). However, Gressmann and Mowinckel have drawn criticism from some scholars, of which the details are beyond the scope of this work.[52] Chester confirms that these ideas were never "sustainable in anything like the form in which they presented it, although in spite of that Mowinkel's view in particular has been influential."[53]

---

46. Smith, "Day of Yahweh," 505–33.

47 Gressmann, *jüdisch-israelitischen Eschatologie*, 142–44. Cf. Lindblom, *Prophecy in Ancient Israel*, 316–17.

48. Hasel (Understanding *the Book of Amos*, 109) also affirms Gressmann's position.

49. Cathcart ("Day of Yahweh," 84) notes this criticism in his studies as well as on in Lindblom, *Prophecy*, 316–17. Lindblom tenaciously argues that "what (some) scholars call eschatology is not eschatology at all. A theophany has itself nothing to do with eschatology. The oracular style, frequently used by the prophets, gives heir utterances an irrational character, in some measure reminiscent of eschatological sayings. Purely historical events are often clothed in the methodological garb."

50. Mowinckel, *He That Cometh*, 145.

51. Hasel, *Understanding the Book of Amos*, 109.

52. For some of these criticisms, see Barstad, *Religious Polemic*, 98–102; Udoekpo, *Re-thinking the Day of YHWH*, 48–49.

53. Chester, *Future Hope*, 12.

Other influential scholars on this subject include Robinson, Černý, von Rad, and Roland de Vaux. In de Vaux's view, the psalms that are part of Mowinckel's proposal do not concern the enthronement of YHWH as a king, in the sense of the human-king. In Israel's religious mind, the all-powerful YHWH does not need human enthronement. Moreover, in those ancient Near Eastern texts, the expression "Marduk is king" is not a formula of enthronement but of acclamation, recognizing Marduk's power to act as a king.[54] Robinson also argues with more clarity that, even though the New Year's festival is identified with the enthronement of YHWH as king in Israel, the festival is nowhere named among the three primary Hebrew festivals (Exod 23:14–17).[55]

Černý believes the Day of the Lord touches on the intellectual, emotional, theological, spiritual, ritual, ideological, and social dimensions of the Hebrew religion.[56] It is a day of divine decree (Isa 10:22–23; 28:21; Ezek 39:8; Zeph 2:2; Mal 3:19, 21) and of darkness (Amos 5:18, 20; Joel 2:2, 3:4, 15)—a dreadful day (Joel 2:11; 3:4; Mal 4:5) and a destructive and dangerous day (Ezek 7:25).[57]

In von Rad's view, the Day of the Lord, eschatologically speaking, encompasses pure events of war. It is the rise of YHWH in battle against his enemies and the day of his victory. Von Rad believes that Israel's prophets took the notion of the "Day of YHWH" from the old holy war tradition and broadened it to embrace the universal or cosmic sphere. Von Rad argues that of the several prophetic texts (Isa 2:12; 13:6, 9; 22:5; 35:8 Jer 46:10; Ezek 7:10; 13:5; 30:3; Joel 1:15; 2:1, 11; 3:4; Obad 15; Zeph 1:7, 8, 14–18; Zech 14:1), Amos 5:18–20, which is usually considered the earliest key passage and departing point for the study of the Day of YHWH, offers insufficient definition of the notion and its tradition.[58] In other words, Amos 5:18–20, according to von Rad, has no monopoly on the mention of the Day of the Lord, and neither is it an isolated notion in the Hebrew Bible as a whole.[59]

---

54. De Vaux, *Ancient Israel*, 261–67.

55. Robinson, *Inspiration and Revelation*, 140–43.

56. Černý, *Day of Yahweh*, vii–viii.

57. Ibid, 17–26.

58. Rad, *Heilige Kreig*,; Rad, "Origin of the Concept," 97–108; Rad, *Old Testament Theology*, 119–25.

59. See Chester, *Future Hope*, 12; Udoekpo, *Re-thinking the Day of YHWH*, 59–62.

Meir Weiss believes von Rad's holy war theory is not perfect.[60] Weiss points to biblical texts that have warlike elements without necessarily alluding to the Day of the Lord.[61] Commenting specifically on Amos 5:18–20, Weiss believes that the prophet's audience understood what Amos meant by the Day of the Lord, since he is the one who originated the concept for the first time in the prophetic tradition through his polemics about the manifestation of the Lord on behalf of his people.[62] C. Carniti similarly argues that the Day of the Lord is Amos' theological invention.[63]

There are many competing views regarding the meaning of the Day of the Lord in the prophetic books, including Amos.[64] Hayes, for instance, asserts that Amos has no eschatological history at all.[65] Wolff suggests that the Day of the Lord in Amos is evidence of Amos' thought pattern, which is influenced by clan wisdom and the thought patterns of the wondering shepherd.[66] Scholars who deny the eschatological implications of the Day of the Lord include Schmidt, Trapiello, Everson, Barstad, and Hoffmann.[67]

This survey indicates, among other things, that there are at least three views regarding the eschatological aspect of the Day of the Lord. First, there are those who ascribe to a narrow definition of eschatology and see Amos 5:18–20 as non-eschatological. Second, there are those who think that the passage reflects the popular notion of eschatology, which preceded the time of Amos. Third, there are those who define eschatology in a broad sense with reference to a finality that is the time of God's intervention.[68] Sweeney also sums up these views under the following traditions: eschatology,

60. Weiss, "Origin of the 'Day of the Lord,'" 29–62.

61. See Udoekpo, *Re-thinking the Day of YHWH*, 64–65, for details of some of these texts.

62. Weiss, "Origin," 29–60.

63. Carniti, "L 'espressione 'il giorno di JHWH,'" 11–25.

64. See Udoekpo, *Re-thinking the Day of YHWH*, 67–80, for other views, including those of Cross, *Canaanite Myth*, 88; Cross, "Divine Warrior," 11–30; Miller, "Divine Council," 100; Klein, "Day of the Lord," 517; Everson, "Day of Yahweh," 329–37; Hoffmann, "Day of the Lord," 37–50; Moore, "Yahweh's Day,'" 193–208; Hiers, "Day of the Lord," 82; Cathcart, "Day of Yahweh," 84–85; Ishai-Rosenboim, "Is יום הי (the Day of the Lord)," 395–401; Sobhidanandan, "Day of the Lord in the Book of Joel," 61–69.

65. Hayes, *Amos*, 38.

66. Wolff, *Joel and Amos*, 253–57.

67. See Schmidt, *Alttestamenttilicher Glaube*, 95–97; Trapiello, "La nocien del 'Dia de Yahve,'" 331–36; Everson, "Day of Yahweh," 329–37; Barstad, *Religious Polemics*, 89–94; Hoffmann, "Day of the Lord," 37–50.

68. Hasel, *Understanding the Book of Amos*, 111.

annual New Year festival that celebrates the Lord's kingship and defeat of his enemies, holy war, theophanic, covenant, and treaty curse traditions, as well as various historical settings that involve military action.[69] DeVries believes that the time of God's intervention in human history is common among these views and traditions, with most of the oracles being against foreign nations, particularly Israel's enemies.[70]

Hasel rightly insists, "the idea that 'the day of Yahweh/Lord' (5:18–20) was a part of popular and broad eschatological theology of some Israelites may be sustained."[71] This explains why Amos, within the immediate preceding context of the passage (vv. 18–20), would rework the concept by extending his invitation to the people to mourn and lament over their social, moral, and religious negligence to seek the Lord (vv. 16–17, on the traditional, but false, assumption that the Lord would fight for them since they were the chosen ones).

Amos' Standard Idioms/Traditions

Shalom M. Paul reinforces the backdrop of Amos 5 with what he describes as a "common ideological denominator," which informs not only verses 18–20 but also the rest of the prophecy (vv. 21–27).[72] It is a denominator of abuse of justice and popular belief in election theology, and perhaps "the remnant of Joseph" common in the time of Amos.[73] As previously discussed, during the time when Amos was preaching, Israel did not take advantage of the decline of Assyria and Syria to better itself. Rather, the wealthy of that time preferred to oppress and marginalize the poor (2:6).[74] Unfortunately, some of those poor and voiceless people were abused—to the point of being exchanged for a pair of sandals (8:6). The wealthy also engaged in worship that included idolatrous practices and faithless pilgrimages to various shrines, as well as music and songs that were not pleasing to the Lord (5:21–23).

69. Sweeney, "Amos," 238.

70. DeVries, *Yesterday, Today and Tomorrow,* 47–53; Barstad, *Religious Polemics,* 97, 103–10.

71. Hasel, *Understanding the Book of Amos,* 111.

72. Paul, *Amos,* 182.

73. See Udoekpo, *Re-thinking the Day of YHWH,* 200.

74. See Heschel, *Prophets,* 33.

These abuses were partially a result of their popular belief in election theology, or a misunderstanding of their covenant relationship with their God. The Israelites, as pointed out earlier by Smith and other scholars, viewed the Day of the Lord as a great day of battle when YHWH would resume the position of a military commander and lead the Israelites in demolishing their enemy nations.[75] In response to the Israelites' abuses and misunderstandings, the prophet Amos invited them to lament over their missteps and presumptions (vv. 16–17). Chester notes that whereas the Israelites would expect the response "mediated by the prophet, to be the assurance of divine intervention for them, with deliverance from what afflicts them, and the restoration of peace and prosperity, on the 'Day of Yahweh,' instead, in the prophecy of Amos they are confronted by the very opposite of this."[76] Amos, according to Mays, is known for taking the central themes in Israel's faith and turning them against his audience (3:1–2; 5:4–6; 9:7).[77] Amos discerns the Lord's decision and contests the piety of his audience. He warns against the disastrous outcome of their piety (5:18–20).[78] Hence, the prophet's woe utterances are pronouncements of doom (misfortunes) for those who complacently desired this Day of the Lord.[79]

Summary of Chapter 3

Scholars have long noticed signs of editorial activity that suggest the twelve Minor Prophets should be read as a literary unit. Many literary features, such as repetition, *inclusio,* catchwords, motifs, framing devices, allusions, quotations, and themes are employed to link the prophecy of Amos to the other eleven Minor Prophets.

Given these premises, Amos 5, with its integrated themes of justice, righteousness, mercy, repentance, exhortations to worship the Lord alone, judgment, and broad eschatological hope for salvation enveloped in the notion of the Day of the Lord, forms a profound theological rapport

---

75. Smith, "Day of Yahweh," 511–12.

76. Chester, *Future Hope*, 14. See also Barstad, *Religious Polemics in Amos*, 109, where he states a similar view: "[A]gain we see how the prophet has directed his words against the Israelites, rather than against their 'enemies,' i.e. the group or groups whom they themselves expected to be struck by that terrible 'day of Yahweh.'"

77. Mays, *Amos*, 103; Paul, *Amos*, 185.

78. Mays, *Amos*, 103.

79. Barstad, *Religious Polemics*, 109.

with the other books of the Minor Prophets. Its theological purpose is to bring Israel back to the Lord. The prophecy of Amos 5 consistently seeks to highlight this same goal in conjunction with the overall prophetic/ OT traditions. Such a unified reading of the Twelve also seeks to avoid a fragmented interpretation of Scripture. These conclusions should be kept in mind when reading the literary and exegetical analyses that follows in chapters four and five.

4

The Literary Structure of Amos and Delimitation of Chapter Amos 5

Introduction

So far we have been dealing with a general background survey of Amos' theology, particularly his worship traditions. It was necessary to translate and critically examine the text of Amos 5, discuss its formation history, and address its relationship with the other books of the Minor Prophets. We also highlighted the theme of the Day of the Lord and its trajectories, including a brief summary of scholarly views on the significance of this concept in the Hebrew Bible/Old Testament. The advantages of these discussions cannot be overemphasized. Amos, we know, was deeply influenced by his culture and traditional idioms. He truly adapted his traditional idioms, culture, and language to serve the purpose of his cult critique and theology of worship, which this work investigates as it stresses the unity of the book of Amos.

This chapter specifically examines the literary structure, features, and forms of the entire book of Amos. It delimits Amos 5, offering a brief outline and examining its relationship with the rest of the book. We will also broadly identify features, markers, and genres (such as laments, hymns, exhortations, riddles, proverbs, pronouncements, judgments, woes, and sarcasm) that affect how we understand or interpret Amos 5. The theological effects of these literary identifications and outlines are further developed in the detailed exegesis that follows in chapter five.

Literary Structure of the Book of Amos as a Whole

Amos 5 is located within the broader context of the nine chapters of what has been referred to as the "theological anchor" of the Twelve. As intimated in the first chapter, there are as many divisions and arrangements of the literary components of the book of Amos (ranging from 2–7 divisions) as there are authors and exegetes.[1] The four major components alluded to in chapter one include: (1) series of oracles against nations (Amos 1–2); (2) collections of prophetic sayings (Amos 3–6); (3) visions (Amos 7:1–9:6); and (4) the epilogue, which embraces hope and restoration (Amos 9:7–15). These four components are alternatively classified by Andersen and Freedman as books of doom (1:1–4:13), woes (5:1–6:14), visions (7:1–9:6) and the epilogue (9:7–15).[2]

In offering his insights on the literary structure of the book of Amos, Paul R. Noble compares previous studies by Hayes (*Amos, His Times and Preaching*), Andersen and Freedman (*Amos*), and many others. Noble notes the diversities and the similarities in these studies and draws his own conclusions. He points out that the authors primarily differ in their analyses of Amos 3–6. For example, Hayes splits these four chapters into five smaller units (3:1–11; 3:12–4:13; 5:1–17; 5:18–20; 6:1–14), while Andersen and Freedman break them into two units (1:2–4:13; 5:1–6:14). Noble observes that the only point of consensus among these scholars is that Amos 5:1 begins a new major literary unit that ends in Amos 6:14.[3]

In Noble's view, the main reason for this structural diversity is the inadequate attention given to chosen criteria for making such divisions. He argues that the introductory and closing formulas (formal criteria) have been given much attention, while the palistrophic element of *inclusios* (literary criteria) have been given less attention. Noble thus offers the following analysis of the four divisions of Amos: (1) superscription (1:1); (2) YHWH's words to the nations (1:2–3:8); (3) a palistrophic judgment oracle (3:9–6:14); and (4) the destruction/reconstitution of Israel (7:1–9:15).[4]

Whatever criteria of structuring is adopted, Amos 5 is located within the section of the woe prophetic sayings of the book (Amos 3–6). However, Amos is located in the fifth section of James Limburg's celebrated sevenfold

---

1. Some of these notable authors already extensively discussed in chapter 1, include, Mays (*Amos*); Rudolph (*Joel-Amos-Obadja-Jona*); Koch (*Amos*); Wolff (*Joel and Amos*); Coote (*Amos among the Prophets*); van der Wal (*Structure of Amos*); Garrett ("Structure of Amos"); Limburg ("Sevenfold Structure"); Staurt (*Hosea–Jonah*); Soggin (*Prophet Amos*); Hayes (*Amos, His Time and Preaching*); Andersen and Freedman (*Amos*); Smith (*Amos*); Finley (*Joel, Amos Obadia*); and Jeremias (*Amos*).

2. Cf. Andersen and Freedman, *Amos*, 23–72.

3. Noble, "Literary Structure of Amos," 209.

4. Ibid., 209–10.

literary pattern (1:1–2; 1:3—2:16; 3:1–15; 4:1–13; 5:1—6:14; 7:1—8:3; and 8:4—9:15), with sections marked by divine speech formulas. For the purpose of presenting an accessible and general overview of the place of Amos 5 within the book of Amos, this study adopts, with minor modifications, the following outlines proposed by Sweeney and Finley.[5]

I. Superscription/Presentation of the Words of Amos: Exhortation to Seek YHWH (Amos 1–2).

   A. The Superscription (1:1)

   B. Central Message of Amos: Exhortation to Seek YHWH in Judah (1:2—9:15)

   C. Presentation of Amos' Motto: YHWH's Theophany in Zion (1:2)

   D. The Oracles against the Nations and Israel (1:3—2:16)

      1. The Oracle concerning Damascus/Aram (1:3–5)

      2. The Oracle concerning Gaza/Philistia (1:6–8)

      3. The Oracle concerning Tyre/Phoenicia (1:9–10)

      4. The Oracle concerning Edom (1:11–12)

      5. The Oracle concerning the Ammonites (1:13–15)

      6. The Oracle concerning Moab (2:1–3)

      7. The Oracle concerning Judah (2:4–5)

      8. The Oracle concerning Israel (2:6–16)

         a. Indicting Israel for Oppressing the Powerless (2:6–8)

         b. Indicting Israel for Rejecting the Lord (2:9–12)

         c. Israel Is Being Sentenced (2:13–16)

II. Prophetic Warnings and Woes (Amos 3–6)

   A. Prophetic Sermon concerning Upcoming Punishment of Israel (3:1—4:13)

      1. Call to Attention (3:1–2)

      2. Prophetic Instructions regarding Cause and Effect (3:3–8)

      3. Announcement of Threat against Samaria (3:9–11)

---

5. Cf. Sweeney, "Amos," 195–268; Finley, *Joel, Amos, Obadiah*, 115–16. May I also note that the numbering of this outline with minor adjustments is provisionally mine.

4. Oracle concerning the Punishment of Israel (3:12)

5. Call for Witness against Israel (3:13–15)

6. Punishment of the Women/Cows of Samaria (4:1–4)

7. Instruction and Punishment of Beth El (4:4–13)

B. Prophetic Call to Seek YHWH and Reject Beth El (5:1—6:14)

1. Call to Seek YHWH and Reject Beth El (5:1–17)

   a. Dirge of the Fallen Israel (5:1–3)

   b. Call to Seek YHWH on the Basis of Judgment (5:4–6)

   c. Rebuke of Israel's Perversion of Justice (5:7)

   d. YHWH's Song as the Judge (5:8–9)

   e. Rebuke of Israel's Oppression of the Poor (5:10–13)

   f. An Invitation to Seek Righteousness (5:14–15)

   g. Lamentations (5:16–17)

2. Woe Speech against the Cultic Leadership (5:18–27).

   a. Pronouncement of Woe (5:18–20)

   b. YHWH's Rejection and His Judgment (5:21–27)

3. Woe against the Political Leadership of the Nations (6:1–14)

III. Five Visions of Judgment and Salvation and Hope for the South (7–9)

A. The First Four Visions (7:1—8:14)

1. First, Vision of the Locust (7:1–3)

2. Second, Vision of Fire (7:4–6).

3. Third, Vision of the Plumb Line (7:7–17)

4. Fourth, Vision of the Basket fruits (8:1–14)

B. The Fifth Vision: Downfall of Beth El, Rise of David (9:1–15)

1. Fifth, Destruction of the Temple (9:1–6)

2. The Lord Stands in the Altar (9:7–10)

3. The Lord Restores His People (9:11–15)

When this outline is closely examined in connection with the previous comments on the literary approaches to Amos, there is clear evidence of a deliberate and purposeful arrangement of the materials in it. Blocks and units of materials have been assembled together with repeating patterns of themes, catchwords, formulas, and other literary markers.

Apart from the third-person superscription, which provides valuable information about Amos and the contents of his book (1:1), the expression "for three transgressions/crimes and for four . . ." (1:3—2:16) occurs eight successive times, which emphasizes Israel's guilt and judgment and gives a sense of separate literary units with editorial activities. According to Wcela, this expression is an ancient literary device used in the recitations of poems.[6] A line of poetic speech often moves forward by mentioning a number and then increasing it by one. In this instance, three plus four equals seven, a biblical number of perfection. Therefore, in Wcela's opinion, the nations are condemned because the cup of their transgression is filled up "perfectly with evils."[7] Pointing to further editorial or literary evidence in this unit of judgment upon the kingdoms, some scholars have also argued that it is unusual to have a series of eight nations rather than seven. Based on this, some see the seven speech addresses to Judah (2:4–5) as an addition.[8] These three speeches, beginning with "Hear this word," can also be put together (3:1; 13; 4:1; 5:1; 8:4) to mark the end and the beginning of a unit.

Other popular markers of deliberate arrangement observed by scholars include the "yet you did not return to me" refrain (4:6, 8,9,10, 11); warnings introduced by "alas" (5:18, 6:1, 4); and the vision unit, which begins with "this is what the Lord showed me" (7:1, 4, 7; 8:1). The woes and judgments concerning the Day of the Lord are also arranged together (5:18–20; 8:9, 13; 9:11; 9:13).[9]

Studying the above outline, one notices an *inclusio:* the book begins with an emphasis on Zion/Jerusalem/Judah (1:2) and concludes with a focus on Judah, the house of David (9:11–15), which many scholars consider to be an editorial addition. As mentioned previously, those who hold this view find the optimism and sense of restoration of fortunes in Amos

6 Andersen and Freedman (*Amos*, 144–49) has an impressive treatment of "the use of poetry and prose in the book of Amos."

7. Wcela, *Prophets*, 18.

8. Andersen and Freedman (*Amos*, 142–43) has an extended list of Amos texts and units commonly doubted or regarded as additions. They include,1:2; 1:9–10; 1:11–12; 2:4–5; 2:10; 3:7; 3:14b; 4:13; 5:8–9, 13, 14–5, 26–27; 6:2, 6; 8:8, 11–12,13; 9:5–6, 8–15.

9. Leclerc, *Prophets*, 126.

9:11–15 as a departure from the strong sense of judgment and doom in the rest of the book.[10]

Judgment and Hope in Amos' Literary Structure

The above mentioned literary *inclusio* in Amos has contributed to the debate of whether the prophecy of Amos 5 communicates any sense of hope. Hasel, who offers a good summary of this debate,[11] notes that a number of scholars, going back to the time of Julius Wellhausen (1892), think Amos 9:11–15 does not belong to the prophet of Tekoa but to Deuteronomistic theologians prior to Amos who were interested in the message of hope and salvation. These scholars feel that the message of salvation in Amos 9:11–15 simply presupposes the fall of Jerusalem (in 586/7 BCE).[12] On the contrary, Wolff and Soggin attribute the passage to a literary redactor not seen before in the book of Amos.[13] Peter Weimar situates this passage into the larger redactional framework of the book of Amos. That is to say, after the compilations of an oral and written tradition, an editing process took place during which a final editor combined these various elements and pieces of traditions (oral and written) to form a whole or a cohesive unity of the present text of Amos.[14] Nel argues that the passage is an unconditional prophecy of salvation to the Judeans during the exile.[15] Childs, a champion of canonical criticism, recognizes the predominant message of doom in Amos and suggests that the final canonical editor placed this passage in the overall eschatological framework of the message of Amos.[16]

Rendtorff, an advocate for the unity of the Twelve, insists that no part of the text of Amos should be interpreted independently from the overall book nor the context in which it is placed. For Rendtorff, as far as Amos 9:7–15 is concerned, "the proclamation of doom is integrated into the

---

10. Cf. ibid., 127–28.

11. Hasel, *Book of Amos* (166–20) has details of this debate.

12. Kellermann ("Amoschluss als Stimme," 169–83) as well as Hasel (*Book of Amos*, 116-18) have lists of notable scholars who prefer to attribute a Deuteronomistic voice to Amos 5:11–15.

13. Wolff, *Joel and Amos,* 353; Soggin, *Amos,* 149–50.

14. Weimar, "Der Schluss des Amos-Buches," 60–100, particularly as cited in Hasel, *Book of Amos,* 117.

15. Nel, "Amos 9:11–15," 81–97.

16. Childs, "Die theologische Bedeutung," 251.

eschatological proclamation of salvation as in all other prophetic books."[17] Most scholars, including those who deny that Amos himself composed the concluding section, recognize the hope inherent in the unique promise made to the southern kingdom: "on that day I will raise up the fallen hut of David, I will wall up its breaches, raise up its ruins, and rebuild it as in the days of old" (9:11).[18] In rearranging the sequence of visions in Amos, Ebo argues that judgment cannot be the end in the prophecy of Amos otherwise "how exactly is it to be executed without infringing on the covenant between Yahweh and Israel?"[19]

Although speaking of prophets in general, Leclerc believes that the task of announcing judgment reveals the prophets' moral courage in standing up against the ruling elite and the people at large. But judgment, he stresses, testifies to the ethical nature of God, his love, and his mercy. According to Leclerc, to "punish sin would be a failure of justice."[20] In this regard Leclerc cautions against overlooking the double-sided nature of divine judgment. When God acts to punish oppressors (like in the case of Amos), "God is simultaneously delivering the oppressed; when God condemns the wicked, God thereby vindicates the righteous . . . Both sides of judgment are characteristic features of the 'Day of the Lord' in Amos."[21]

On this note, Hasel affirms that various interrelated literary forms and topics, such as the Day of the Lord, the woe-cry (5:18–20), the exhortation to seek the Lord, goodness, justice and righteousness (vv. 4–5, 15–16, 24), the remnant of Joseph (vv. 14–15), and lamentation (vv. 16–17) make Amos a prophet of "eschatological doom and eschatological hope.[22] For him, this prophecy is also "determined by moral demands from a covenant in which the divine-human relationship [is] at the center, . . . giving continuing direction to the life of God's people."[23]

In sum, the preceding literary overview of the book of Amos, which has been the main focus of this chapter, gives birth to the following tripartite presentation of the book of Amos as a coherent text. First is

17. See Rendtorff, *Das Alte Testament*, 234, as cited in Hasel, *Book of Amos*, 117.

18. See Hasel, *Book of Amos*, 118, where there is a long list of those who support the unity of Amos and the authenticity of 9:11–15.

19. Ebo, "Re-ordering," 67.

20. Leclerc, *Prophets*, 111.

21. Ibid.

22. Hasel, *Book of Amos*, 119–20.

23. Ibid.

the central message of Amos, condemning the nations and Israel (1–2). Second is the attack of corruption and warning of the Day of the Lord (3–6). Third is the five visions of judgment and hope for the restoration of the Davidic dynasty (7–9). The initial two chapters are clear reminders that the magnitude of Israel's and Judah's sins against the covenant cannot go unpunished (2:4–5, 6–16). Nations such as Damascus, Philistia, Tyra, Edom, the Ammonites, and Moab are equally subject to judgment (1:3—2:16). This is followed by a warning against the breach of covenants, lack of repentance, injustice and corruption, as well as a pronouncement of woes against those who worship without ethics. The following section (3–6), in which the organizational structure of Amos 5 is located, is clearly encircled by the theology of five visions, with the implication of judgment and hope of restoration for those who repent, especially the remnant and descendants of the house of David (7–9).

Delimitation of Amos 5

In addition to the preceding analysis, and in order to facilitate the exegesis that follows in the next chapter, it is necessary to delimit Amos 5. Amos 5 begins a separate theological and literary unit, which functions best within the overall context of the book of Amos. It consists of messenger formulae, exhortations, pronouncements of judgment, laments, woes, disputation sayings, riddles, proverbs, and accusations concerning ethical and worship behavior in Israel.

A. Vanlier Hunter reviews the scholarly comments on the peculiarity of verses 1–17 as a rhetorical unit. Hunter notes that the various sayings of this unit, which begins with "seek" (דרש), were expected to stay together but were placed in different locations (vv. 4–6; 14–15).[24] Many scholars have noticed that, after the introductory phrase "hear this word" (שמעו את־הדבר), as was the case in previous chapters (3:1; 4:1), the unit proceeds with a funeral dirge and prophecies of destruction (vv. 1–3), followed by exhortations (vv. 4–6). Verses 8–9 are the second hymnic and doxological fragments of woe arranged to follow verses 10–12, which are suspected to contain foreign material.[25] As a hymn or doxology, verses 8–9

24 Hunter, *Seek the Lord,* 56–57.

25 See Hunter, *Seek the Lord,* 57, for these views drawn from Berg, *Die Sogenannten;* Crenshaw, *Hymnic Affirmations,* 147–58; Cripps, *A Critical and Exegetical Commentary,* 183; Myers, *Hosea, Joel, Amos, Obadiah, Jonah,* 125; Wolff, *Joel and Amos,* 246–49.

are surrounded by the first hymn (4:13) and the third doxology (9:5–6). Scholarly debates surrounding these passages touch on the issues of literary genre, dates, origin, and unity. Hasel, for instance, believes there is a general consensus that these three passages (4:13, 5:8–9; 9:5–6) are related.[26] Those who regard these passages as later additions or foreign materials argue that they do not flow smoothly from their contexts and they have an elevated theology of God as creator and Lord of Hosts.[27]

In terms of dating the hymns, Crenshaw is not decisive whether they are pre-exilic, exilic, or early postexilic.[28] The hymns may even antedate Amos.[29] However, there are those who argue for an early dating and Amos' authorship of the hymns.[30] McComiskey in particular, while arguing on the basis of elements of style and form, insists that the passages are consistent with the rest of the book of Amos. McComiskey insists that "the doxologies are poetic representations of theological truth written by Amos himself to give awesome validation to the content of the oracle that precedes each doxology."[31] Finley, on the other hand, stresses the importance of understanding how the various hymnic portions relate and interact in the rest of the book of Amos. Finley is convinced of "tight interrelationships of these pieces, both poetically and semantically."[32]

In Amos' text, the first hymn serves as a "climax to the first 'word' that Amos invites the people to hear (4:13). The second hymn serves as the center that holds the first rhetorical unit (5:1–17) in the second 'word' (vv. 5–6, 8–9), while the third hymn serves as a climax of the vision of the Lord destroying the altar and temple in Bethel (9:1–4; 5–6)."[33] Regarding the third hymn—the specific hymn of our focus (5:8–9)—Andersen and Freedman believe the hymn is misplaced or a gloss in the book of Amos, though its

---

26. Hasel, *Book of Amos*, 84.

27. Smith (*Amos*, 140) has the details of this argument and supports the authenticity of this hymnic material.

28. Crenshaw, *Hymnic Affirmations*, 143.

29. Andersen and Freedman, *Amos*, 5.

30. Watts, "An Old Hymn," 33–99; Mays, *Amos*, 84; Rudolph, *Joel-Amos-Obadja-Jona*, 1181–83; Hammershaimb, *Amos*, 150; McComiskey, "Hymnic Elements," 139–57.

31. McComiskey, "Hymnic Elements," 120.

32. Finley, *Joel, Amos and Obadiah*, 332.

33. Ibid., 333.

theology of praising God as the Lord of heaven and earth remains the same, irrespective of its location in the text.[34]

Hunter also points out that there is an overwhelming consensus that verse 13 is a gloss.[35] That being the case, it is here that we encounter the second exhortation (vv. 14–15) followed by the announcement of judgment (vv. 16–17), which should have been attached integrally to verse 12.[36] Hunter also indicates that, over the years, several suggestions have been proffered in an attempt to account for the seeming "odd placement" of the hymns (vv. 8–9) and other materials in the book of Amos (vv. 1–17).[37] Karl Marti, for instance, postulates that a later scribe inadvertently omitted verses 14–15 after verses 4–6 and then reinserted them when he realized his mistake.[38] Artur Weiser and Wolff attribute the growth of Amos 5 as a whole to the influence of non-Amos materials.[39] Rudolph assumes that the final structure of vv. 1–17 is the product of several layers of redaction.[40] Karl Neubauer assigns verses 14–15 to the prophet Amos himself, arguing that he purposefully used verses 7 and 10–12 to shed light on the exhortative meaning of verses 4–6 and 14–15, which present conditions for life and salvation.[41]

Jan de Waard is critical of any hypothesis that views this section as disjointed or misplaced. He believes the initial discourse in verses 1–17, which begins with "hear this word," is chiastically structured. Verses 1–3 can be seen as an independent sentence, though its unity is not *apriori*, yet the קינה ("lament") not only binds verses 1–2 together but is also in literary harmony with verse 3 through the particle כי ("for/because").[42]

De Waard insists that even though verse 4, like the previous verse, begins with כי, ("for/because"), there are several reasons why it can be considered an opening verse of a new paragraph or subunit (vv. 4–6). First,

34. Andersen and Freedman, *Amos*, 88–89.

35. Hunter, *Seek the Lord*, 57. But in Hammershaimb (*Amos*, 84) verse 13 is interpreted as authentic material.

36. Hunter, *Seek the Lord*, 57. See also, Wolff, *Joel and Amos*, 249; and Mays, *Amos*, 96–99.

37. Hunter, *Seek the Lord*, 58.

38. See Marti, *Das Deodekapropheton*, 187, as cited in Hunter, *Seek the Lord*, 58.

39 Cf. Weiser, *Profetie*, 149; Wolff, *Joel and Amos*, 237, as referenced in Hunter, *Seek the Lord*, 58.

40. Rudolph, *Joel-Amos-Obadja-Jona*, 184.

41. See Neubauer, "Erwägungen," 316, as cited in Hunter, *Seek the Lord*, 59.

42. De Waard, "Chiastic Structure, 170.

although the particle כי ("for/because") often links paragraphs to one an-other, the setting clearly changes from that of war (v. 3) to that of sanctuaries and exiles (vv. 4–5). Second, the exhortation given in the previous sentence (v. 4b) turns to warnings (v. 5a) and then to an invitation to seek the Lord and not Bethel or Gilgal (vv. 5b–d). This is followed by the prophetic saying (v. 6) that builds on the previous sayings (vv. 4–5), forming a chiastic struc-ture that introduces the hymnic section (vv. 8–9). There is a brief interrup-tion (vv. 7, 10), which serves as the prophetic description of the people.[43] This is followed by the next subunits (vv. 10–13 and vv.14–15), which share at least some semantic relationship. For example, verses 10–13 reject the oppression of the poor, express hatred for acts of injustice, sins, crimes, and bribery, and foreshadow the punishment, doom, and impending lamenta-tion of verses 16–17, which begin with לכן ("indeed"). Still, according to de Waard, the exhortation in verse 14, "seek good and not evil, that you may live; then truly will the LORD, the God of hosts, be with you as you claim," forms a break. Also, this verse is not only thematically close to verses 4–6, but parallel to verse 15, which says, "hate evil and love good, and let justice prevail at the gate. Then it may be that the LORD the God of hosts will have pity on the remnant of Joseph." On this note, de Waard concludes that verses 1–17 have an overall character of judgment and mourning. For him, it is a separate discourse, chiastically amplified, with the closing paragraph (vv. 16–17) taking up again the opening lamentation (vv. 1–3).[44]

In Hunter's view, de Waard's analysis lends important support to see-ing purposeful ordering and structuring of this rhetorical unity (vv. 1–17). Yet it does not demonstrate enough how the structure contributed to the meaning of the whole, which this present study pursues.[45] However, credit must be given to de Waard for identifying the middle point of the unit (vv. 8–9), which holds together the two sections (vv. 1–7, 10–17) that are chiastically connected.[46]

In his famous work *The Religious Polemics of Amos*, Barstad affirms the literary and thematic independence of this unit (vv. 1–17) despite its function within the overall book. For him, verses 18–27 contain the fa-mous judgment formula of יום יהוה ("Day of the LORD," vv.18–20), among

43. De Waard, "Chiastic Structure," 172.

44. Ibid., 173–76.

45. Hunter, *Seek the Lord*, 59.

46. See Hasel, *Book of Amos*, 87, where similar credit has been given to de Waard in detail.

other themes. He believes the import of verse 26 is very cryptic, with terms such as Sakkuth (סכות) and Kaiwan (כיון). In spite of this "crypticness," the thematic and literary nature of the overall section (vv. 18–26) serves to shed light theologically on the distinctive unit of the preceding rhetorical unit (vv. 1–17). With this argument, Barstad, like de Waard, rejects any fragmentary reading of the text of Amos 5. In Barstad's opinion, it does not matter whether the message of Amos is cryptic, redacted, or inserted. Amos' prophecy is basically directed toward the one and same audience.[47]

Duane A. Garrett, like Barstad, also comments on the editing and the question of the authenticity of the text of Amos (vv. 10–13). Garrett draws attention to the rhetorical features in Hebrew poetry, including chiasmus and parallelism. He warns that, even though scholars may have reason to doubt the authenticity of this text (vv. 10–13) based on breaks in the flow of a given passage, challenging the integrity of an acrostic poem or this specific text (vv. 10–13) might be very difficult. Moreover, it is chiastically structured. Garrett dismisses the proposal that Amos 5:10–13 is a later insertion.[48]

Andersen and Freedman consider Amos 5 as a distinct unit in the Books of Woes (5:1–6:14). They argue that Amos 5 not only has inner or-ganization and structure but an *inclusio* with the repetition of "the house Israel" (vv. 1, 25). An *inclusio* also supports the unity of Amos, as a similar *inclusio* is inherent in the entire book of Amos with its initial reference to Judah (1:2) and the mention of hope for the house of David in the conclud-ing chapter (9:11). However, regardless of the literary creativity of others, Andersen and Freedman believe and affirm that Amos 5 is an independent unit of exhortations for Israel and Judah. They proposed the following out-line, which is adopted in this study with only minor changes and additions:

I. Exhortation to the House of Israel (vv. 1–6)

    A. The Fallen Virgin (vv. 1–2)

    B. Decimation (v. 3)

    C. The Sanctuaries (vv. 4–6)

        1. "Seek the Lord" (vv. 4–5)

        2. Threat against Bethel (v. 6)

47. Barstad, *Religious Polemics*, 76.

48. See Garrett ("Structure of Amos," 275–76) for a full discussion and chiastic rep-resentation of Amos 5:10–13.

II. First Woe (vv. 7–13), and the Second Hymn (vv. 8–9)

    A. First Woe (v. 7)

    B. Second Hymn (vv. 8–9) and vv. 10–12, continuing the First Woe

    C. The Wise Man (v. 13)

III. Exhortation and lamentation (vv. 14–17)

    A. Repentance (vv. 14–15)

    B. Lamentation (vv. 16–17)

IV. Warning and Woe (vv. 18–27)

    A. The Day of the Lord (vv. 18–20)

    B. Justice and Righteousness (vv. 21–24)

    C. Threat of Exile (vv. 25–27).[49]

This outline, together with the preceding literary opinions, is not dramatically different from Noble's literary judgment on the book of Amos. In sum, Noble considers Amos 5 part of the palistrophic structuring of the overall text, which is chiastically patterned as follows:

A   Rejection of Israel's Cult (4:4–5)

    B   The Final Judgment (4:6–12)

        C   Lamentation of Israel (5:1–3)

            D   Seek the Lord (5:4–6)

                E   The Corruption of Justice (5:7, 10)

                    F   Hymn of the Lord (5:8–9)

                E′   The Corruption of Justice (5:11–13)

            D′   Seek the Lord (5:14–15)

        C′   Lamentation of Israel (5:16–17)

    B′   The Final Judgment (5:18–20)

A′   Rejection of Israel (5:21–27).[50]

---

49. Andersen and Freedman, *Amos*, 469–70.

50. See Noble ("Literary Structure," 211) for a detailed palistrophic presentation of the book of Amos.

Summary of Chapter 4

A few conclusions can be drawn on the basis of the preceding discussions. First, the book of Amos is shown to be part of the Minor Prophets thematically, rhetorically and literarily. Secondly, various units of Amos 5 (vv. 1–17, [vv.4–6, 14–15], vv.21–27) function as a whole for the purpose of inviting Israel to repent and receive salvation. Even though there might have been some deliberate literary arrangement or editorial activities in the text, this study stresses the unity of the text in its present form as the Word of God. Thirdly, the importance of this chapter for the theology of worship in Amos cannot be overemphasized. The preceding discussion—particularly the delimitation of the literary structure of Amos 5, with the identification of various forms and features (messenger formulae, woe-cries, announcements of judgment, hymns, exhortations, didactic questions, lamentations, riddles, proverbs, etc.) supports a comprehensive understanding of the meaning of Amos 5. It also demonstrates the homogeneous structure and inner organizational integrity of Amos 5.

Even when some later additions are identified in the text, its theological beauty must not be ignored. As suggested by Leclerc, the editorial activities (i.e., additions and redactions) have rescued the book of Amos from being "merely a historical record and a time bound-message. The editor's theological conviction is that God's word is timeless and has the power to address more than one audience in one place or at one time."[51] In other words, Amos 5, among other purposes, aims at exhorting and soothing the remnant of Joseph (v. 15) of every culture, and it dashes the false hopes of those who take comfort in the unconditional assurances of salvation that emanate from empty worship (vv. 21–27).

Finally, irrespective of minor differences of opinion with regard to the structure, stylistic features, and proliferation of forms (including laments, exhortations, hymns, and doxologies), a full exegetical analysis and discussion of the theological potential of this unit (which is the focus of the next chapter) can best be achieved when it is discussed within the broader socio-historical context of the prophetic traditions, especially the Twelve and the book of Amos in particular.

---

51. Leclerc, *Prophets*, 129.

5

Exegetical Analysis and Exposition of the Theology of Worship in Amos 5

Introduction

THIS CHAPTER FOCUSES ON the exegesis of Amos 5. In doing so, it builds on previous conclusions, with emphasis on the need for ethical worship of God. It stresses love, judgment, repentance, justice, and righteousness. This is not done in isolation, but inclusively within the broader context of the entire book of Amos (Amos 1–9).[1] For instance, Amos 2:8 offers a critique of unrighteous behavior at worship centers, where the elites stretched out on the garments of the destitute while drinking wine obtained by extortion. This foreshadows the later cult critique (Amos 5) and call for repentance and hope for salvation (Amos 6–9).

As intimated in the previous four chapters of this work, Nolan P. Howington and others observe that Amos' cult polemics have been wrongly criticized as judgmental, dooming, and lacking hope. The upshot of all this according to Ebo, is "that although Israel's guilt is as indisputable as Yahweh's right is to inflict punishment is incontestable, still Yahweh is limited in His choice of punishment so as not to run foul of his covenantal responsibility to Israel, who quite rightly, has no legitimate claim to life, but is totally dependent on Yahweh."[2] Additionally, some scholars have judged the section that offers some measure of hope (9:11–15) as a later addition to the book. Howington insists that the somber fact of judgment that is ubiquitous in Amos is a conditional judgment,[3] though Hunter argues that

---

1. Jeremias, *Book of Amos*, 101.
2. Ebo, "Re-Ordering," 67.
3. Howington, "Ethical Understanding of Amos," 411.

Amos is fond of placing condition on salvation rather than on judgment.[4] His severest message of judgment upon Israel, Howington concludes, is designed to induce penitence and a reversal of behavior.[5]

Howington's observation is affirmed in this chapter, which strongly demonstrates the boldness of Amos' preaching against the altars in Bethel (3:14). This study further theologically and exegetically emphasizes Amos' mockery of Israel's misdirected religious worship in Gilgal (4:4–5). Importantly, Amos exhorts Israel to seek the Lord (5:4–5, 14–15) and never to rely falsely on the notion of the Day of the Lord (vv. 18–20). These exhortations are heightened by the prophet's critique of offerings and sacrifices, which the Lord rejects in favor of justice and righteousness (vv. 21–27). Familiar with his cultural traditions, Amos skillfully relates his prophecy of true worship (Amos 5:1–27) to what precedes (Amos 1–6) and to what follows (Amos 7–9). This is evidenced in the literary, linguistic, and theological interrelationship of the texts (3:1; 4:1; 5:1, 7, 18; 6:1).[6]

This chapter, which focuses on exegesis of Amos 5, is sensitive to the previously discussed literary blocks, opinions, and outlines. It is also conscious of the overall prophetic traditions, especially that at of the Twelve, upon which Amos stood to prophesy. In order to be accessible to readers, this exegetical enterprise is methodologically carried out in three sections. Its theological dividends are adapted in the final chapter in order to interact with contemporary worship issues in Africa and North America.

Exegetical Analysis of Amos 5:1–17

The subunit of Amos 5:1–17 mostly features elements of exhortation and lamentation, along with an invitation to the house of Israel to refocus attention on seeking the Lord. Issues of accusation, judgment, and appeal also appear in this unit and are intentionally designed to convince the audience to "seek the Lord" and reject sanctuaries of worship outside Judah, especially those located in Bethel, Gilgal, and Beersheba.[7]

---

4. Hunter, *Seek the Lord*, 122.

5. Howington, "Ethical Understanding of Amos," 411.

6. Amos' use of Israel's tradition is further discussed in Hasel, *Book of Amos*, 71–81.

7. Sweeney, "Amos," 232.

Laments over the Fallen Virgin (vv. 1–3)

Verse 1 begins with an invitation to the house of Israel to hear God's word (v. 1a). As the conscience of the people and God's mouthpiece, Amos uses the genre of lamentation (קינה, *qînā*) to poetically invite Israel to listen to God. Several exegetes delight in this verse and seem to pay particular attention to it. For instance, Sweeney sees קינה (*qînā*) as a technical expression for a formal dirge or lamentation. Sweeney gives the examples of David's funerary laments over Saul and Jonathan (2 Sam 1:17–27) as well as Ezekiel's laments over the princes of Israel (Ezek 19:1–14) and Pharaoh (Ezek 32:1–16).[8] These chanting activities were not only restricted to kings like David or prophets like Jeremiah (Jer 9:10) and Ezekiel. Others, including women, were also invited to participate in funeral dirges (Judg 11:39–40; Jer 9:17).[9] Literally, a formal "dirge" (קינה) typically consists of three beats followed by two. This is evident in Amos 5:2a: "fallen-to rise-no more, -O virgin Israel."[10]

Niehaus identifies four inherent and contextual parts of these laments: (1) the tragedy (vv. 2–3); (2) a call to react (vv. 4–6; 14–15); (3) address to the fallen (vv. 7–13); and (4) summons to mourning (vv. 16–17).[11] In his article "Teaching Amos in the Churches," Clyde T. Francisco discusses "the perils of Institutionalism" and "the essence of true religion." Commenting on this passage (vv. 1–3), he notices that prophets prior to Amos had not really condemned the nation of Israel. Rather, they focused on groups and rulers. For him, this partially explains why the prophet Amos calls Israel "virgin" (בתולה): the nation of Israel had never before been conquered or humiliated. In Amos' theology, Israel is bound to fall as a result of her misunderstanding of the nature and essence of true worship.[12]

Finley insightfully observes that Jeremiah, preaching in the late preexilic period, uses the phrase "virgin Israel" (בתולת ישראל) while promising future restoration to Israel, noting that "there shall be a day when sentinels will call in the hill country of Ephraim, 'Come, let us go up to Zion, to the Lord our God'" (Jer 31:6). Finley believes that Jeremiah here is simply

---

8. Ibid., 233.

9. Finley, *Joel, Amos, Obadiah*, 224.

10. For extensive and useful demonstrations of a "dirge," see Finley, *Joel, Amos, Obadiah*, 224; and Sweeney, "Amos," 233.

11. Niehaus, "Amos," 409.

12. Francisco, "Teaching Amos in the Churches," 413–19.

reinterpreting Amos in light of the hope for the remnant of Israel who would seek the Lord in Judah. He adds that Amos addresses Israel in this manner because, like death, it is a tragic situation wherein a young woman has been cut down in the prime of her life.[13]

Shalom M. Paul sees the "young woman" in this context as representing Israel, who is still in its infancy and enjoying its political, social, and economic prosperity during the reign of Jeroboam II, to the detriment of the poor and the negligence of true worship. It is in the midst of this immaturity that Israel's demise tragically comes.[14]

In Niehaus' view, Amos addresses Israel as a "virgin" to affirm her as the bride of YHWH. The grammar of the text, with the terms "fallen" and "forsaken," is a "prophetic perfect," which presents Israel as a nation that has already hopelessly collapsed with no one to raise her up except the Lord. Thus, this passage may point to the fact that the Lord alone restores life to the righteous and to those who turn and seek him.[15] Underlining these various interpretations is a God who controls the destiny of Israel.

Verse 3, which begins with the particle "for" (כי), offers reasons for this lamentation (vv. 1–2)—namely, the impeding military havoc. Israel will suffer unimaginable military defeat (2:14–16; 4:10; 7:11). Finley suggests that the military sense of this verse is shown by the term "thousand" (אלף) and by the expression "that goes out" (היצאת), both of which indicate a military battalion on the move for war (2 Sam 18:4).[16] That is to say, of an Israelite contingent arranged in a thousand that goes out (Exod 18:21; Deut 1:15; 1 Sam 10:19; 1 Chr 27:1 2 Chr 25:5), only one hundred shall be "left" (תשאיר). Likewise, of a contingent of one hundred on the battlefront (Judg 7:16; 1 Sam 22:7; 2 Sam 18:1, 4), only ten shall be "left" (תשאיר).[17] Although Israel suffers defeat because of their covenant breaking, it is the Lord who raises up those in trouble (1 Sam 2:6–8; Hos 6:2; Amos 9:11–15).[18]

Birch sees in Amos 5:1–3 elements of misunderstanding, misconception, judgment, powerlessness, and vulnerability in the affairs of "virgin

---

13. Finley, *Joel, Amos, Obadiah*, 225.

14. Paul, *Amos*, 160.

15. Niehaus, "Amos," 411.

16. Finley, *Joel, Amos, Obadiah*, 225–26.

17. For extensive commentary on the semantics of this verse, see Hayes, *Amos*, 156–57; Finley *Joel, Amos, Obadiah*, 226; Paul, *Amos*, 161; Niehaus, "Amos," 411–12; and Sweeney, "Amos," 233–34.

18. Birch, *Hosea, Joel, and Amos*, 212.

Israel." He thinks that by establishing shrines outside Judah, Israel unethically risks worshiping other gods in those shrines. Birch also detects an implicit element of hope for life that underlines the following prophetic plea and the invitation to seek the Lord (vv. 4–6).[19] The question that remains to be answered is whether today's attitude toward the sacred or worship centers, especially in Africa (Nigeria) and America (the USA), reflects a contemporary misconception and misunderstanding of true religion, or vice versa.[20]

Seek Me and Live (vv. 4–6)

The lamentation over the fallen house of Israel (vv. 1–3) is followed by an invitation to seek the Lord (vv. 4–6). This comes with some implications of judgment and hope for salvation. As mentioned in the previous section, some scholars consistently see doom in the message of the prophet Amos, while others, including Howington and Ebo, see hope or a "silver lining" in Amos' message of judgment.[21] Abraham J. Heschel sees hope in Amos' message, noting that there is not only an invitation to repentance in every disaster, but "there is always a dimension of God's perverting affection where compassion prevails over justice, where mercy is a perpetual possibility."[22] Heschel's observation is in close affinity with the view of Karl Neubauer, who affirms the intention of Amos (vv. 4–6, 14–15) to offer a critique of worship without obedience to the covenant and love of one's neighbor. This critique leads to Amos' exhortation of Israel "to seek the Lord."[23]

Verses 4–6 use verbs that are of great theological significance, offering hope on the condition that Israel will listen to the Lord's exhortation "seek me and live" (דרשוני והיו)), which is communicated through his messenger Amos (vv. 4a–b). In light of verses 4–6, it has been widely recognized that the verb, דרש (drš) in this phrase, "seek the Lord," is Semitic in root and can be used synonymously with בקש (bqš) in biblical theology. While דרש (drš) in its various forms appears around 165 times in the OT, בקש (bqš) is found about 220 times in various contexts, but always in connection with

---

19. Ibid., 212–13.

20. This question and many more will be addressed in chapter 6.

21. Hunter (*Seek the Lord*, 60–67) has details of these reviews.

22. Heschel, *Prophets*, 43.

23. Neubauer, "Erwägungen," 292–316.

God.[24] In Amos, what stands before and after the imperative phrase "seek the Lord" is not only lamentation (vv. 1–3) and judgment (vv. 18–20), but also the exhortation with its intrinsic message of hope (cf. vv.14–15, v.24; 9:11–15).[25] Its theological function is to remind Israel that they were not committing themselves to the Lord himself, but to empty forms of worship without morality.

In Finley's opinion, this is one of the rare moments that Amos opens the window of hope in his prophecy. Amos does so in conformity with the Lord's graciousness, kindness, steadfast love, and mercy, which he has shown throughout his relationship with Israel.[26] Therefore, the expression "seek me and live" is exhortative, not ironic, since it has been repeated thrice (vv. 4, 6, and 14).[27] Modern exegetes consistently stress its invitation to repent and to have life.[28]

Niehaus admonishes that it is important to appreciate the theological concept of life, which is expressed in the command "seek the Lord that you may live." This imperatival phrase implies different things to different people in OT studies. For instance, in the legislative texts of the Pentateuch (Lev 18:5, 28; Deut 30:16–18), it represents a viable rediscovery of the lost promised inheritance: Israel lost the promised inheritance because they disobediently sought things rather than God. The prophet Amos, therefore, believes the Israelites' hope and national pride will be restored if they seek the Lord.[29] Furthermore, one seeks the Lord by desiring his oversight of one's life based on his graciousness—a message evident in other OT texts (Deut 30:6), particularly the prophetic books (cf. Hos 2:4–5;4: 15; 6:6; 10:12; 12:7; 14:2–4; Mic 6:8; Isa 1:16–17; Zeph 2:1–3; Ezek 34; 37; 40; 47).[30]

---

24. Wagner ("בקש biqqēsh; בקשה; baqqāshāh,"229–41) and Wagner ("דרש ʿ dārash; מדרש midhrāsh," 293–307) have different and synonymous ways these notions are used in diverse contexts in OT studies.

25. Hunter (Seek the Lord, 71); Wagner ("דרש ʿ dārash; מדרש midhrāsh," 299) have records of impressive views on whether the context in which דרש (drš) occurs in Amos 5:4–6; 14–5 is cultic in connection with Wisdom traditions.

26. Finley, Joel, Amos, Obadiah, 227.

27. See Paul, Amos, 162–63, for details of these scholarly opinions.

28. Wagner ("דרש ʿ dārash; מדרש midhrāsh," 298–99) affirms these modern views, including that of Wassermann, who prefers to interpret this passage in light of Jeremiah and Ezekiel.

29. Niehaus, "Amos," 414.

30. Ibid.

The prophet Zephaniah, for instance, found it necessary to respond to the rampant idolatries, syncretism, and corruption among leaders—including religious officers in Jerusalem (Zeph 1:4–10)—and the influence of foreign nations on Judah (1:8–13) by inviting the people to "seek the Lord" (Zeph 2:1–3). Zephaniah reminds the nations and Jerusalem of the God of Israel and the everlasting covenant relationship that has long been established between him and them. Zephaniah also stresses obedience and faithfulness to God as important ingredients for this relationship. He exhorts not only the nations, but also the rich and the poor in Judah, to seek the Lord so as to evade the impending judgment (1:18–20). Like Amos, Zephaniah's intention is not just to declare judgment, but also to universally inspire repentance, humility, faith, hope, and righteousness.[31]

Ezekiel expresses hope for the future restoration of Israel with the metaphor of the good shepherd (Ezek 34), the vision of the dry bones (Ezek 37), and the vision of the restored temple, city, and land (Ezek 40–42; 47). In Ezekiel 47, the river starts at the temple and flows below the threshold from the east toward the south (47:1–12). Leclerc affirms that this river of life, coming from the sanctuary, "is a potent symbol of the divine life that comes from God and rejuvenates the land, the sea, creatures, plants, and humans." Here, the people's life is once again restored by God, who dwells in the temple or in the sanctuary, where the people gather in times of need and trouble (cf. Ps 24:6; 27:8).[32]

In the Psalter, Israel is constantly encouraged to "seek the Lord" in praise and prayer based on their reflection of what God has historically done for Israel.[33] Both verbs דרש (*drš*) and בקש (*bqš*) occur in Psalm 105. As in Amos, these verbs are used exhortatively in the Psalter (cf. Pss 105: 4–5; 9:11; 69:33).

In my judgment, the word of the Lord in Amos is contingent upon the worshipers' response and change of heart or direction. Repentance has the power to abrogate the death sentence (vv. 1–3) and judgment (vv. 18–20) upon both the individual and the entire nation. Amos has invited the people to seek the Lord (v. 4a–b) and cease worshiping in Bethel, Gilgal,

31. Hunter (*Seek the Lord*, 260–70) carries a detailed study of this exhortation to "seek the Lord" in Zephaniah.

32. Leclerc, *Prophets*, 298–99.

33. Kraus (*Theology of the Psalms*, 11–15) discusses extensively the significance of "Israel in the presence of Yhwh." Metaphorically, "presence" (*pānah*), literarily "face," especially in the Psalter, refers to seeking God's help, blessings, his love, and recognizing his sovereignty and how limited we are as God's creatures.

and Beersheba (vv. 4b–6c) in order that they may have life. Seeking external shrines would bring death (vv. 1–3) and doom (vv. 18–20).

Verse 5a like the overall chapter, is connected to what precedes it (4:4–5). The exhortations in this verse are thoughtfully crafted. In Wolff's brilliant opinion, the prohibition "do not seek Bethel" (ואל־תדרשו בית־אל) is crafted antithetically to the command in verse 4b "seek me and live" (דרשוני והיו) as earlier mentioned. In verse 5b, Israel is further strictly warned "not to come to Gilgal nor to Beersheba" (והגלגל לא תבאו ובארשבע לא תעברו). Wolff believes Amos' artistry is further evidenced in the "distinction between אל; ('not') with the jussive as a vetitive and לא ('not') with the jussive. This prohibitive would allow one to recognize an artful intensification in verse 5a."[34]

Amos also judges that "Gilgal shall go to exile" (v. 5c, כי הגלגל גלה יגלה), while "Bethel shall become nothingness" (v. 5d, ובית־אל יהוה לאון). In this regard, several scholars, including Shalom M. Paul, believe Amos cleverly employs geographic paronomasia as well as alliterative repetition to demonstrate that "Gilgal" (הגלגל) "shall go into exile" (גלה יגלה).

In a way, this is a pun used by the prophet in order to emphasize the severity of God's judgment upon those who hide behind Gilgal to practice injustice. In addition to the use of pun to mock the false sense of security in Gilgal, the prophet Amos also plays on the nothingness of Bethel (ובית־אל יהוה לאון). Amos interprets און as "nullity" and אל as "god." He playfully reads "Beth-el" ("house of god") as "Beth-al" ("house of nothingness"). This house, when unethically approached or used as a center for injustice, will become nothing except nullity.[35]

Amos' audience must have been startled and shocked that a man like Amos, who was familiar with his native culture and tradition, would say this about Bethel, Gilgal, and Beersheba.[36] Historically, these shrines were important religious sanctuaries for the people, and Amos and his contemporaries were fully aware of this.[37]

Bethel was the main sanctuary for the northern kingdom of Israel (1 Kgs 12:28–32). It was also associated with the patriarchs Abraham, Jacob, and Isaac. Abraham sacrificed and called upon the name of the Lord at Bethel (Gen 13:3–4), and Jacob received revelation from "the

---

34. Wolff, *Joel and Amos*, 239.

35. Paul, *Amos*, 163–64.

36. Finley, *Joel, Amos, Obadiah*, 226.

37. Niehaus, "Amos," 414.

God of Bethel" (הָאֵל בֵּית־אֵל) when he was departing from Laban's family (Gen 31:13–14). Earlier, he had come to Bethel as a wanderer without any certain future (Gen 28:10–22). He also returned to Bethel after his reconciliation with his brother, Esau (Gen 35:1–15).[38] During Jacob's second visit to Bethel, God changed Jacob's name from Jacob to Israel: "Your name is Jacob, and no longer shall you be called Jacob, but Israel shall be your name" (Gen 35:10). This name change reassured Jacob and renewed his hope in God's blessings and prosperity. As such, Bethel was symbolically a center of hope and renewal. This traditional symbolism would have contributed to the shocking response Amos' words would have evoked from his original audience. Yet, as Motyer rightly observes, "There was something about the whole Bethel syndrome which inhibited the pilgrims from experiencing the reality which Bethel was supposed to be all about, namely the life-giving presence of the Lord."[39]

It was at Beersheba that each of the patriarchs received God's assurances of protection and companionship on their various journeys. Abraham made his first call to the Lord at Beersheba, and it was here that his dispute with Abimelech was reconciled. Abraham made a covenant with Abimelech and dug a well in Beersheba ("well of seven"/ "well of oath,") "because both of them swore an oath." In Beersheba Abraham planted a tree "and called there on the name of the LORD, the Everlasting God" (Gen 21:21–33). It was also in Beersheba that the Lord assured Isaac, saying, "I am the God of your father Abraham; do not be afraid, for I am with you and will bless you and make your offspring numerous for my servant Abraham's sake" (Gen 26:23–25). And in Beersheba the Lord said to Jacob, "I am God, the God of your father, do not be afraid to go down to Egypt" (Gen 46:1–5).

Given the historic significance of the ancient shrine at Beersheba, Amos' prophecy must not only have been challenging but also an indication that, like Bethel, Beersheba was abused. It was no longer representing the repository of God's love and the sacrament of his living companionship—a temptation that contemporary worshipers are yet to completely overcome.[40]

Gilgal was also a holy place with long-standing tradition. It was associated with Israel's entry into the land (Josh 4–5), and it was at Gilgal

---

38. Motyer, *Message of Amos*, 106; Niehaus, "Amos," 414.

39. Motyer, *Message of Amos*, 106; Birch, *Hosea, Joel, and Amos*, 203.

40. Motyer, *Message of Amos*, 106. See also Niehaus, "Amos," 415. See also 1 Sam 8:1–2; 2 Kgs 22–23.

that the first king of Israel, Saul, was anointed (1 Sam 11:14–15).[41] As with Bethel and Beersheba, Amos' prophecy "that Gilgal shall go to exile" (v. 5c; 5:27) must have sparked some unbelieving fears in the ears of Amos' contemporaries, especially those who ignored ethical justice while taking for granted worship and pilgrimages to these sanctuaries, even though they were not able to keep the fundamental promises and faith inheritance for which such sanctuaries originally stood.

Hunter notes that "the mention of these three is not restrictive but representative of all the sanctuaries and cult places."[42] Even though Amos was a native of Tekoa in the south, he did not specifically say when he preached in the north "seek me in Jerusalem," as some critiques would suggest. It is evident from the entire prophecy of Amos that the brunt of Amos' critique of worship is the syncretic element of the YHWH cult at these old sanctuaries (vv. 4–6; vv.14–15).[43]

Amos theologically and skillfully seeks to remind his audience that the sanctuaries have become ends in themselves instead of a means to God. Traveling to these shrines (Bethel, Gilgal, and Beersheba) with offerings, gifts, songs, and dances in ways that had very little to do with the moral life God demanded in daily life for those who seek him was not good enough (vv. 4–6). Amos believes that those who seek the Lord at these worship centers are called to a responsible life of covenant obedience that extends beyond the altars and into the market squares. Unless Israel seeks the Lord (vv. 5–6), every self-serving sanctuary in the house of Joseph (v. 6b) would be reduced to nothingness by exile and fire.[44] In these verses (vv. 4–6), it

---

41. Birch, *Hosea, Joel, and Amos*, 203.

42. Hunter, *Seek the Lord*, 70.

43. Kapelrud, *Central Idea of Amos*, 37. Also, see Wolff (*Amos*, 44–45) where the question is also raised of "whether the particular form of exhortation speech used by Amos does not spring from the same roots in wisdom." For Wolff, "very rarely does this prophet exhort."

44. Sweeney (*Prophets*, 234) also makes an insightful comment on the imagery of the "house of Joseph" and "fire" breaking out here. He says, "the imagery of fire breaking out against the 'house of Joseph,' is a very real threat at the time of Sukkoth, as the transition from the dry to the rainy season approaches. Indeed, the prophet's vision of fire consuming the land (Amos 7:4–6) may recall just such an outbreak of fire prior to the rains." Also, "the designation of Israel as the 'house of Joseph,' is particularly pertinent as Joseph is the father of Ephraim and Benjamin, the two tribes that populate the central hill country of Israel and in whose territory the sanctuary at Beth El is located."

seems that Amos is not ready to let go of hope for life, which he believes is a better alternative to a hopeless death.[45]

Rebuking Injustices (v. 7)

In verse 7, Amos explains how the Israelites have not sought the Lord. This negligence leads to attacks, which begin with "woe to you . . ." (v. 7) and are followed by threats and punishments (vv. 8–9).[46] Sweeney notices that these attacks, threats, and punishments are directed toward the leaders of Israel, who have "turned (ההפכים) justice (משפט) into wormwood (ללענה)" and "thrown (הניחו) righteousness (צדקה) to the ground" (5:7)[47]

Philip J. King notes that wormwood (ללענה) is "a dwarf shrub some-times used for healing in folk medicine."[48] He stresses that the shrub is aromatic and bitter.[49] Mays likewise notes, "Wormwood, a Palestinian plant of exceedingly bitter taste (cf. 6.12b), was frequently used in metaphors to describe the bitterness of calamity (Jer. 9.15; 23.15; Lam. 3.15, 19)."[50] Israel's leaders and their collaborators had distorted justice to the level of a bitter poison (v. 7a).[51] By and large, Amos is warning against and detesting the fact that the Israelites have hurled righteousness violently to the ground (v. 7b).[52] They have neglected the requirements of the Mosaic Law (Deut 25:1) while creating bitterness and suffering among the citizens.[53]

In verse 7, the prophet Amos condemns unequivocally and idiomati-cally the oppression and subjugation of the poor and the needy in society. He sees injustice as this bitter wormwood. He also uses the genre of hymn/doxology to heighten his critique of the unethical behaviors of society (vv. 8–9). Even though, logically, this genre (vv. 8–9) sounds like an interruption

---

45. Simundson, *Hosea, Joel, Amos, Obadiah, Jonah, Micah,* 194.

46. See Anderson and Freedman, *Amos,* 483–87, for extensive comments on this first woe in the book of Amos.

47. Sweeney, "Amos," 235.

48. King, *Archaeological Commentary,* 124.

49. Ibid.

50. Mays, *Amos,* 91.

51. Niehaus, "Amos," 418.

52. See also Mays, *Amos,* 91–92, and Branick (*Prophets,* 47–48) for a detailed study of the terms משפט and צדקה and their use in Amos within the context of the judicial proceedings. This will be expanded in our exegesis of Amos 5:21–27.

53. Niehaus, "Amos," 418.

from verse 7 that is better connected to verse 10, theologically it gives "a good summary insight of Amos' critique of all that was wrong in Israel's society."[54] It also highlights how perverted and contemptuous of truth the people are. Commenting on the significance of this, Branick says, "Amos 5:7, 10–13 is the heart of the sermon."[55] Verse 7 contains God's words of woe condemning the oppression of the weak and the poor. What God expects from Israel is "fair judgment" (*mishpat*) and "justice" (*tzedeqah*). This message runs throughout Amos 5 connecting it with the rest of the book of Amos and of the Minor Prophets.

Even though *mishpat* literally means "judgment" in the legal sense of the word, biblically it is what leaders, or Israel's judges (*shophtim*), are supposed to carry out in the community in order to support the weak, the wounded, the voiceless, and the marginalized. Righteousness (*tzedeqah*), on the other hand, describes the rightness of God, his fidelity to his covenant, and his "justice."[56] In Amos' mind, both are connected to the worship of God. There is a close juxtaposition of injustice and false worship, since seeking the Lord is concerned with justice (cf. 5:14–15, 24).[57]

Hymn and Doxology of Praise (vv. 8–9)

Verses 8–9 are widely regarded as the second of the three hymns in Amos.[58] This hymn serves to bring the Israelites into direct relationship with the Lord, whom they have refused to seek, in order to find life. The Israelites have incurred punishment by relying on a pseudo-form of worship and by mocking justice.[59] This hymn (vv. 8–9) as a whole describes God as the creator of the heavenly bodies, the one who takes charge of the daily transition from day to night and night to day, and the God who provides the rain and the water that nourishes plants, animals, humans, and every other living

54 See Simundson, *Hosea, Joel, Amos, Obadiah, Jonah, Micah*, 195; Finely, *Joel, Amos, Obadiah*, 229, for samples of a detailed discussion on the break in flow of the context at verse 7, Cf. Paul, *Amos*, 166–67.

55. Branick, *Prophets,* 47.

56. Ibid.

57. Finley, *Joel, Amos, Obadiah*, 230. Again, exegesis on this theme will be expanded when we take up verses 14–15, 24.

58 The style in grammar and the recurring phrase "and his name is Lord" identify this hymn with similar hymns, the first and the second in Amos 4:13; 9:5–6 (Simundson, *Hosea, Joel, Amos, Obadiah, Jonah, Micah*, 195).

59. Ibid, 231.

thing.[60] This hymn portrays God as the sovereign of all creation—a concept also found in other prophetic books.[61] Shalom M. Paul describes this hymn as "a declaration of the power and majesty of the Lord, who will bring the threatened punishment upon those who defy his will. Those who are guilty of social inversion shall now witness and suffer cosmic inversion."[62]

Amos' choice of the words "Pleiades" (כימה) and "Orion" (כסיל) is significant (v. 8a).[63] Similar words of creation are found in Wisdom texts (Job 9:9; 38:31), where they are also associated with the New Year (Nisan) and the change of weather between winter and summer. This hymn in Amos' prophecy praises God as the creator and regulator of natural order[64] who turns darkness into light (vv. 8b–c) and controls the waters of the sea and the earth (vv. 8d–e). YHWH's action, as presented in the hymn (vv. 8–9), foreshadows Amos' notion of the Day of the Lord (vv. 18–20), just as the concluding doxology "and his name is the LORD" (v. 8f) fits the pattern already common and familiar in Amos (4:13; 9:6).

Amos uses these hymns to remind his audience of the importance of seeking the Lord (v. 6).[65] He expands on his praises of the power of God, who brings destruction upon the threshold and can also bring down the fortress, no matter how strong it might seem (v. 9). Sweeney, commenting on this hymn's role in Amos' theology, argues that "the motif of bringing destruction upon the strong and upon the fortress conveys YHWH's power to bring security of the state and its leaders to an end."[66] Sweeney also posits that verse 9 builds upon the portrayal of YHWH in verse 8.[67] God acts universally. He can do and undo, and he can administer justice to those who attempt to downplay justice and truth and oppress the poor (vv. 10–13) while proceeding to the altars.

---

60. Ibid., 195.

61. See Leclerc, *Prophet*, 112–13, for a good summary of the theme of the Divine Sovereignty in the prophetic books.

62. Paul, *Amos*, 167–68.

63. Finley (*Joel, Amos, Obadiah*, 232–34) has additional commentaries on "Pleiades" (כימה) and "Orion" (כסיל).

64. Paul, *Amos*, 168.

65. Sweeney, "Amos," 434–35.

66. Ibid.

67. Ibid., 435.

Rebuking Oppressors of the Poor (vv. 10–12)

In verses 10–13 Amos rebukes those who oppress the poor. He speaks words of woe to those who mock justice, oppress the poor, and indulge in corruption. In so doing, Amos revisits the theme addressed earlier in his prophecy (v. 7).

In verses 10–13 Amos singles out those who "hate the one who reproves the gate" (v. 10a) and "abhor the one who speaks the truth" (v. 10b). An understanding of Amos' historical context can illuminate the meaning of these phrases. King notes that, prior to the time of Amos, city gates were constructed in ancient Israel for defense and protection (שער).[68] The city gate was also a place of assembly and—more importantly—a place where legal affairs were conducted, presided over by the elders and the judges of the community (Deut 21:1–9; 25:7; Ruth 4:1–12).[69]

In Amos' day, city gates were the places where public hearings took place and where justice was administered (Amos 5:10, 12, 15).[70] The person "who reproves at the gate" (מוכיח) was responsible for dispensing justice, recognizing injustice, and raising awareness and crucial questions in the courts. These people were thus hated by those elites who were primarily concerned with their own selfish interests (cf. Gen 31:37, 42; 1 Chr 12:17; Isa 2:4; 29:21; 11:3).[71] The selfish and indifferent elites likewise abhorred those who spoke the truth in legal settings (v. 10b).

Some commentators regard verse 11 as an addition because it begins with the term "indeed" (לכן).[72] For instance, Wolff sees verse 11 as "an independent and differently motivated threat of punishment."[73] As maintained throughout this study, the conjunction "indeed" in Amos 5 serves to prepare judgment or punishment for the unjust, who "abhor" and "hate" justice (vv. 10a–b) and "trample" and "levy" the poor" (vv. 11a–b). This term also looks back at the offenses of those who acquire their wealth in an unjust manner and looks ahead to their punishment (vv. 11c–f).

---

68. King (*Archeological Commentary*, 74–76) has a detailed description of the city gate during the time of Solomon, including the architectural plan of the gate.

69. King, *Archaeological Commentary*, 75; Finley, *Joel, Amos, Obadiah*, 236; Sweeney, "Amos," 236.

70. Paul, *Amos*, 170–71.

71. Finley, *Joel, Amos, Obadiah*, 236; Sweeney, "Amos" in *the Twelve Prophets*, 236.

72. See Paul, *Amos*, 171, for a comprehensive list of these commentators especially those that sees it as a continuation of vv. 7, 10.

73. Wolff, *Joel and Amos*, 247.

Following this conjunction, Amos proceeds rhetorically to convince the corrupt leaders that even though they have built their houses with stones (v. 11c), they shall not live in them (v. 11d). Neither will they enjoy the wine from their vineyards, though they planted them with delight (vv. 11 e–f). Shalom M. Paul calls this rhetoric a "retaliatory punishment, in the form of a 'futility curse' . . . that describes the reversal of one's expectations."[74] Such rhetorical curses can be found in ancient texts outside of the Bible, especially in ancient Near Eastern treaties. A typical example is the eighth-century BCE Sefire treaty conducted between two minor kings, Barga'yah and Matti'el, who hailed Arpad. In the following text, Matti'el swears to accept dire consequences for himself and his cities should he violate the stipulations of the treaty:

> A treaty of Barga'yah, king of Ktk, with Matti 'el, the son of 'Attarsamak, king of [Arpad a t]reaty of the sons of Barga'yah with the sons of Matti 'el. . . . As this wax is consumed with fire, thus Arpad [and its dependencies] shall be consumed ext[ensively]. Hadad shall sow in them salt and water cress. And it shall not be mentioned (ever after). As this wax is consumed by fire, thus Ma[tti 'el] shall be consumed [by fi]re. As this bow and these arrows are broken, thus Inurta (Ninurta) and Hadad shall break [the bow of Matti 'el] and the bows of his nobles. As the man of wax is blinded, thus Matti 'el shall be blinded.[75]

Upon close examination, this treaty describes punishment in the form of reversal for those who do not keep the stipulation treaty. Similar reversals are also found in biblical texts outside of Amos (Deut 28:30–39; Mic 6:15; Zeph 1:13). In the context of Amos, the upper class' ill-gotten possessions will be taken away from them because they have enlarged their property and wealth at the expense of poor.[76] Niehaus stresses that this threat is based on the Lord's knowledge of the people's sins, as captured in the expression "for I know (כי ידעתי) how many your crimes are" (v. 12a).[77]

Sweeney suggests that the prophet uses the initial "for" (כי) in verse 12 in order to skillfully and logically reinforce his previous judgment (v. 11). Amos is asserting that the Lord knows the sins of the corrupt leaders as well

---

74. Paul, *Amos*, 173.

75. See the "Sfire treaty" in Pritchard, *ANET*, 659–60; Simundson, *Hosea, Joel, Amos, Obadiah, Jonah, Micah*, 196–97.

76. Paul, *Amos*, 173

77. Niehaus, "Amos," 421.

as their oppression of the righteous (v. 12c).[78] Finley highlights the effect of the participle "oppressing" in the expression "oppressing the righteous" (צררי צדיק) to characterize how the wicked conduct themselves daily. They would regularly use the courts to fake legal bases for their crimes against the poor and the helpless. Their behavioral pattern includes taking bribes (כפר) and subverting (הטו) the needy at the gate (vv. 12c–d).[79]

Prudence, or Passivity (v. 13)

In verse 13, Amos moves from challenging those who worship falsely, oppress the poor, and abhor justice at the gate (vv. 10–12) to those who are passive and indifferent (v. 13). Amos calls such people "prudent": "indeed the prudent man is silent at this time (v. 13a), for it is an evil time" (v. 13b). Scholars differ in their understandings of the term "prudent" here. Some scholars think it is the language of an outsider commenting on the prophecy of Amos.[80] For instance, Mays believes the expression reflects a late genre of Wisdom literature, pointing to the similar expression "the prudent man" (המשכיל) in the book of Proverbs (e.g., Prov 10:5, 19; 17:2; 21:11).[81] Wolff, on the other hand, thinks this is a misplaced gloss and thus additional material.[82] Barstad acknowledges that the entire verse (v. 13) is a crux but insightfully warns against seeing any difficult text in Amos as a late addition. In his view, the problem of verse 13 could be the result of modern interpreters' failure to uncover its full meaning within the ancient literary context of Amos' prophecy.[83] Similarly, Simundson believes these suggestions can only be left at the level of possibility, particularly that of Wolff, since he is not certain.[84]

78. Sweeney, "Amos," 236.

79. Finley (*Joel, Amos, Obadiah*, 239) explains that "taking bribes" (()כפר) usually means ransom paid as a substitute for one's life (Exod 21:30; Num 35:31, 32), but in Amos the term may have a more general sense of money accepted to influence justice in the court, just as the participle "subverting" (הטו) would reflect the general condition of constantly harassing the poor.

80. Simundson, *Hosea, Joel, Amos, Obadiah, Jonah*, 197.

81. Mays, *Amos*, 98.

82. Wolff, *Joel and Amos*, 248–50.

83. Barstad, *Religious Polemics*, 81.

84. Simundson, *Hosea, Joel, Amos, Obadiah, Jonah*, 197.

In Finley's view, although prudence is a virtue, the prophet Amos is not condoning silence in the face of evil, since he himself spent his prophetic mission openly challenging evil, injustice, and worship without morality (e.g., 7:10–17). Rather, abhorring justice, milking the poor, corrupting the socio-political systems, and remaining passive in the face of injustice are "unwise." According to Finley, these seem to be the conditions prevalent in what the prophet Amos idiomatically characterizes as "an evil time."[85] The question left for contemporary religious societies, therefore, remains whether it is prudent or wise to remain silent, indifferent, or passive in the face of injustice, or whether we must instead seek righteousness in the way we treat one another, especially the poor.[86]

Exhortation, Repentance and Life Seeking (vv. 14–15)

From his warnings against indifference in the face of injustice (v. 13), Amos advances to demonstrating his bravery. His prophecy shows consistency in its message: he repeatedly challenges Israel's bad behaviors, including their syncretism (vv. 4–6). Amos intensifies his exhortations that the community should seek good (דרשו־טוב) and not evil (ואל־רע) so that they may live (v. 14a).

Many scholars see verses 14–15 as a continuation or an intensification of Amos' earlier exhortation (vv. 4–6). For instance, Mays insists that "the opening sentence takes up the form of 5:4b and 6a."[87] Hasel also calls verse 14 "a commentary on the earlier exhortation to seek the Lord" (vv. 4–6). For him, the Lord cannot be found in sanctuaries alone, but through seeking righteousness and justice, even in the marketplaces.[88] Hunter describes verse 14a as an imperatival transformation of Yahweh's call to "seek me and live" (v. 4b).[89] Seeking God in Amos' theology (v. 4b) is not for nothing. It has a goal, a finality, and a purpose. It bears the sense of hope for life, as demonstrated by the renewed rendering "so that" (למען) "you may live" (תחיו) in verse 14a.

85. Finley, *Joel, Amos, Obadiah*, 239–40.

86. See the recent cautions against indifference toward the difficulties facing humanity in Pope Francis' New Year Message for the celebration of the world Day of Peace, 1 January, 2015, titled, "No Longer Slaves, But Brothers and Sisters."

87. Mays, *Amos*, 99.

88. Hasel, *Remnant*, 196–97; Sweeney, "Amos," 236.

89. Hunter, *Seek the Lord*, 80.

In this section, Amos reiterates the call to "seek good and not evil" with a slight variation (vv. 14–16). In the earlier text (vv. 4–6), God ("me") was the object of seeking. Hunter observes that in verse 15, the expression "hate evil, love good" (v. 15a) replaces the verbs "seek" and "live" (vv. 4–6) with a new interpretation.[90] Where Amos previously exhorted the people to seek the Lord and live, he now exhorts them to seek good and not evil so that they may live.[91] In this context, goodness is the result of seeking or knowing God.[92] Besides the desire to live in goodness, justice must prevail or be manifested at the gate (והציגו בשער משפט) and law courts (v. 15b). Therefore, goodness, righteousness, prosperity, good health, and fear of the Lord are the ingredients of a just and faithful society.

Some scholars see in Amos 14–15 wisdom elements similar to those found in Wisdom literature, particularly the book of Proverbs and the Psalter. Wolff, for instance, points to the coupling of positive and negative exhortations (Prov 24:21; 25:9), the antithetical pairs (Prov 1:22; 9:8; 12:1), and the concern for life (Prov 4:4; 11:19; 12:28).[93] Mays observes that two wisdom poems in the Psalter (cf. Pss 34:12–14; 37:3, 27) parallel the style of Amos (5:14–15).[94] Samuel Terrien argues that Wisdom influence can be seen in Amos' moralistic conception of salvation. In this case, Amos makes ethical behavior the prerequisite for divine favor.[95] However, Hunter cautions that the Wisdom-element theory must not be taken too far, since contrasting pairs (e.g., love/hate) are so essential to the life experience that they cannot be monopolized by a single tradition.[96]

Hunter further highlights the debate over whether the phrase "the Lord God of Hosts" (יהוה אלהי־צבאות) in v.14 is a cultic epithet.[97] He suggests the qualifier "perhaps" (אולי) serves to reject the notion that in Amos, salvation from God can only be given through cultic worship. This is to

---

90. Ibid.

91. Cf. Mays, *Amos*, 100, for additional discussion on the significance of these exhortations.

92. Niehaus, "Amos," 423.

93. Wolff, *Amos the Prophet*, 45; Hunter, *Seek the Lord*, 81.

94. Mays, *Amos*, 100.

95. Terrien, "Amos and Wisdom," 108–15.

96. Hunter, *Seek the Lord*, 81.

97 Hunter (*Seek the Lord*, 83–84) has details of this debate.

say that the adverb reminds the community of the conditionality of God's promises on their seeking the Lord.[98]

The meaning of the phrase "the remnant of Joseph" (שארית יוסף) in verse 15d is not unconnected from the preceding text (vv. 15a–c). Hunter offers additional insight into the interpretative aspects of this phrase, as scholars attempt to draw a line between exhortations and the prophecy of unconditional judgment. He observes that the argument concerning Amos' prophecy often rotates around the premise that the prophet proclaims doom and the unconditional disintegration of Israel and seeks to attack the elites of Israel and the political, social, and economic institutions (including the iron palaces, cities, and temples) that support their hegemony. Amos, however, does not envision a complete annihilation of every Israelite. Rather, some people will survive the collapse of the nationhood. The remnant will consist of those who seek not only the Lord, but also pursue his justice and righteousness. Hence, Amos' prophetic message has elements of both judgment and salvation, as is emphasized throughout this study.[99]

James M. Ward similarly sees dual elements in Amos' prophecy. He believes the kingdom of Jeroboam was annihilated alongside his cultic establishment, yet the people of God were spared and survived the fall of the monarchy, perhaps as a result of their response to Amos' invitation to seek the Lord.[100] Hasel insists that this remnant motif bridges the tensions that exists between Amos' message of doom and the salvation it generates.[101] Hasel also notices that, historically, the remnant motif in Amos has been used both negatively and positively: negatively, it is used to intensify the judgment message of Amos (3:12; 4:1–3; 5:3; 6:9–10; 9:1–4). In a positively sense, the remnant motif holds out hope for the faithful within the nation (5:3; 14–15; 9:11–12) and defines theologically the implication of the message of judgment in Amos.[102]

The implication of these arguments is that Amos is attacking the popular dual conceptions of the phrase "remnant of Joseph": first, that on the Day of YHWH nations other than Israel would be destroyed,[103] and second, the hope that the remnant shall survive any catastrophe to carry on

98. Ibid., 85.

99. See ibid., 85–86.

100. Ward, *Amos and Isaiah*, 58.

101. Hasel, *Remnant*, 203.

102. Hasel, *Book of Amos*, 113–14.

103. Ibid., 201.

the hope of the chosen people.[104] Amos counters the first conception with the argument that Israel as a whole will not survive, only the remnant. He counters the second conception with the belief that the precondition for a possible remnant is not cultic justification, but ethical righteousness. Such arguments concerning the reversal of a popular notion of the remnant are in line with Amos' habit of attacking complacency based on election theology (3:1–2; 9:7) and challenging the people for taking the Day of the Lord for granted (5:18–20; 8:9–10; 9:10).[105]

In line with Hasel and Hunter, we can conclude that Amos is not necessarily countering a popular eschatological interpretation of the "remnant of Joseph" (v. 15 d). There is no additional word to clarify what Amos had in mind (v. 15d), as was the case for the election theology (3:1–3) and the Day of the Lord, which Amos changed from light to darkness (5:18–20). Hunter believes Amos is simply taking over the phrase "remnant of Joseph" from popular and cultic usage, where it had positive and sentimental connotations for Israel. The Israelites expect from the cult the reassurance that God will grant his continual blessings and favor to the descendants of Joseph.[106] Perhaps by "descendants" Amos was referring to the northern kingdom, since he knew that the patriarch stood under the blessings of the Lord and preserved the remnant (שארית) of Israel during a devastating threat to their existence (Gen 45:47).[107] Hasel ultimately concludes, "a positive remnant idea is present in 5:14–15 and 9:11–12. It is an eschatological idea located right at the center of the Book of Amos."[108]

Niehaus supports this approach and argues that the prophet Amos theologically speaks of the people through whom God continues to carry out his promises.[109] These people are not limited to northern Israel; everyone is universally exhorted to repent, seek good, and hate evil. For Amos, everyone is under the divine radar of judgment and salvation, irrespective of their region, nation, or culture (vv. 4–6, 14–15).[110]

---

104. Cf. Müller and Preuss, *Vortstellung*, 59.

105. Hunter, *Seek the Lord*, 87.

106. Ibid., 93–94.

107. Hasel, *Remnant*, 201; Finley, *Joel, Amos, Obadiah*, 242.

108. Hasel, *Book of Amos*, 116.

109. Niehaus, "Amos," 423.

110. Birch, *Hosea, Joel and Amos*, 214. See also Hunter, *Seek the Lord*, 101–5, for a detailed discussion on the intention and relationship between vv. 4–6; 14–15, within the overall larger unit of vv. 1–17. The intention remains not only that of exhortation and lamentation over sins, but motivation to seek the Lord or call to repentance and

Invitation for Lamentations (vv. 16–17)

In an effort to further remind his eighth-century BCE community of the implications of judgment and salvation, Amos in verses 16–17 returns to the theme of lamentations (vv. 1–3), which began the entire unit (vv. 1–17). Sweeney thinks that this text (vv. 16–17) plays an important role in pointing to the consequences of failing to heed the prophet's warning and exhortation (vv. 1–15) and introducing the woes (5:18–27; 6:1–14) that describe the consequences in detail.[111]

The conjunction "indeed" (לכן) in v.16a is of particular significance. It introduces the announcement of judgment (3:11; 4:14; 5:11; 6:7; 7:17) and connects the passage with verses 10–13.[112] The messenger formula: כה־אמר יהוה אלהי צבסות אדני("thus says the Lord, God of Hosts"), which is repeated in verse 17b, indicates that God approves of the consequences for sins, which include lamentations and mourning in every street, field, vineyard, and city (vv. 16–17).[113]

Barstad argues that, as a unit, verses 1–17 summarize the prophet's core message. Whereas previous pronouncements (vv. 2–3, 11) caution Israel against worshiping other deities at shrines located in Bethel, Gilgal, Dan, and Beersheba—thereby challenging their social and moral/religious behavior—verses 16–17 as a subunit both combine and intensify the cult polemics, highlighting the relationship between social life, economics, and worship. Through verses 16–17, Amos stresses God's role in providing Israel's farm produce and giving them abundant fertility. The Israelites must faithfully follow and seek the Lord in order to evade the impending doom (vv. 18–20).[114]

Exegetical Analysis of Amos 5:18–20

This section (vv. 18–20) builds on the preceding conclusion that the initial unit (vv. 1–17) points to the judgments or consequences of refusing to

obedience, so as to have life.

111. Sweeney, "Amos," 237.

112. Finley (*Joel, Amos, Obadiah,* 243) argues that "indeed" introduces the fact that "inexcusable injustices throughout the land fully justify what the Lord will do."

113. For detailed commentary on verses 16–17, see also Sweeney, "Amos," 237; Andersen and Freedman, *Amos,* 512–18.

114. Barstad (*Religious Polemics,* 82–88) discusses extensively the role of the deities and YHWH as sources for rain and fertility is extensively discussed.

seek the Lord in the right place and manner. These consequences are well expressed in Amos' prophecy of judgment (vv. 18–20), which begins with these words: הוי המתאוים את־יום יהוה ("Misfortunes for you who desire the Day of the LORD") . Significant in this prophecy is the notion of Day of the Lord. The following exegesis amplifies the history of research on the Day of the Lord and the role it plays in uniting Amos 5 to the rest of the Twelve as examined in the previous chapters.

Darkness of Misfortunes (v. 18)

Verse 18a begins with the interjection of a pronouncement of "misfortune" (הוי).[115] This is followed by Amos' participial expression: המתאוים את־יום יהוה ("those who long for this day of the LORD"), which describes the conduct that attracts the lamentation in the first place (cf. 5:7; 6:1).[116] This type of woe-cry or "cry of misfortune" directed to a living audience is common in prophetic books, especially in funeral contexts. In such contexts, Israel's prophet presumes to be familiar with the conduct of his audience and makes commensurate pronouncements.[117] The participial expression "you who desire (המתאוים) the Day of the LORD" also seems to challenge those who maintain that Amos' audience had no preconception of the idea of the Day of the Lord. Wolff notes that Amos evidently grapples with this

---

115 Udoekpo (*Rethinking the Day of YHWH*, 203) translates הוי in v. 18a as "misfortune" for the following reasons: First, it seems to covey better all the woes of a contemporary audience as equally expressed in *Rogets' 21st Century Thesaurus in Dictionary Form*. Here the following synonyms for misfortune are listed: "bad luck," "disaster," "accident," "adversity," "affliction," "annoyance," "anxiety," "bad break," "bad news," "blow," "burden," "calamity," "casualty," "cataclysm," "catastrophe," "contretemps," "cross," "crunch," "debacle," "hardship," "harm," "inconvenience," "misadventure," "mischance," "misery," "reverse," "trouble," etc. Second, scholars do not agree on the original *Sitz im Leben* of this form of "woe" (הוי). Some trace it to the Wisdom tradition, while others trace it to the funeral laments. For instance Gersternberger ("Woe-Oracle of the Prophets," 249–63) argues that the woe article came from the wise men's reflection about the vicissitude of life. For him it is a wisdom saying. While Westermann (*Basic Forms of Prophetic Speech*, 190–94) sees it as a curse form Clifford ("Use of Hôy in the Prophets," 458–64) traces it to the lament over the dead. Wanke ("*ōy und hōy*," 215–18) argues that "*ōy*" is a cry of dread, peril, and lament, while "*hōy*" is lament for dead. I do not think the meaning should be confined to these distinctions, as "woes" can take any form of "misfortune" or its synonym.

116. The interjection of misfortune used to refer to dead was used in 1 Kgs 13:30 (הו אחי), "Misfortune, my brother!" and in Jer 22:18.

117. Mays, *Amos*, 103.

expression, since it is repeated many times in this short oracle (5:18a, 18b, and 20)."[118]

Verses 18b and 20a present rhetorical questions such as, "what is this Day of the Lord for you?" (למה־זה לכם יום יהוה), which also undermines the popular hope and optimism of the community. Amos uses this type of rhetoric to exhort, challenge, and invite his audience to self-introspection on the true meaning of the Day of the Lord (cf.5:4–5; 14, 20; 8:11; 9:4). According to Finley, Amos' question also highlights the amazement of the questioner: It suggests the shock of seeing unjust people who also deny God. They live in ignorance, asking for God's blessings while at the same time practicing injustices in the community. Amos believes that, to such people, the Day of the Lord will be a day of darkness rather than light (הוא־חשך ולא־אור). Darkness here symbolizes judgment, while light represents salvation.[119] Amos uses these symbolic motifs to warn Israel of the impending calamity, doom, and exile that awaits those who do not seek the Lord (5:27).[120] As an anchor of other prophetic books, especially the Minor Prophets, these motifs are also relationally vivid and theologically evident in other prophetic books (e.g., Isa 13:10; Ezek 30:3; Joel 2:1–2; Zeph 1:15).[121]

Irony of Humor (v. 19)

In verse 19, Amos resorts to his usual repertoire of linguistic and metaphorical expressions (2:13; 3:12; 6:12; and 9:9) to convey his message. Finley describes verse 19 as Amos' use of "masterful irony and humor" to paint the picture of a hopeless situation.[122] Amos compares the Day of Lord to the experience of a man or a person who escapes from the lion (הארי) only to get attacked by a bear (הדב). He also compares the Day of the Lord to the experience of a man who comes home to lean his hand on the supposedly safe walls of his house and is bitten by a snake (הנחש). These comparisons

---

118. Wolff, *Joel and Amos*, 255. Outside prophetic texts the phrase appears only once in Lam 2:22 (ביום אף־יהוה), "on the day of the wrath of the Lord."

119. Cf. Leclerc, *Prophets*, 110, where it is rightly observed that besides darkness and light, "the prophets use a wide range of images and metaphors to describe impending judgment, for example, a boiling pot (Jer 1:13–14), surging waters(Isa 8:7–8; Jer 46:7), a devouring sword (Hos 11:6; Isa 1:20), a cutting razor (Isa 7:20), a trap (Jer 48:43–44), a plague (Zech 14:12–18), and invasion of locusts (Joel 1:2–4)."

120. Chisholm Jr., "Minor Prophets," 406.

121. Paul, *Amos*, 185.

122. Finley, *Joel, Amos, Obadiah*, 247.

evoke emotion and paint a vivid threat, as an actual encounter with these deadly creatures is never pleasant (1 Sam 17:34, 36–37; 2 Kgs 2:24; Hos 13:7–8; Prov 28:15; Num 21:6).[123]

Under these circumstances, Amos reminds Israel that misfortunes can occur when least expected. Relying on the laurel of momentary success, as did Jeroboam II (2 Kgs 14:23–29) after defeating Damascus, could be an illusion. Amos advises that even if Israel had escaped death during previous battles, they could not expect deliverance because they had returned to practicing injustice, extortion, fraud, and unrighteousness (Amos 5:21–27). The coming of the Day of the Lord (יום יהוה) will be as fatal as an encounter with a deadly lion (הארי), violent bear (הדב), or poisonous snake (הנחש).

Repeating the Darkness of Misfortune (v. 20)

In verse 20a–b, Amos employs an *inclusio* that began in verse 18a–c with the negative and antithetical notes of darkness without light. Amos employs synonymous parallelism by repeating in an intensive way ואפל ולא־נגה לו ("gloomy and no brightness") to stress the misfortunes of the Day of the Lord.[124] In other words, in verses 18–20, Amos skillfully and rhetorically confronts the fundamental theme of Israel's faith—election, exodus, and salvation history—and turns it against the community of Israel (3:2; 9:7; 2:9–11).

Amos believes that if God is coming in judgment on his day (5:18–20) against his people, it is to redress the injustices. This includes the abuse of power, wealth, cult, religious mediocrity, class distinctions, and the interrelationship of all things in creation, which makes the universe an enduring and functioning entity. This judgment calls for justice that touches the lives of all men and women, including aliens, orphans, and widows.[125] In Amos' theology, the Day of the Lord brings justice (*misphat*) that surges like water. It also offers righteousness (*sedeqah*) like an unfailing/ever-flowing stream (5:23–24). These elements form the basis of the next section, which also vigorously stresses the Lord's rejection of false worship.

123. Udoekpo, *Rethinking the Day of YHWH*, 206; Niehaus, "Amos," 428.

124. For the meaning and detailed treatment of parallelism, see Kugel, *Biblical Poetry*, 1–58; Berlin, "Parallelism," 155–62; Berlin, "Reading Biblical Poetry"; Alonso Schökel, *Manual of Hebrew Poetics*, 48–68; Soulen, *Biblical Criticism*, 133–34.

125. Reid, *What Are They Saying?*, 78.

Rejections of False Worship (vv. 21–27).

Taking a cue from his prophecy of judgment on the Day of the Lord (vv. 18–20), the prophet Amos presents the Lord's critique of worship activities. He observes that Israel's worship is not accompanied by justice and respect for the dignity of all human persons, especially the poor (vv. 21–27).[126]

Amos relates his critique to what precedes (1–5:20) and follows it (5:21–9:15). Literary (3:3; 4:1; 5:1, 7, 18; 6:1; 9:11–15) and theological features that show how the texts are related include the highlighting of the sins of oppression (2:6–7; 5:7–13; 8:4–7), calls for repentance, and invitations to Israel to seek the Lord so as to evade judgment and have life (4:13; 5:8–9; 9:5–6).[127] Although Amos' challenge of the worthlessness of hypocritical religions (4:4–5; 5:5–6, 14–15, 21–27) was initially directed at his contemporaries, the verse by verse exegesis that follows foreshadows the benefits of Amos' theology of worship for contemporary society today, particularly in Africa and North America.[128]

Israel's Rejected Festivals (v. 21)

Amos methodically challenges the essential elements of the Israelites' worship, starting with their festivals (v. 21), sacrifices (v. 22), and noisy music (v. 23) and moves on to the proliferation of the cult and the exilic consequences of empty sacrifices (vv. 25–27).[129] Amos' God both hates (שׂנאתי) and despises or rejects (מאסתי) the empty festivals, sacrifices, melodies, and songs that accompany Israel's external assemblies of worship which lack ethical conviction.

---

126. See Sweeney, "Amos," 239.

127. For some significant literary and theological studies on Amos 5:21–27, see Mays, *Amos*, 105–13; Wolff, *Dodekapropheton*; Ward, *Amos and Isaiah*; Vollmer, *Geschichtliche Rückblicke*, 39; Willi-Plein, *Vorformen de Shriftexegese*, 37; Kraus, "Hôj als prophetische," 24–25; Berridge, "Zur Intention de Botschaft des Amos," 333; Markert, *Struktur und Bezeichnung*, 160; Fohrer, *Einleitung in das Alte Testament*, 478; Barstad, *Religious Polemics*, 76–126; Finley, *Joel, Amos Obadiah*, 248–51; Klingbeil and Kleingbeil, "Prophetic Voice of Amos," 171; Rector, "Israel's Rejected Worship," 161–75, esp. 162–63; Hyatt, "The Book of Amos," 341–42; Weiss, "Repudiation of the Cult," 199–200.

128. As stressed earlier focusing study contextually on Africa (Nigeria), my native birthplace, and the United States of Americ,a where I am currently ministering and lecturing, does not limit the relevance of the theology of Amos to these regions.

129. Mays, *Amos*, 106.

These strong verbs of warning and condemnation ("hate" and "refuse/reject") demonstrate Amos' prophetic courage and zeal. They also demonstrate God's anger over Israel's empty and idolatrous worship. The root word "to hate" (שׂנא) is found in various theological contexts in the Hebrew Bible,[130] including the hatred of the human person, one's enemy (Gen 26:27), idolatrous places, assemblies (Hos 9:15) or offerings, and festivals loathed and spurned by God (Amos 5:21). Amos used the term "to hate" in verse 10 in reference to those who practice injustice (v. 7). By implication, these violators of justice hate those who reprove the gate (champions of justice). Amos exhorts these violators not only to seek the Lord (vv. 4, 6, 14) but also "to hate evil and love good" (v. 15).[131] In this context (vv. 21–27), the Lord is the one who hates the festivals (חגיכם) of hypocritical worshipers (5:21a; 6:8; cf. Pss 5:6; 11:5).[132] Their proliferated religious assemblies (עצרתיכם) in Gilgal and elsewhere are also not pleasant to God (v. 21b).[133]

The Lord refuses what is unpleasant and rejects what he has already hated. The basic meaning of the root verb "to reject/refuse/despise" (מאס) is equally applicable to diverse theological contexts in the OT.[134] For example, in one instance wicked people are rejected (Num 14:31), while in another people and lands are despised for breaking the Lord's commandments (2 Kgs 17:15). In Amos 5:21a the Lord strongly rejects and despises Israel's worthless festivals and assemblies (cf. Hos 4:6; Ps 78:59, 67).

Wolff confirms that these two verbs (שׂנא and מאס) are usually used in prophetic contexts to describe unified actions that are often juxtaposed

---

130. See *BDB*, 971; Jenni ("שׂנא Sn' to hate,"1277–79) and Holladay (*Hebrew and Aramaic Lexicon,* 353) for further distributive usage and semantic theological scope of the word "to hate" (שׂנא).

131 Cf. Finley, *Joel, Amos, Obadiah,* 249.

132. Notice that the expression "your festivals" (חגיכם) is the object of God's rejection and hatred. According to Mays (*Amos,* 106–7) "it is a term used in old festival lists as the common name for Unleavened Bread (*maṣṣoth*), Weeks, and Harvest, the three annual pilgrimage festivals (Ex. 23.15–18; 34.22,25; Deut. 16.10–16." In other words, it also "represents the days fixed by law that are traditionally kept by the people," according to Weiss, "Amos' Repudiation of the Cult,"203. See also Botterweck and Kopsftein, "*ḥaḡ*," 730–44.

133. Here, according to Mays (*Amos,* 107), "your assemblies" (עצרתיכם) clearly refers to "festive times (Isa. 1.13; Joel 1.14; II Kings 10:20) when the people took a holiday from work to celebrate (Lev. 23–26; Deut. 16.8; Num. 29.35)." In other words, it refers to religious gatherings on those days of festivals. See also Barstad (*Religious Polemics,* 111); Weiss ("Repudiation of the Cult," 203); Sweeney ("Amos," 240) for additional analysis of the expression "your assemblies" (עצרתיכם).

134. See *BDB*, 549; *HALOT* 2:540–41

asyndetically.[135] In this case, the unifying action is against Israel's unethical proliferation of religious places, lavish ceremonial cult, worthless pilgrimages, and misdirected festivals that do not delight the Lord (v. 21b).[136] Anticipating the relevance of Amos' rejection of false worship for today (which will be extensively discussed in the next chapter), Niehaus rhetorically asks, "How much does the church today need to learn the lesson? How many attend 'solemn assemblies,' falsely believing that their ritual attendance pleases God? But now, as then, God desires not only our attendance, not even our empty pilgrimages, but ourselves."[137]

Israel's Rejected Sacrifices (v. 22)

In addition to their festivals (v. 21), God also rejects Israel's sacrificial forms (v. 22),[138] including the "burnt offering" (עלה), "bloodless sacrifice/gift or cereal offering" (מנחה), and "peace offering," (שלם).[139] Usually עלה refers to a burnt offering in which the whole animal is offered on the altar and is burnt up completely.[140] The term מנחה refers to the bloodless sacrifice, or sacrifices requiring just cereals. The term עלה refers to an offering wherein the fat part of the animal was placed on the altar while the remaining part was consumed by those who sacrificed the animal.[141] In the book of Leviticus (Lev 1:13; 3:9; 3:16), each of these offerings are described as "a sweet-smelling oblation to the LORD" (ריח ניחח ליהוה).

The verb translated "sweet-smelling" (ריח) in Leviticus is rendered as "to make specious" (אריח), with reference to assemblies, in Amos 5:21b. Finley thinks this suggests that the abused sacrifices Amos condemned

135. Wolff, *Joel and Amos*, 258. Similar expressions are found in Hos 9:9; Zeph 3:7.

136. Paul, *Amos*, 188.

137. Niehaus, "Amos," 431.

138. See Mays (*Amos*, 106) where he rightly contends that in vv. 21–23 the essential elements of Israel's worship are taken up one after another: festivals, sacrifice, and praise.

139. See *BDB*, 750, 585, where the nouns מנחה, עלה, and שלם are basically affirmed as "whole burnt offering," "gift, tribute, offering," and "sacrifice for alliance or friendship; peace offering." See also *HALOT* 2:828–31 for extensive entries of the verb form of עלה, e.g., as "ascend," "go up" (Jer 4:7), "make one's way up" (Exod 12:38) in *qal* form. In the *hiphil* it is "to make someone climb up" (1 Kgs 20:33).

140. This type of burnt offering is also very common in the Chronicler's history (1 Chr 16:2, 40; 21:24, 26; 23:31; 29:21; 2 Chr 1:6; 8:12; 23:18). See Wolff, *Joel and Amos*, 259.

141. Hammershaimb, *Book of Amos*, 89–90.

were initially known and "commonly thought of as pleasing to God" (cf. Isa 1:11–17; Jer 7:21–22; Hos 6:6).[142]

The prophets' rejection of festivals and sacrifices has raised questions concerning the relationship between Israel's prophets, particularly Amos, and the cult. Some scholars argue that Amos was anti-cult,[143] while others maintain that he was a cult prophet whose mission was to condemn the misdirected use of cult.[144] Others argue that Amos based his views on the tribal wisdom tradition.[145] Each of these opinions (anti-cult, cultic, or sapiential) is valuable since none of them fully captures the complex nature of Amos' approach to the cult. Roberts insists that the insights of each of these interpretations should be maintained where possible, though it is obvious that Amos' worship innovation was Deuteronomic, humanitarian, and ethical.[146]

Amos' critique was meant to remind his contemporaries that traditional worship functioned to maintain the rapport between Israel and God. When worship was conducted properly and devotedly with a sense of love, gratitude, justice, righteousness, and respect for the dignity of people—especially the weak and the poor—it was acceptable to God for the atonement of sins (Lev 1:4).[147] Finley cautions that this is not to say there are no differences between the older traditional forms of worship (Amos or Leviticus) and gestures of worship today in the New Testament period. Whatever the form in each given time, God would rigorously reject and refuse those of-

142. Finley, *Joel, Amos, Obadiah*, 250. For me, just as Leclerc (*Prophets*, 135), whether the verb is the same or not is immaterial to the fact that Amos as a whole was trying to improve or innovate a longstanding tradition of worship in Israel.

143. This view goes back to Wellhausen (*Israelitisheche und jüdische Geschichte*, 110–13). Lafferty ("Priority of Cult," 5–7) has more details on Wellhausen's comments on Israel's cult and the role of Amos.

144. Even though extensive discussion on this is beyond the scope of this work. Some of the studies who maintained that Amos a cult prophet include: Kapelrud, "Cult and Prophetic Words"; Rowley, "Ritual and the Hebrew Prophets," 338–60; Hentsche, *Die Stellung*,; Kapelrud, *Central Ideas in Amos*, 68–78; Würthwein, "Kultpolemik," 115–37; Buss, "Meaning of 'Cult,'" 317–25; Rector, "Israel's Rejected Worship," 172–73; Barstad, *Religious Polemics*, 77–126; Finley, *Joel, Amos, Obadiah*, 250.

145 Wolff (*Amos' geistige Heimat*) holds this view, which later appeared under *Amos the Prophet*. Cf. Hasel, *Amos*, 77–79.

146. Cf. Roberts, "Recent Trends," 15–16; Rector, "Israel's Rejected Worship," 173; Barstad, *Religious Polemics*," 117–18; Finley, *Joel, Amos, Obadiah*, 250; Hasel, *Amos*, 77–89; Klingbeil and Klingbeil, "Prophetic Voice of Amos,'" 171–76; Carroll R., "Can the Prophet Shed Light," 216–27.

147. For further details, see Wenham, *Leviticus*, 55–66.

ferings and sacrifices if worshipers oppress their neighbors and refuse to seek justice.[148]

In regard to these divine rejections, Wolff advises that we not take for granted the prophetic words that are uniquely selected since Amos' mission is that of innovation, aiming at challenging the outdated *status quo* of worship without justice. For example, regarding the "gift offering" (מנחה), Amos cautions against sacrifice that may be presented with spiritual ignorance and a false sense of security. Amos uses its plural form מנחתיכם ("your gift[s] offerings") to refer to all forms of empty sacrifices that the Lord has rejected from the community (v. 22b–c) and would never look at (לא אביט).[149] Moreover, the root נבט ("to look at") is not attested elsewhere in a cultic context. In Amos, it clearly refers to the unacceptability of the unethical sacrifices in question.[150]

The Lord's rejection is emphasized by the use of כי־אם ("even if"), which is often used as a single expression ("but," or "unless"), generally following a negative clause.[151] This study views this term in its emphatic sense "even if" for several reasons. First, it emphasizes God's negative attitude toward the misdirected festivals and unethical assemblies that are not part of the long established practice of offerings and sacrifices (burnt, gift/ cereal, or peace). Second, it clarifies that God's rejection is related to their immoral way of life and the idolatrous practices associated with such sacrifices and offerings.[152]

Israel's Rejected "Noisy" Songs (v. 23)

In addition to sacrifices and offerings, Amos criticizes idle songs (v. 23). Amos' God rejects Israel's empty praises and forcefully demands that their songs (שיר) accompanied with harps (נבל) be taken away or tuned down (סור) in his presence.[153] In his criticism, Amos bravely declares, "take away from me the noise of your song and I will not listen to the melody of your

---

148. Finley, *Joel, Amos, Obadiah*, 250.

149. Wolff, *Joel and Amos*, 263.

150. Paul, *Amos*, 190.

151. Ibid., 190.

152. Mays (*Amos*, 107) also rightly reiterates the point we have been making that there are "no hints that the ritual was regarded as irregular or pagan. The sacrifices were for Yahweh." Koch (*Prophets*, 55–56) holds similar views.

153. For a detailed study of שיר, see Ficker, "*šīr*," *THAT* 2:895–98.

instrument" (v. 23a–b).[154] Finley notes that music was a regular means by which worshipers expressed devotion to the Lord (cf. Exod 15:1–18, Deut. 31:30–32:43; Judg.5). He points out that Amos later makes a connection between music and David (Amos 6:5). Music, as in David's case, should be a spontaneous expression of love, not a hypocritical show of zeal for the Lord wherein the worshipers' everyday behavior lacked genuine commitment.[155] That is to say, he who sings should not only praise but should also love the God about whom he is singing. This resembles St. Augustine of Hippo's (+430) statements *"Qui bene cantat bis orat"* ("he who sings well prays twice") and *"Cantare amantis est"* ("singing belongs to the one who loves").[156]

Like the rest of the prophecies of Amos, this verse (23a) could be initially misleading, especially for church musicians and lovers of music during worship. In his article "A Church Musician's Journey with Amos," Paul Westermeyer offers his initial impression of Amos 5:23: "Was not Amos' point to get rid of music in church? Yet, in my own circles there was this stunning contradiction: somehow what Amos said did not apply to Protestant churches. I found it hard to sort this out, but Amos' words seemed applicable only to churches whose music was wrong—to Roman Catholics (and maybe Orthodox). This was one of those unchallenged assumptions in the woodwork."[157] Westermeyer says that over time, he realized that the problem was not about "Catholic and Protestant" music. Rather, "sacrifice and works of righteousness were at issue here." The problem, Westermeyer stresses, was "the absence of justice using idle songs to console those who hide from their wicked ways."[158]

While reflecting on this same subject, Weiss notes that the "idle songs" are so displeasing to God that he demands their immediate removal. The use of the verb הסר ("you take away") underscores the intensity of God's rejection of their "empty sound" or "noise" (המון).[159] According to Birch,

---

154. The grammatical transition from second person plural in the preceding verses to singular imperative in verse 23 (הסר, "take away" and שריך, "your song," in the singular) is provocative to grammarians and scholars. This justifies the MT's suggestion that it was probably meant to be read, הסירו ("Take away" [pl.]), שיריכם ("your songs"), and נבליכם ("your jars/harps"). See Paul, *Amos*, 191–92, for these scholarly debates.

155. Finley, *Joel, Amos, Obadiah*, 250.

156. See *Catechism*, 1156; St. Augustine, *En. In Psalmum* 72.1 (PL 36:914); Pinto, "*Catare Amantis Est*," lines 1–16.

157. Westermeyer, "Church Musician's Journey," 151.

158. Ibid., 151–56.

159. Weiss, "Repudiation of Cult," 207. Cf. Isa 1:14.

the songs are not only idle but so bad that they are described as "noise."[160] This form of rejection is not limited to the prophecy of Amos. The prophet Isaiah similarly speaks of God's rejection of personal prayer: "when you stretch out your hands, I will hide my eyes from you; even though you make many prayers, I will not listen" (Isa 1:15; cf. Mic 6:6).[161]

Amos declares that Israel's tumultuous "empty sound" (המון) was irritating and repugnant to the divine ears.[162] Niehaus has described this sound as "a 'din,' the sort of noise made by torrential waters or the thundering wheels of an army's chariots."[163]This sound needed to be replaced, flavored, or replenished with the higher standard of religious activities that would promote justice and righteousness.[164] The stringed instrument (נבל) that accompanied this tumultuous "empty sound" (המון) was also unworthy of God's attention.[165] In Amos' view, that which is pleasing to the Lord does not just consist of long processions to shrines, festivals, sacrifices, offerings, noisy songs, and rituals, but rather of humility, compassion, justice, righteous acts, oneness, charity, and ethical conduct. These things are also needed more than ever in our contemporary society.

God's Demands of Justice and Righteousness (v. 24)

Amos moves from discussing Israel's rejected festivals (v. 21), sacrifices (v. 22), and idle songs (v. 23) to highlighting Israel's urgent and commensurate needs—namely, justice and righteousness (v. 24). Amos insists that in order for their worship to be acceptable to God, the Israelites must practice justice (משפט) and righteousness (צדקה). While insisting on these ethical demands, Amos proclaims: (ויגל כמים משפט וצדקה כנחל איתן)"let justice roll along like water and righteousness like ever flowing stream."

---

160. Birch, *Hosea, Joel and Amos*, 220.

161. Ibid.

162. Paul (*Amos*, 192) contends that לא אשמע ("I will not listen to" in v. 23b) means a total anthropomorphic disapproval of Israel's act of worship by shutting down his senses of sight (v. 22) and now of hearing in verse 23.

163. Niehaus, "Amos," 432.

164. Weiss, "Repudiation of Cult," 207.

165. This is a stringed instrument of a certain shape mentioned in various situations in the Bible (cf. 1 Sam 10:5; 2 Sam 6:5; Pss 32:2; 57:9: 81:3: 92:3; 108:3; 150:3; Isa 5:12; Neh 12:27).

Justice is vital for all generations and groups who have labored to define not just its meaning but also its importance for healthy society. Ancient
philosophers in particular sought to define its meaning or essence. Some
defined it as an objective practical moral concept needed for a healthy, political, and humanitarian society.[166] Cephalus saw justice as the speaking of
the truth and payment of one's debt, while his contemporary Thrasymcus
saw it as the interest of the ruler.[167] Plato understood it as a virtue whose
fundamental nature and structure was as much in the life of an individual as
in the way in which a society is organized; he also posited that the just man
is the one in whom part of the soul is harmoniously governed by reason.[168]

Aristotle conceived of justice as the greatest virtue whereby one does
the right thing, believing in the right conduct, wishing what is right, and
wishing above all, that the law should be maintained and treat equals equally.[169] St. Augustine defined justice as the "habit of the soul, which imparts
to every man the dignity due to him."[170] St. Thomas Aquinas, on the other
hand, defined justice as "a habit whereby a man renders to each one his
due by constant and perpetual will."[171] The many other philosophical views
on justice among modern and contemporary philosophers are beyond the
scope of this work.[172] Whether some of them were influenced by Amos'
theology of worship is a subject for further reflection, which is also beyond
the perimeter of this theological exegesis.

In biblical theology, justice (מִשְׁפָּט) and righteousness (צְדָקָה) are two
important concepts that can generally be used interchangeably.[173] Heschel
believes that if justice is seen as judgment given by a judge in the court, a
norm, a legal right, a law, or the bestowal to each person of his or her dues,

---

166. Udoekpo, "Unen (Justice) in Annang," 1.

167. Ibid., 1; Plato, *Republic*, 64–74.

168. Plato, *Republic*, 74.

169. Udoekpo, "(Unen) Justice in Annang," 2.

170. Cf. Stumph, *Philosophy*, 157.

171. Aquinas, *Summa Theologica*, 1429.

172. See Udoekpo ("(Unen) Justice in Annang," 10–17) for further lists, studies, and
classification of justice, which includes: "commutative" (advocating for a fair stand of giving and receiving what is assigned to a person); "distributive" (classification of goods and
resources equally and fairly to all); "retributive"(having as its ends and finality correction,
restoration, and restitution of offences and damages done); and "social justice"(general
justice requiring general good in all its aspects with regard to the needs of everyone in
the society, poor and rich).

173. Holladay, *Hebrew and Aramaic Lexicon*, 221, 303.

then righteousness goes beyond justice.[174] While justice tends to be strict, righteousness connotes compassion, charity, kindness, and generosity. What both have in common, according to Heschel, is an ability to discern between good and evil.[175]

Based on this theological climate or context (v. 24), justice and righteousness are consistent with the prophet's language and reaction to the people in Bethel (5:7, 14–15).[176] Justice and righteousness represent the highest values for the human and divine realms.[177] They are recognized as being of central importance in Amos critique of worship (5:21–27).[178] In Kapelrud's view, they are also key demands in every ethical religion, and they are particularly opposed to what people were doing prior to or within the context of Amos' critique on worship.[179] This may be why, for Jeremias, justice and righteousness remain the vital embodiment of the prophetic words within the context of an announcement of disaster and judgment on Israel's unjust and bad behavior.[180] In fact, in the beginning, justice (משפט) and righteousness (צדקה) were expected from the people within the context of God's covenant with Israel (Isa 3:18; Mic 7:9).[181]

In Amos' theological inquiry, justice (משפט) also encompasses reparation for the defrauded, restoration of fairness to the less fortunate, and the bestowal of dignity and compassion to the needy. Righteousness (צדקה) refers to the conditions that make justice possible: attitudes of mercy and generosity and honest dealings that imitate the character of God.[182] In Amos' theology of worship, one can conclude that justice must flow from righteousness. The former is the fruit of the latter (Amos 6:12). As Birch notes:

> Righteousness is not the fulfilment of some list of rules or adherence to a set of standards. Righteousness is a relational term. It refers to the expectation in relationships that persons will, in their

174. Heschel, *Prophets*, 256.

175. Ibid., 256–57.

176. Birch (*Hosea, Joel and Amos*, 220) describes verse 24 as "the climax of this passage and one of the best-known lines in all prophetic literature."

177. Koch, *Prophets*, 58.

178. Hayatt, "Meaning of Amos 5:23–24," 17; du Preez, "Let Justice Roll," 96.

179. Kapelrud, *Central Ideas in Amos*, 65.

180. Jeremias, "Amos 3–6," 221–22.

181. Kapelrud, *Central Ideas in Amos*, 65; du Preez, "Let Justice Roll," 96.

182. Mays, *Amos*, 92–108.

intentions and actions, seek the wholeness of the partner in that relationship. Thus, righteousness can refer to a relationship to God or any of the many human relationships that make up our lives. Doing justice is one of the ways in which we might seek to fulfill our obligation to righteousness in the relationships of neighbor, community, and nation.[183]

The prophetic pairing of the words "justice" and "righteousness" (v. 24) in this passage is not accidental. These terms are closely interconnected as part of the concept of covenant faithfulness, which the prophets turned to in order to confront those in Israel who denied ordinary citizens justice and who corrupted righteousness.[184] Birch describes this verse as a "dramatic divine call to moral commitment rather than empty pious ritual."[185] The images of water and liquid in this verse are also powerful.

Commenting on this powerful and dramatic prophetic presentation, Weiss notes that "this hendiadys positively expresses the idea of justice that is righteous and a justice on which a society ought to be founded and which Amos blames Israel for trampling upon (5:7; 6:12)."[186] Weiss also perceives that the entire pronouncement, "let justice roll along like water and righteousness like ever flowing stream" (ויגל כמים משפט וצדקה כנחל איתן), figuratively captures what he calls a "theological metaphor." By implication, just as water (מים) would flow and roll permanently in the wadi (כנחל איתן) for the common good, human, animals, and plants, justice and righteousness must be parts of the spiritual nutrients for the living and worshiping community.[187]

The message of Amos 5:24 contrasts the behavior of the "fat cows of Bashan" and their elite husbands mentioned in previous sections (4:1ff). These "fat cows" often rolled insensitively and indifferently to the sanctuaries for their selfish purposes after practicing corruption and eating sumptuous meals. The Israelites understood that the divine power and support of justice and righteousness received during worship strengthens them like

---

183. Birch, *Hosea, Joel and Amos*, 216.

184. Ibid.

185. Ibid., 220.

186. Weiss, "Repudiation of the Cult," 209.

187. See ibid., 210, where details of the permanence of this flowing water is highlighted. But interestingly Berquist ("Dangerous Water," 56–57) stresses that this is a reference to the flood myth as a time of disaster and destruction, as connected to the motif of *uhheilseschatoligie* (Isa 10:22), as well as a motif of comfort, healing, constancy, and dependability (cf. Job 12:9; Jer 49:19).

fresh drinking water.[188] Importantly, these divine gifts were meant to be lived and allowed to flow on the altar of life in the marketplaces, on the ordinary streets, plazas, and outside the confines of those shrines, as discussed in previous chapters.

Reflecting further on the images of water and liquid contained in verse 24, Finley rightly observes that Amos, being a sheep dealer and a professional farmer, was aware of the importance of water for land irrigation. The prophet witnessed the devastating nature of drought (1:2; 4:7–8, 7:4) as well as the life-giving properties of hills that are saturated with water from springs and streams (9:13). Therefore in Amos, justice and righteousness are poetically and figuratively made liquids that bring healing to the wounded and broken land (v. 24).[189]

Adele Berlin insists that in poetic and biblical literature, water can serve as a symbol of a life-sustainer as well as of hope. The psalmist, for instance, compares the deer's taste for water with human beings' thirsting for God (Ps 42:2).[190] The prophet Ezekiel uses the image of the river flowing from the restored temple in a passage that could be likened to the demanded flow of justice and righteousness in Amos. Regarding this passage in Ezekiel, Leclerc notes that the water flows from the new temple of hope below the threshold from the east and heads south (Ezek 47:1–12). As it flows from the source, it grows stronger and mightier. As fresh as it is, this water brings life wherever it flows—even down to the Dead Sea. It refreshes the areas where it flows to allow fish and other living creatures to thrive and causes trees to grow along the banks of the river. These trees bear abundant fruits, and every month their leaves and roots are used for food and healing.[191] Leclerc concludes that this river of life that gushes from the temple is a sign of hope and divine life, which rejuvenates land, the sea, plants, creatures, and humans, both rich and the poor.[192] Ezekiel's vision affirms Amos' teachings as well as those of Israel's other prophets (Isa 1:10–17; Jer 6:20–21; Hos 6:4–6; Mic 6:6–8; Zeph 2:1–3). This life sustainer (justice and righteousness) historically stands parallel with God and his values.

Amos' overall understanding of the God of Israel can provide insights into Amos as a prophet (vv. 21–27). For Amos, God is not only the creator

188. Koch, *Prophets*, 59–61.

189. Finley, *Joel, Amos, Obadiah*, 251.

190. Berlin, "Biblical Poetry," 25–36.

191. Leclerc, *Prophets*, 298

192. Ibid.

and sovereign of all creation. He is the covenant maker. Amos' God is the subject and object of worship, including religious songs. He stands for the poor, being concerned with their economic and spiritual needs. Many scholars have acknowledged this aspect of Amos' theology.

In his impressive article "Amos Economics," Robert R. Ellis stresses that a major focus of Amos is the issue of economic justice. He points out how the prophecy of Amos depicts Israel's political stability and material prosperity, which has already been highlighted in this study. Ellis further observes that the wealth of the nation was hoarded in the hands and the basements of the elite, while the majority of the population lived in abject poverty. And the elite did not stop there: they sucked from the poor the little they had. Uniquely, Ellis elaborates on different ways through which the elites abused the poor economically: through debt slavery, harsh taxation, marketplace robbery, and injustices in the court. He also emphasizes that the overarching concern that guides Amos' economic issues, as with the other social ills addressed in this study, is the principle encapsulated in the moral appeal: "Let justice roll down like water, and righteousness lie an ever-flowing stream" (v. 24).[193] It is with this appeal that Amos' God guides Israel through the events of the exodus to the conquest of the land (Amos 2:9–10). We must remember today that Amos' God is our God, and he prefers obedience to sacrifice in order that we may have life.

Sacrifice Alone Is Not Enough (vv. 25–27)

Amos highlights that sacrifices alone are not enough. Verse 25 in particular points to the exodus with the phrase "that era of forty years" (ארבעים שנה); this phrase also points to Israel's liberating experiences and the subsequent establishment of a covenant relationship with God.[194] During this period, Israel is said to have enjoyed divine grace and benefited from God's protection (Amos 2:10). Such divine care had no preconditions of abstaining from unethical cultic worship or performing ritual prescriptions.[195] Rather, as attested by the Deuteronomistic historians (Deut—2 Kgs 25), God endorses obedience over sacrifices, which are

193. Ellis, "Amos Economics," 463–71.

194. Begg ("Class Lectures") also stresses that "forty years" (ארבעים שנה) in the language of the Deuteronomistic Historian is a period of change.

195. Paul, *Amos*, 193.

intended mostly for gratitude and humanitarian purposes.[196] This is further evidenced by the following rhetorical question, "Sacrifices and offering did you bring to me in the wilderness for forty years, house of Israel?"
(הזבחים ומנחה הגשתם לי במדבר ארבעים שנה בית ישראל).

This rhetorical question no doubt poses an interpretative challenge
to all of us. Does verse 25 suggest that sacrifices and offerings were unnecessary at that time in the wilderness? Birch argues that there was some
worship life among the Israelites at that time and that Amos was probably
referring to the lack of established and furnished "sanctuaries with their
control of ritual observance and their tendency to draw loyalty to themselves rather than God."[197] Some scholars consider this whole section (vv.
25–27) to be a secondary addition.[198] Others debate whether the -ha (ה) in
the Hebrew word הזבחים, plural of זבה ("sacrifice"), should be taken as the
definite article "the" or as an "interrogative" הֲ or even as an "exclamatory
הַ."[199] If taken as an interrogative, should the answer be in the affirmative or
in the negative?[200]

There are no quick monophonic fixes to these questions. Hayes suggests (albeit unsatisfactorily) that Amos was referring only to cereal offerings and "well-being" offerings. He argues that other types of offerings were
not brought to the Lord during the forty days in the desert.[201] Yet verse 22
mentions the burnt offering. According to Hans Wilhelm Hertzberg, the
issue at stake is that of the legitimacy of sacrifices per se, and not whether
they should be made to the Lord or to other gods.[202] Feinberg argues that
the Pentateuch (Exod 24:4–6; Num 7; 19) holds the answers. There, the
Israelites offer sacrifices several times to God as well as to other gods.
Therefore, by raising the question "sacrifices and offering did you bring to
me in the wilderness for forty years," "Amos is charging Israel with observ-

196. See Barstad (*Religious Polemics*, 10) where it is stressed that, "whereas the sacrificial cult according to the Priestly Code is something which should be practiced for its
own sake, in order to please the deity, Deuteronomy holds that the godhead has no need
of sacrifice." In fact, "Deuteronomy holds the view that the offering should be consumed
by the offered in the sanctuary and shared by the needy, the poor, the alien, the orphan,
the widow and the Levite."

197. Birch, *Hosea, Joel and Amos*, 221.

198 See Soggin, *Prophet Amos*, 97; Mays, *Amos*, 113.

199. Soggin, *Amos*, 98.

200. Feinberg, *Minor Prophets*, 106.

201. Hayes, *Amos*, 175.

202. Hertzberg, "Prophetische Kritik am Kult," 219–26.

ing the ritual of Mosaic Law, while at the same time worshipping other gods."[203] Mays believes that Amos is not only mocking Israel, but denying the efficacy of unethical sacrifice in the relationship between God and Israel. Consequently, the disobedient Israel will be dominated by foreign empires for some time (v. 26); they will be sent into exile (v. 27).[204]

These opinions notwithstanding, I believe the question in verse 25 is rhetorical, with an anticipated "no" answer.[205] This makes sense since, as we saw in the beginning of this study, Amos followed the tradition of many pre-exilic prophets and the Deuteronomistic Historian, who consistently and prophetically stressed the Lord's preference for obedience over sacrifice. Hosea reflects this pre-exilic prophetic tradition when he says, "For it is loyalty that I desire, not sacrifice, and knowledge of God rather than burnt offering" (Hos 6:6).[206]

The meaning of verse 26 ("you shall take up Sakkut your king and Kaiwan your images, your star god which you have made for yourselves") is also debated.[207] Wolff thinks it is not out of place since its subject and tense correspond to those in verse 25.[208] The crux of the matter lies not only with the proper meaning of *sikkūt* (סכות) and *kîyyūn* (כיון), but also with the initial expression "you shall take up" (נשאתם). Mays suggests it could be read as "you take up (נשאתם)."[209] Since it is a perfect tense, N. Schmidt argues the meaning should be read with reference to the past forty years (v. 25c).[210] Others suggest devocalizing the text in the *niphal*, ונשאתם." ("You will be carried along with"). Stanley Gevirtz prefers the *piel*, "ונשאתם" ("But now you carry").[211]

For theological reasons, this study follows the future translation "you shall take up."[212] With this rendering, this passage offers a window of hope or serves as a reminder of the blessings that await those who persevere in justice. It also reflects an anticipation of the punishment in verse 27 (cf.

---

203. Feinberg, *Minor Prophets*, 106–7.

204. Mays, *Amos*, 111.

205. Similar rhetorical devices are found in Amos 2:11; 3:3–8; 5:18; 8:8; 9:7.

206. See also Mic 6:6–8 and Jer 6:20; King, *Archaeological Commentary*, 89.

207. See Soggin, *Amos*, 98, for various interpretations.

208. Wolff, *Joel and Amos*, 265.

209. Mays, *Amos*, 112.

210. Schmidt, "Text and Interpretation," 11.

211. Gevirtz, "New Look at an Old Crux," 267–76.

212. Barstad (*Religious Polemics*, 121) also keeps to this form of translation.

4:2–3; 6:7; 7:11; 9:4), necessitated by the worship of false gods, *sikkūt* (סכות) and *kîyyūn* (כיון).[213] It is a reminder that idolatry, syncretism, and unethical behavior are punishable by God.[214]

Amos goes on to declare that God, the sovereign of all creation, will bring those who practice empty rituals "into exile across Damascus." Many have seen the phrase "into exile across Damascus" as an allusion to the Babylonian and Assyrian exiles (cf. 2 Kgs 17:6).[215] This study considers it a metaphor of punishment of evildoers or an alienation of people from the love and goodness of God, their creator. This God of hosts (אלהי צבות) is the only one who can do and undo history and who can bless those who ethically/faithfully and obediently worship him in every time, place, and culture.

Summary of Chapter Five

Given the preceding discussion, it seems that God does not find all forms of worship useless and objectionable in themselves. Neither does God seem to declare that rituals and religious songs as a whole have no value. They have value but must conform with a spirit of prayer, justice, and charity to one's neighbor. Also, although Amos' prophecy focuses on the indictment of Israel's worship, the context of its exhortation must be taken into consideration. In the preceding analysis, it does not seem that God is unhappy with all forms of festivals or sacrifices per se. As Birch well articulates, "it is the notion of these rituals as sufficient in and of themselves in order to establish a relationship to God that is objectionable."[216] In other words, in Amos, the sanctuaries are not the main object of worship; God is. If the Israelites' behavior in the marketplaces were characterized by love, justice, righteousness, and compassion, then their festivals, offerings, pilgrimages, and songs would be an ideal of authentic worship dedicated to God. In Amos' view,

213. Mays (*Amos*, 112) interestingly observes that "the forms of *sikkūt* and *kîyyun* is a result of pronouncing their consonants with the vowels of 'abomination' (*siqqūṣ*), a scribal device for derogating names of false gods . . . *Sakkūt* and *Kaiwan* are both known from Babylonian sources as names of the astral deity Saturn."

214. Birch (*Hosea, Joel and Amos*, 221) has also cautioned that "in verse 26 there is a clear reference to idolatry although the exact details are obscure because the verse is difficult to translate . . . his problems with Israel's worship life have more to do with its separation from lives lived in obedience to covenant moral demands."

215. Paul, *Amos*, 198; Soggin, *Amos*, 101.

216. Birch, *Hosea, Joel and Amos*, 222.

dedication and devotion to God must flow from the socio-political and economic services rendered to our neighbors. For Amos worship and justice are intimately conjoined in God's Covenant with God's people. This teaching is particularly applicable today to the situations in Africa (Nigeria) and in the United States of America.[217] Such an application is the focus of the next chapter.

217. Commenting on this, Birch (ibid.) rightly recalls Pss 15:1–15; 24:3–6, which says, "O LORD, who may abide in your tent? Who may dwell on your holy hill . . . those who walk blamelessly, and do what is right . . . those who do these things shall never be moved."

6

Relating the Message of Amos 5 to Contemporary Religious Communities in Nigeria and in the United States of America

Introduction

THE PURPOSE OF THIS final chapter is to address the remaining aspect of the question raised at the beginnings of this study. It is an honest and simple effort to relate the theology of Amos 5 to our contemporary life situations, using Africa (Nigeria) and America (the United States of America) as case studies. As mentioned in the introductory section of this work I choose to focus on these two nations for a few reasons. First, as a Nigerian-born theologian ministering and teaching in the USA for years it is easier to draw strong and compelling parallels, with less speculation, from these two contexts (Nigeria and the USA) with the prophecy of Amos 5. Of course, the parallel lies mainly in the chasm that separate worship from justice and righteousness. Second, Nigeria has been widely known and described as the giant of Africa, or one of the foremost countries in Africa, for many reasons, including geography, demography, natural and human resources as well as prominent in area of biblical studies.[1] The same sense of "foremost" or "notable" among all the nations could be said of the United States of America within the continent of North America and beyond. Third, in his preaching Amos repeatedly refers to the Israel of his time as the notable among

1. For recent (2007) extended geopolitical, historical, demographical, and cultural and socioeconomical heritage of Nigeria within the context of Amos' study, see Iroegbu, "*Let Justice Roll Down*," 261–29. In areas of biblical studies, at least from the 1960s to 2000, see numerous works compiled in Holter, *Yahweh in Africa*; and Holter, *Old Testament Research for Africa*.

the first of the nations (Amos 6:1) Their elites drink wine from bowls and anoint themselves with finest oils (Amos 6:6). They also became the first to go into exile (Amos 6:7), demonstrating that to "whom much is given much is expected." The situation in Nigeria and the USA, both "foremost" nations, can be related to the pungent and graphical message of Amos 5. This task can be challenging since each culture exposes moral failure in seeking to address its ongoing social, economic, political, ethical, and religious issues. Certainly, while reader-oriented critics (who base their interpretation solely on "the world in front of the text") may find this task less compelling, this study is consistently mindful of the relevance of the Old Testament as a whole, of which Amos forms a part. It is also cautious, so as not to tendentiously read contemporary ills back into Amos' theology of worship.[2]

Relevance of the OT and Amos in Particular

Harrington's comments on the relevance of the Old Testament (of which the prophecy of Amos is a part) for Christian worship are worth recalling here. According to Harrington, the OT and the prophetic books in particular have a prominent place in the liturgical cycles of Scripture readings for daily, Sunday, and occasional worship gatherings in both Catholic and non-Catholic churches. This goes back to the early church, where Scripture basically consisted of the OT with its prophetic books. Thus, in the early church, the OT was the most formative document and an integral part of worship.[3] For Harrington, Amos 5 offers worthy and indispensable material for contemporary worship. Walter Brueggemann communicates a similar belief in his work *Prophetic Imagination*, where he argues that the study of the prophets must take into account the contemporary situation of the church today.[4]

In her discussion of the relevance of Amos for us today, Joan C. Cook affirms the observations made by Harrington and Brueggemann. She notices that both in Year B and C, Amos appears about five times in Sunday Lectionary for Mass (LM) and three times in the Revised Common

2. See also Carroll R., (*Amos—the Prophet,* 3–72), for an elegant discussion of the history of research on Amos with various interpretative approaches from Wellhausen to the twenty-first century.

3. Harrington, *Interpreting the Old Testament,* 122–23.

4. Brueggemann, *Prophetic Imagination,* 1.

Lectionary (RCL) in relation to other biblical texts.[5] Cook points out that in the Weekday Lectionary for Mass in Year B, the texts of Amos are read for six days of the Thirteenth Week in Ordinary Time. These readings, according to Cook, "are a representative sample of Amos' message, including 2:6–10, 13–16, the announcement of judgment against Israel; 3:1–8; 4:11–12, rhetorical questions that highlight the impending destruction because of the people's sins; 5:14–15, 21–24 . . . and 9:11–15, the final hymn."[6]

The "people's sins" that Cook refers to here alludes to the social character of our faith. Harrington also mentions this social character when he speaks of the use of the OT and prophetic books: "even when God is presented as dealing with individuals in the Old Testament, the individual is significant only in relation to the fortunes of God's people."[7] That is to say, the idea that "God exercises a special concern for the 'have-nots' of society—widows, orphans, strangers, and others in economic need" is central to the message of the prophet Amos.[8] Preaching the relevance of Amos 5 to modern society during the Wednesday liturgy of the Thirteenth Week of Year C, Walter J. Burghardt said:

> Thank God, millions of America's Catholics live that link between worship and justice, move from church to the world, from altar to people, from the Eucharistic Christ to the Christs pinned to contemporary calvaries. The Problem? Uncounted Catholics who don't believe this, resent "politics" from the pulpit, or simply have enough troubles of their own without taking St. Christopher's Christ on their shoulders. Here is our challenge: how to get all our believing worshippers to listen to Amos and respond with fire in their bellies, "This is the Word of the Lord!"[9]

Honeycutt similarly argues that prophets are contemporary no matter how long the distance between their social, political, and religious interests and ours. As God's mouthpiece, they still speak the word of God with notes of relevance, authenticity, and power that thousands of years have failed to diminish.[10] Amos 5 forms an ever-relevant theological part of God's Word

---

5. See Cook (*Hear O Heavens*, 66) for details.

6. Ibid., .

7. Harrington, *Interpreting the OT*, 123–124.

8. Ibid.

9. Burghardt, "Mercy, Not Sacrifice," 103.

10. Honeycutt, "Amos and Contemporary Issues," 411.

(cf. 1sa 40:8' 1 Pet 1:23–25).[11] Amos can speak to people in Africa and North America today since the challenges he encountered in the eighth century BCE—including idolatry, socio-political issues, and economic injustices—are still prevalent in our society today. What follows is an attempt to relate the message of Amos to the life settings of Africa (Nigeria) and the United States today.

Amos 5 and the African (Nigerian) Socio-Political Situation

In regard to politics, economics, and society as a whole, the situations of African countries—particularly Nigeria—are similar to the socio-historical situation of Amos' time. He lived in a paradoxical period: on the one hand, there was great material prosperity; on the other, social and religious corruption.[12] In Iroegbu's words, at this time, "judges are criminals, oppressing the just, accepting bribes, repelling the needy at the gate (Am 5:12)."[13] The teachings in Amos' prophecy were thus "meant for all times."[14]Amos was an exemplary prophet in challenging the political situation of his time, as previously discussed in chapter one. He did so by vigorously denouncing every form of political injustice: abuse of power, selfishness, inhumanity of foreign nations (1:3–15), cruelty, corruption, and bribery (2:4–7; 3:10; 5:9–12; 6:1–11). These political injustices are endemic to contemporary African political structures.[15]

In most African societies today, particularly Nigeria, stable political leadership is still in its infancy.[16]As these societies attempt to govern themselves, the situations rejected in the prophecy of Amos often occur in the form of incessant tensions, rivalries, Boko Haramism, drugs and child trafficking, abduction of Chibok school girls, tribalism, military intervention, abuse of office, bribery and corruption and the widespread violation

---

11. Cf., *Dei Verbum*, nos. 12–26; *Verbum Domini*, no. 1, on the ongoing relevance of the Bible as the Word of God.

12. Burghardt, "Mercy, not Sacrifice," 100.

13. Iroegbu, *"Let Justice Roll Down,"* 259.

14. Cf. Hardon, *Lifetime Reading Plan*, 12.

15. See Cohen, "Political Background," 153–60; Howington, "Ethical Understanding," 407–8; Udoekpo, *Corruption in Nigerian Culture*; Udoekpo, "Moral," 44–47.

16. For an extensive and impressive discussion on the present sociopolitical and economic situation in Nigeria, see Iroegbu, *"Let Justice Roll Down,"* 275–300.

of fundamental human rights.[17] Just as Amos vigorously rejected the broken political structure of his time, our hope is that the Nigerian electorate of all groups would opt for positive and conscientious ethical changes. My hope is that the message of Amos would heal the broken political culture in Nigeria and the related broken economic situation of Nigeria's citizens.

Amos 5 and Economic Injustice in Africa

Apart from the rejection of broken political structures, Amos also criticized the economic inequalities of his time. The poor of his day suffered from indebtedness (2:6), excessive taxation (5:11), and robbery in the market-places (8:4–6). They also experienced injustice in the courts by the very rulers who took seats at worship centers (5:10–12). The poor were also economically victimized by cunning and dishonest business elites, who would use false weights and inaccurate measures to sell inferior products to the poor (5:7; 8:4–6).[18] Amos rebuked these practices.

Situations similar to those Amos courageously critiqued in his day are common in Africa today, particularly in Nigeria.[19] With the fluctuating economic gains in Nigeria from natural resources, minerals, and crude oil, ethical failures and unjust economic situations are at a record high. The Nigerian currency, "Naira," is highly devalued compared to the dollar or euro. This is partly due to the excessive importance placed on material wealth, which seems to be the measure of one's success. Those who strive to meet this measure often engage in the embezzlement of public funds to the detriment of the poor, who attend the same worship assemblies as the perpetrators. Employers in this culture act like the merchants rebuked by Amos by grossly underpaying their poor employees, who have already become accustomed to months of work and labor without receiving a salary.[20]

This economic situation in Nigeria has become the focus of many articles in economic social journals. For example, in his article "The Ministry of Amos in Israel and Its Socio Religious Implication for the Nigerian

17. Udoekpo, "Prophet Zephaniah," 39. For details on the injustice of kidnapping of the Chibok School Girls in Borno State, Northern Nigeria see the *Wikipedia* article, "Chibok School Girls."

18. Howington, "Ethical Understanding," 406.

19. For some contextual studies on Amos and economic justice, see Howington, "Ethical Understanding," 405–7; Ellis, "Amos Economics," 463–76.

20. Cf. Udoekpo, "Liberation," 33–38.

Society," Timothy Agboluaje affirms that Nigeria is plagued with economic injustices of all forms. Agboluaje particularly mentions corruption, which breeds disparity between the poor and the rich, which Amos condemned in his prophecy (Amos 2:6–7; 5:12 8:6).[21] A local Nigerian journal also notes that, despite its being one of the world's major oil producers with a potential for economic ascendency, Nigeria is rated by the United Nations Development Program as one of the poorest nations of the world, with widespread greed.[22] In Nigeria poverty is a reality that depicted by lack of food, clothes, education and other basic amenities.[23]

As acknowledged in the preceding chapters, Amos presumed that the Israelites knew God's moral demands, as listed in the covenant code (Exod 20–23), which include justice, righteousness, mercy, humanitarianism, respect for the Sabbath, sexual ethics, honesty, and truthfulness (cf. Deut 12–15).[24] To his disappointment, those moral demands were absent from the worship centers and marketplaces of his day, especially in Bethel, Beersheba, and Gilgal. Ethical injustices—including maltreatment of the poor, dishonesty, and incest—became the order of the day (2:6–16; 4:6–13; 5:21–27).

African countries, particularly Nigeria, seem to be swimming in an ocean of ethical issues similar to those that Amos challenged centuries ago. In addition to the difficulties cited above, these countries also face such issues as child trafficking, tribal conflicts, discrimination, intolerance, unemployment, general insecurity, and economic violence against the poor and the weak.[25] Exploitation is unknown in Nigeria since the society can be classified as that of the oppressed and oppressor.[26]

To countries plagued by these injustices, Nigeria in particular, the book of Amos offers good news in its ethics of obligation rooted in God's graciousness and reconciliatory and redemptive activities. As noted throughout this study, and particularly as reiterated by Howington, "Sin is therefore a rebellion against God . . . the prophet's repeated demand for repentance contains both the threat of judgment and the hope of mercy

21. Agboluaje, "Ministry of Amos," 6.

22. See Deji, "Corruption and National Rebirth," 99.

23. Uche, "Poverty in Nigeria," 47.

24. See Kalperud, *Central Ideas in Amos*, 60–61; Ska, *Pentateuch,* 40–41.

25. See Achebe, *Trouble with Nigeria*; Udoekpo, *Corruption;* Obinwa, "*Shepherd Motif in Ezekiel 34,*" esp. 16, where some of these sociopolitical issues are extensively discussed.

26. Folarin and Olanisebe, "Threat of Judgment," 257.

(5:4–7, 14–15, 24; 9:8).[27] The preaching of Amos' ethical texts on Sundays and weekdays, especially in local languages, didactically invites today's contemporary Nigerian population to return to God's moral and authentic religious paths.[28]

In other words, constant and effective preaching of Amos 5 can make a huge difference in the Nigerian church and society. As Mary Healy puts it, "it is difficult to exaggerate the importance of good preaching in the life of the Church. All the great waves of revival in Church history can be traced at least in part to exceptional preaching."[29] Drawing from the *Verbum Domini*, she concludes from the Christian's point of view that good homilies of biblical texts must be Christocentric, kerygmatic, and realistic. Most importantly, preachers of Amos 5 must "display a profound unity between what they preach what they live."[30]

Amos 5 and the Religious Situation in Africa

Amos offers some irony in that some of the people who indulged in the unethical behaviors described above were actively involved in religious syncretism. They made religious pilgrimages to Bethel, Gilgal, and Beersheba, where they took part in festivals and offerings (vv. 1–17, 5c, 27). This suggests that ethical religion during Amos' time was lacking but also at its peak. This is why Burghardt notes that, "how well the Jew related to God depended in large measure on how the Jew related to fellow members of the covenant community. But what was the actual situation in Amos' time? The merchants were impatient for the holy days to pass, so they could resume their fraudulent business."[31] In Howington's words, Israel's gifts matured through the long struggle of the nation's moral leaders and prophets to keep the faith and to promote worship of the one true God of the covenant.[32] Amos and other prophets accomplished this through criticizing Israel's unethical and unjust gestures, idolatry, and acts of worship. For instance, Amos challenged and mocked his contemporaries' unjust worship (4:4–5). He declared unequivocal rejection of their hypocrisies (5:18–20, 23) with

27. Howington, "Ethical Undertanding," 411.
28. Cf. Udoekpo, "Moral," 38–44.
29. Healy, "Biblical Peaching," 109.
30. Ibid., 122.
31. Burghardt, "Mercy, Not Sacrifice?," 101.
32. Howington, "Ethical Understanding," 409–10.

the aim of inviting Israel to the true religious path of seeking the Lord alone (vv. 4–6, 14–15, 21–24).

Generations of global religious bodies have inherited the religious enthusiasm that goes back to the time of Amos. On the African continent, religion remains an exciting phenomenon for both the poor and the rich.[33] Today, Nigeria, in particular, is witnessing a proliferation of churches, as well as a pluralism of religions (in particular Christianity, Islam, and African Traditional Religion [ATR]). Worship centers are spread out predominantly in northern and southern Nigeria, as was true in the time of Amos. In these centers, tension and occasional violence that sometimes results in the kidnap of children, loss of lives and property have been recorded.[34] Those who promote this violence justify their unethical actions as "worship of God" (Allah, *Oludumare, Chukwu,* or *Abasi Ibom*), their Supreme Being.[35] To this situation we find relevance in Amos' hearty denunciation of violence, syncretism, and abusive use of religious power (1:3, 6, 9; 5:11–12). As far as Amos was concerned, no matter how physically flourishing religion may seem, religion without love for fellow human, compassion, and justice, and religion that is characterized by destructive ideology, becomes unethical in itself.[36] In fact, Abraham Joshua Heschel in his "No Religion Is an Island," expressed this fifty years ago:

> To meet a human being is a major challenge to mind and heart. I must recall what I normally forget. A person is not just a specimen of the species called *homo sapiens.* He is all of humanity in one, and whenever one man is hurt we are all injured. The human is a disclosure of the divine, and all men are one in God's care for man. Many things on earth are precious, some are holy, and humanity is holy of holies. To meet a human being is an opportunity to send the image of God, the presence of God."[37]

33. Nwanunobi, *African Social Institutions,* 162–63.

34. See Udoekpo (*Limits of A Divided Nation,* 31–46) for impressive analysis on war in religious family" as well as Mbiti (*African Religions & Philosophy*); Idowu (*African Traditional Religion,* 106); Megesa (*African Religion*) and Agibi ("Still Searching: The Quest for Justice in Nigeria") for additional studies on ATR and abuse of Religion.

35. There are many more names, but these are some of the names given to the Supreme Being by Christians, Muslims/Hausa, Yoruba, Igbo, and Efik/Ibibio/Annang speaking groups of Nigeria, respectively.

36. Howington, "Ethical Understanding," 409.

37. Heschel, "No Religion Is an Island," 121.

Among the three major religions flourishing in Nigeria, Christianity (particularly Catholicism) is at its peak. This is noted in one of the documents of the First Synod for Africa. Areas where Catholicism flourishes in Africa, particularly include: (a) a remarkable increase in the number of Catholics, priests, and consecrated persons; (b) a remarkable number of missionaries who serve beyond the shrines, temples, and borders of Africa; and (c) a remarkable continental consultation platform created for them.[38] Pope Benedict XVI (now Emeritus), during his inaugural homily at the Second Synod for Africa, described this flourishing church as "an immense spiritual lung" for people who face several faith and religious challenges.[39]

One challenge or abuse at worship centers that we often ignore—perhaps due to indifference to poverty or to greed—is the distribution of cash, cars, and expensive material items to a few religious leaders by public office holders in the name of worship, when teachers and civil servants in their counties, local government areas, states, and nations have not been paid basic salaries for months. Amos does not disdain offerings to the church and support of religious centers and their prosperity per se. Yet he does reject the misplacement and abuse of these offerings and gifts (v. 22).[40]

In his exhortations (vv. 4–6, 14–15; 24), which are read in the church during the weekday Masses of ordinary season in Year B, Amos indirectly invites contemporary worshipers to make ethical offerings and to faithfully use sacred space for worship. It is within this context of the proper use of the sacred place that Niehaus rhetorically asks: "How much does the church today need to learn the lesson? How many attend 'solemn assemblies,' falsely believing that their ritual attendance pleases God? But now, as then, God desires not our attendance, not even our pilgrimages, but

---

38. See *Lineamenta*, no.6

39. See Soédé, "Enduring Scourge of Poverty," 181–90, and particularly Odozor ("Foreign Religious, Ethical Ideologies," 214–25) for details of this imagery of the church in Africa as a "spiritual lung" for humanity as well as the challenges facing her.

40. Again, I do not by this suggest that charitable donations to the needy church and the poor are not important. But this must be done bearing the messages of Amos and Malachi 1:6–14; 3:7–12 in mind. Although Malachi seems to insist on the customs (cf. Lev 27:30; Num 18:21–32; Deut 12:6–18; Neh 13:10–13), the overall context of covenant-breaking must be considered. Repentance and worship of God with one's whole heart is at stake. Even in Matt 23:23 and Luke 11:42 these donations are not enough, but justice, mercy, righteousness, and deep faith are needed. Offerings must be done freely, with love and trust in God and his teachings, for God loves a cheerful giver (cf. 2 Cor 9:7; Deut 15:7–11; 25:13–16; Sir 35:1–12).

ourselves."[41] In sum, Amos' rejection of festivals and sacrifices (vv. 21–22), as well as his prophetic and religious zeal, can serve as didactic lessons for religious societies today, especially where individuals flock, some less then wholeheartedly to religious centers in the continent of Africa.

Amos 5 and Worship Issues in Africa (Nigeria)

It is important to reiterate that just as Amos does not hate festivals and offerings *per se*, he does not hate music as such; his critique is of the manner in which the music is rendered. What is the function of music in worship? The *Catechism of the Catholic Church* (CCC) describes the function of music in worship as follows:

> Song and music fulfill their function as signs in a manner all the more significant when they are "more closely connected . . . with the liturgical action," according to three principal criteria; beauty expressive of prayer, the unanimous participation of the assembly at the designated moments and the solemn character of the celebration. In this way, they participate in the purpose of the liturgical words and actions: the glory of God and the sanctification of the faithful.[42]

The *Instrumentum Laboris* of the Second Special Assembly for Africa emphasizes that the worshiping assemblies in Africa are sustained by the vitality of their liturgies and living ecclesial communities.[43] African worship and liturgical settings are unquestionably unique, lively, and joyful, being flavored with songs and hymns. The New Testament authors and the council fathers bestowed praises upon such songs, hymns, and the use of instruments. They also emphasized appropriate enculturation, adaptation, contextualization, reverence, holiness, and prayerfulness (Eph 5:19; Col 3:16).[44] St. Augustine, in his *Confession*, is noted to have said of religious songs that come from the heart:

> How I wept, deeply moved by your hymns, songs, and the voices that echoed through your Church! What emotion I experience in them! What emotion I experienced in them! Those sounds flowed

41. Niehaus, "Amos," 431.

42. *Catechism of the Catholic Church*, no. 1157.

43. *Instrumentum Laboris*, no. 7.

44. Vatican II, *Scrosanctum Concillium*, nos. 112–21.

into my ears, distilling the truth in my heart. A feeling of devotion surged within me, and tears streamed down my face–tears that did me good.[45]

The harmony of these songs, signs, words, music, and actions is even more fruitful when expressed in the cultural richness of the people of God.[46] Elochuckwu E. Uzukwu, an African theologian, applauds this emphasis. He notes that "body language" or gestures of praise, adoration, contemplation, and ritual assemblies with dances and movements are a means through which African people worship and joyfully express their Christian faith.[47] Uzukwu also emphasizes the obligatory nature of enculturation for African worshipers, insisting that Africans "must maintain and work toward such a legitimate pluralism not only in cult and discipline, but also in the theological expression of the received Christian faith."[48] Uzukwu's insistence is in line with the faith traditions of the Catholic Church on the theology of enculturation, which may also be relevant to other Christian faith communities.[49]

The Church endorses creative enculturation of songs and dances into liturgy, provided it does not change the essential and ethical elements of worship.[50] Worship songs must be theological such that the faithful and worshipers, poor and rich, can better understand and live the meaning of liturgical celebrations, even in marketplaces.[51] During Amos' time, some of these qualities were scarce and hard to find, as is true today in some assemblies of worship across Africa, particularly Nigeria. A typical example can be drawn from the context of the Church in my native and home diocese of Ikot Ekpene. Although liturgical music is well rendered here, in some cases there is need for improvement. In light of this, Immaculata Offiong called for training of African (Nigerian) choristers in the teachings of the

---

45. St. Augustine, *Confession* 9.6.14; PL 32:769–70.

46. *Catechism of the Catholic Church*, no. 1158.

47. Uzukwu, *Worship as Body Language*, 1–33.

48. Ibid., 1–33, 323.

49 For an extensive and very basic study on enculturation, its emergence, theological import, role in the mission of the Church, the teachings of the Vatican II on it, and its challenges, see Onwubiko (*Theory and Practice of Inculturation*), which I consider a masterpiece on enculturation.

50. Komonchak et al. (*Dictionary of Theology*) consider these elements as Trinitarian, paschal, ecclesial, sacramental, ethical, and eschatological.

51. *Lineamenta*, no. 27; John Paul II, *Ecclesia in Africa*, nos. 59–64.

Church.[52] She proposes the establishment of local liturgical-music guidelines that would highlight issues of doctrine and morals, adaptation and use of stringed instruments, and enculturation and checking of external influences.

As an African musician, Offiong is worried about liturgical syncretism. She is also rightly concerned about some Church musicians' inability to differentiate between music from secular settings, African Traditional Religion (ATR) settings, and the Church's theological settings. The inability to differentiate between secular and sacred music settings introduces the threat of performing the very idle songs and noise (המון), rejected by the prophet Amos: "Take away from me the noise of your song, and I will not listen to the melody of your instrument" (v. 23). For Amos, liturgical music must be lived out in acts of justice and righteousness, words and actions.

Let Justice Roll With Ever-flowing Righteousness

In Amos' view, and as stressed throughout this study, what is pleasing to the Lord is not just processions to modern shrines, festivals, sacrifices, noisy songs, and rituals, but justice and charity. How we treat one another is important for Amos. At worship, silence, proper musical tones, and disposition of justice to ones' neighbor should be observed. Such dispositions, acts of kindness, justice, and righteousness must not be limited to the temples, but must be extended and allowed to flow constantly and everlastingly, like a stream, to marketplaces and the margins of the society (v. 24).[53]

To summarize, the subjects of Amos' critique of shallow worship, threats of exile, and prophetic-mockeries are endemic in contemporary religions, especially in the three major religions across the continent of Africa. As in Amos' time, syncretism, fragile faith and trust, intolerance, and lack of dialogue between religious groups are challenges faced by the Church in Africa today.[54] In Nigeria, where religion has been repeatedly used as an instrument of oppression and characterized by religious violence, division, and acts of injustice rather than redemption, unity, and salvation, citizens should turn to the prophecy of Amos.[55]

---

52 Offiong, *Lineamenta-First Synod Ikot Ekpene*, 95–96.

53. Ibid., 98–102.

54. I have already summarized this in Udoekpo, "Prophet Zephaniah," 38–39.

55. See, Udoekpo, "Moral," 48–58; Udoekpo, *Limits of a Divided Nation*, 31–47.

In Amos' view, sacrifices alone are not sufficient (vv. 25–27). Religion must contain the basic elements of obedience to God, dialogue, justice, righteousness, unity, peace, forgiveness, and ethics of love, mercy, and compassion for the poor. Each of these elements (economic, ethical, political, social and religious) is related to the broader social fabric, since the community that goes to worship is a web of human relationships with needs. Within Israel's covenant tradition, upon which Amos stood and which we (the Church in Africa) are invited to renew in Christ, the overarching principles of social order include justice, righteousness, love, and mercy.[56]

Besides reading, preaching, singing, and reflecting on the texts of Amos in local African languages, perhaps the following liturgical material of the Psalm tradition upon which Amos stood, which ties authentic worship to the moral qualification of the worshipers, needs to be recited and lived on daily basis;

> O Obong Abasi, anie edidung ke tent [atayat]?
>
> Anieditie ke edisana obot fo?
>
> Owo ke asagnade nte ofonde ama,
>
> onyung odohode akpaniko ke esit esie
>
> Owo ke midoke edidok ke edeme esie;
>
> minyung inamke ufan esie idok;
>
> minyung itingke iko but idian mbohoudung esie.
>
> Enye ese oburobut owo ke ndek,
>
> edi okpono mmo eke ebaked Obong Abasi.
>
> Enye onwongo se itukde idem esie, ndien ikpuhokede.
>
> Enye ibuotke inyene esie idia udori ikaha,
>
> inyung iboho eno ituk owo eke miduehe isop.
>
> Owo eke anamde Nkpo emi idisehekede ke nsinsi.
>
> (Ps 15:1–5.cf. Ps 24:3–6).[57]

56. Howington, "Ethical Understanding," 408.

57. This text is my translation adopted from the *Efik* Bible, *Edisana Nwed Abasi Ibom*. But the text is represented in the NRSV as "O LORD, who may abide in your tent? Who may dwell on your holy hill? Those who walk blamelessly, and do what is right, and speak the truth from their heart; who do not slander with their tongue, and do no evil to their friends, nor take up a reproach against their neighbors; in whose eyes the wicked are despised, but who honor those who fear the LORD; who stand by their oath even to their hurt; who do not learn money at interest, and do not take a bribe against the innocent. Those who do these things shall never be moved." This Efik text is the Scripture used in

The Relevance of Amos 5 for the United States

When we leave the shores of the African continent and turn to the United States, we also encounter challenges regarding how to read, preach, study, reflect on, and apply the theological message of Amos for our daily living. Just as we examined contexts for Africa, and Nigeria in particular, this section addresses the socio-political, economic, ethical, and religious contexts of the church in the United States in light of Amos 5.

Amos 5 and the Socio-Political and Economic Situation in America

Amos can significantly speak to all people of all cultures and to diverse worship situations in our contemporary world. His prophecy can be reinterpreted and made accessible to particular socio-political groups in the United States of America that are relatively separate and unique with its diversities and pluralism of migrants. This is why Cook insists that the socio-economic situations of Amos' time and setting are very familiar to Americans in the United States today, citing the widening gap between the "haves" and the "have-nots" and its implications for daily living. Cook also cites issues with unequal access to housing, food, education, and medical care, which are viewed as basic necessities of life in the United States. She notes that while limits and conditions can be related to one's industry, location, and earning potential, they are also affected by factors that transcend human control, such as language barriers or family history. This is especially true for those who migrate to the United States. The daily problems of immigrants are exacerbated by the individualism that pervades American socio-political life today.[58]

It is worth noting that prior to Cook the question of proper handling of immigrants, drug trades, recycling of illicit funds, corruption, violence, arm race and racial discrimination were listed in *Ecclesia in America* as some of the issues that cry for the message of Amos preached in the Church.[59] This same document stresses that it is the duty of the Church, in

---

my native place, the Calabar region of southern Nigeria. Apart from this text, the reading and teaching of the book of Amos in the language of the *Efik* Bible is one effective way of communicating the message of Amos to the people.

58. Cook, *Hear O Heavens*, 67.

59. John Paul II, *Ecclesia in America*, nos. 56–65.

the United States to see that immigrants are defended against oppression and lack of hospitality.[60]

Building on Cook's views and that of the *Ecclesia in America* Kenneth Long presents a list of socio-political and economic troubles in America, including pride, selfishness, consumerism, materialism and ignorance of other people's cultures. He also mentions abuse of guns, drugs, greed, and a false sense of nationalism.[61] Regarding the idea of nationalism, M. Daniel Carroll R. notes that Christians in America can benefit from Amos in learning discernment in cases when faith is closely tied to national ideology. Carroll R. singles out for comment Jim Wallis book *God's Politics*, which discusses the division of Christian faith in America based on party lines (Democratic/Republican).[62] Carroll R.'s assessment of Wallis' work reflects on how a biblically grounded worldview should engage systemic issues of economics and social policy, as well as evaluate objectively international political realities and initiatives. Carroll R. believes that Wallis' warning is akin to the presumptuous behavior of the Bethel's priest Amaziah, who while serving confused Jeroboam II and his kingly sanctuary (Amos 7:10–17).[63]

When we consider economic and socio-political situations in the United States in the light of those in Amos, Ellis further suggests a need to recall those unfair lending practices uncovered in the recent economic crash, which revealed widespread predatory loans that led some into insurmountable debt. We also need to recall those sweat factories in underdeveloped nations that enslave labor pools to produce cut-rate products for discount merchandisers in the U.S. and other industrialized nations.[64]

In addition, Ellis notes, "loopholes in the U.S. tax system and dysfunctional politics sometimes enable those most able to bear the cost of the economic 'safety nets' designed to project the poor to pay the least amount of tax proportionally." Ellis further draws attention to the paucity of market outlets in poor urban areas, which often make residents victims of predatory pricing. And he observes that "the poor, especially African American males, know all too well that it can be quite difficult to find

---

60. Ibid., no. 65.

61. Long, *Trouble with America*, xvii–89.

62. Carroll R., "Worship Wars," 222; Wallis, *God's Politics*, 1–35.

63. Carroll R., "Worship Wars," 222.

64. Ellis, "Amos Economics," 473.

the same level of justice in the U.S. court system as Anglo [white] males, especially wealthy ones."[65]

In the light of Amos' economics, Birch further says regarding contemporary American economic injustices:

> Reading about such flagrant abuses in the Israel of Amos, can of course, remind us that the poor are most vulnerable to abuse in our times as well. Misleading bait-and-switch advertising, high-pressure sales tactics, misrepresentation of inferior goods, loans made at exorbitant rates, complex credit schemes for purchase of high-price goods, high prices for doing business in the inner city, redline real estate practices–all these practices and more find a disproportionate majority of their targeted population among our society's poorest by the well-to-do and the influential, with the economic burden of these practices falling most heavily on the lowest levels of income. By contrast white-collar fraud on income tax returns . . . .has reached record levels. Such continuing practices truly "bring to ruin the poor of the land."[66]

Birch's economic illustration, as well as those of Ellis, Long, Cook, Carroll R., and Wallis, depict specific circumstances and contexts that are different from those of Amos. But their examples serve to rebuke and reject all forms of injustices and exploitation under the principle of justice and righteousness championed by the prophet Amos. As Ellis states, the church in America "needs the clear word from Amos about pressing issues of economic injustices in our world and the responsibility of those who have the resources to act with justice and compassion on behalf of those who do not."[67] That is to say, the rich as well as the church must show solidarity with the poor. This is true, since "by her social doctrine the Church makes an effective contribution to the issues presented by the current globalized economy . . . [Which] must be analyzed in the light of the principles of social justice, respecting the preferential option for the poor who must be allowed to take their place in such an economy."[68]

At the dinner table at Sacred Seminary and School of Theology on November 29, 2014, one of the issues discussed among my colleagues was how wealthy the church is in the West, yet some members of the church,

---

65. Ibid.

66. Birch, *Hosea, Joel and Amos*, 245.

67 This impressive quote is from Ellis, "Amos' Economics," 475.

68. *Ecclesia in America*, no. 55.

particularly those who work in catholic institutions, are still victims of economic injustices.[69] This is not to deny that many within the American church are sacrificing and courageously making a real difference in the daily lives of the poor and needy as noted earlier by Burghardt.[70] A good example is the work of the Catholic Charities in the United States. Yet we must admit that there are also those within the church in America and elsewhere (e.g., Africa) who have succumbed to the siren song of cultural voices that praise self-centered wealth and unbridled wealth accumulation, and whose goals have stopped short of compassion for the poor. They pile up earthly treasures and, in Ellis' words, "their default moral position is admiring the rich and despising the poor."[71] It is just such a moral default that Amos rebuked and rejected throughout his prophecy. Amos' defense can thus serve as a template for those who seek and champion justice and righteousness within and outside religious communities in the United States of America and beyond.

Amos 5 and the Religious/Worship Situation in America

In addition to relating Amos prophecy to the socio-economic and political situation in the United States, we can also relate the worship issues addressed in Amos to the worship in United States churches. Even though debates over worship styles or the relationship between worship and ethics have been heard perennially throughout Christian history, such debates are recently becoming intensified in the United States. Carroll R. remarks on this intensity that today, we "hear many competing voices, churches, and denominations line up with a wide spectrum of views and practice."[72] Amos' prophecy and cult critique (5:21–24) presents a template by which the church in the United States can evaluate its worship practices in relation to justice and righteousness.

Carroll R. offers three valuable points about worship that can help the church in the United States examine the integrity of its worship style: (1) Worship must be willing to question reigning ideologies (Amos 7:9–17; 9:1); (2) worship must engage in the harsh realities of life (4:4–13; 5:4–6);

69. This discussion took place at the Sacred Heart Seminary and School of Theology, located in Milwaukee, Wisconsin, in the United States of America.

70. Burghardt, "Mercy, Not Sacrifice?," 102–3.

71. See Ellis, "Amos Economics," 476.

72. Carroll R., "Worship Wars," 215.

and (3) worship must nurture a commitment to justice of all forms (Amos 5:18–27; 8:3–6).[73]

With regard to the first point, Amos from the beginning to the end of his prophecy champions the cause of Zion: God roars from Zion (Amos 1:2) and must be worshiped centrally in Zion (Amos 5:1–17). Additionally, Zion, the house of David, shall be restored (9:11–15). Amos was also clear that moral laxity, a false sense of security, and exceptionalism were not in the best interest of Israel's nationalistic ideology. As suggested by Carroll R., worshipers in the United States can learn from Amos the necessity of discerning or separating our faith from a false sense of nationalism.[74] Amos challenges Christians in the United States and elsewhere to move beyond self and national ideologies or "self-serving tendencies of our holy places."[75]

Carroll R.'s second point reminds the church in the United States of Amos' message that sanctuaries and places of worship should not become ends in and of themselves. Rather, they were meant to be a means to God (Amos 4:4–13). Amos is both brave and sarcastic in his message. He says, "go to Bethel and sin; go to Gilgal and sin yet no more" (4:4ff). He later continues with "seek me, seek well, avoid evil, seek the LORD and live" (5:4–6, 14–15). Amos was not afraid to startle and shock his audience, nor did he fear embracing the harsh realities of life. He "took the bull by the horns." He knew that, historically, the shrines were important religious sanctuaries for the people. Yet traveling to the shrines with sirens and music while neglecting the poverty and economic, social, and political injustices around them was not good enough. The church in the United States could learn much from Amos' courageous teachings, such as this lesson articulated by Carroll R.:

> In a world driven by entertainment but broken in so many ways (personal trauma, family dysfunction, substance abuse and addictions, sexual perversions, overwhelming personal debt, no sense of direction and purpose), the pull for worship to focus on encouragement and celebration is enormous. Coupled with the drive to grow in attendance, an uplifting service offers the greatest appeal to more people. Nevertheless, if we are not careful, this sort of worship can cut itself off from the hard facts of life, which the church must face and is called to minister to: poverty, hunger,

---

73. For details of these elegant three points, see Carroll R., "Worship Wars," 220–25.

74. Ibid., 222.

75. Birch, *Hosea, Joel and Amos*, 223.

tsunamis, racism, and war, as well a personal brokenness both at home and abroad.[76]

In addition to connecting everyday life with worship, this inclusive passage also calls for a high integrity of worship in American culture, which all too frequently emphasizes entertainment. Amos challenges us "to keep God at the center of our worship life so that our creativity in liturgy and music is directed to praise God and not to entertain."[77] Conscious of the danger of mistaking entertainment for worship, Marva J. Dawn in her book *Reaching Out Without Dumbing Down: A Theology of Worship of this Urgent Time* cautions that although the church uses media for evangelization, its sacred songs and sermons must not be measured by secular media culture, but instead by a spirit-filled exegesis of the Word of God, since worship is about God.[78] Dawn, like Uzukwu and many African theologians cited in this study thus far, affirms Vatican II and the Synod Father's promotion of enculturation and adaptation without diluting authentic worship and Christian identity.[79] She further recommends genuine community gathering, with songs and accoutrements that reflect a true and ethical spirit of worship, which was championed centuries ago by the prophet Amos (5:21–23).[80] Dawn concludes:

> Let us reach out in the Church and to the world with the best music we can offer from the Church's entire history, from the distant past to the present. The congregation can "sing a new song" not because we are trying to appeal to the culture, but because God is present in our midst in new ways. As we respond to God, the subject of our worship, our song will reach out to the culture surrounding the Church with the Church's best gifts—without dumbing down the faith.[81]

Similarly, Austin Fleming reminds ministers and liturgical functionaries that through our rituals and assemblies, God is the object of worship, not cell phones, iPods, and other electronic devices. He calls on Christians to eschew idolatry and all kinds of hypocrisy.[82] He sees the necessity of plan-

76. Carroll R., "Worship Wars," 223–24.

77. Birch, *Hosea, Joel and Amos*, 223.

78. Dawn, *Theology of Worship*, 15–72.

79. Ibid., 138.

80. Ibid., 139–55.

81. Ibid., 204.

82. Fleming and Turano, *Preparing for Liturgy*, 2–26. See also Gusmer, "Is It

ning, honesty, authenticity, integrity, adaptation, and community spirit, as well as the spirituality of inclusivism, at worship. Fleming prefers a situation that does not isolate the poor or trample upon the needy and the weak of society.[83]

In support for the third point raised by Carroll R., that "worship must nurture a commitment to justice," Fleming affirms that the worshiping community cannot isolate itself from the work of justice, peace, and righteousness that is assiduously promoted by the prophet Amos.[84] Another interesting voice in this area is Ron Sider's in *The Scandal of the Evangelical Social Conscience,* which cites statistics regarding the use of money, sexual activity, divorce rates, spouse abuse, concern for the poor, and racism in order to substantiate his argument that, in many ways, the lifestyle and values of evangelical worshipers in the United States are not very different from those of the surrounding secular culture, which is often characterized as individualistic, materialistic, and greedy.[85]

Pope Francis, the leader of the global Catholic Church, in his Apostolic Exhortation *Evangelii Gaudium* ("The Joy of the Gospel") insists on the inclusion of the poor in the socio-economic and religion-political societies around the world. He cautions that the greatest dangers in today's world include the pervasion of consumerism, complacency of the covetous heart, and feverish pursuit of frivolous pleasures, as well as a blunted conscience that leaves no room for the poor.[86] Francis exhorts that everyone today, including worshipers, must be able to say no to the economy of exclusion, the idolatry of money, and a financial system that rules rather than serves, resulting in the inequality, selfishness, spiritual sloth, worldliness, and warring among self and all forms of injustices that Amos espoused.[87]

Worship?," where he acrostically lists elements of authentic "worship" to include: wholeness, organization, ritual, sharing, harmony, integrity, and prayerfulness—qualities that are all found in Amos' theology of worship.

83. Fleming, *Theology and Spirituality,* 27–97.

84. Ibid., 99.

85. Cf. Sider, *Scandal of the Evangelical Social Conscience;* Carroll R., "Worship Wars," 225.

86. Francis, *Evangelii Gaudium,* nos. 2, 53–109.

87. Ibid., nos. 53–109.

Let Justice Roll with Ever-flowing Righteousness

One other way we can see how Amos' message of justice and righteousness applies in North America is by reflecting on the life of an American icon, Martin Luther King Jr.—especially the way he appropriated Amos' theology to address injustices in the United States. Susan Ackerman summarizes King's adaptation of Amos' theology in her article "Between Text and Sermon: Amos 5:18–24."[88] Ackerman observes that in his legendary "I Have A Dream" speech, delivered at the 1963 March on Washington, he drew not only from iconic Western texts such as the Gettysburg Address, the plays of Shakespeare, and the Declaration of Independence, but also from the Bible. King cited many texts from Scripture, particularly Amos 5:24, which he paraphrased as "until justice rolls down like waters and righteousness like a mighty stream," when talking about the lack of civil rights for people of color, especially the blacks in the United States. King also appropriated Amos 5:24 at several other points throughout his career, including a speech in December 1955 at the beginning of the Montgomery Bus Boycott, in a 1961 commencement address at Lincoln University, in his last presidential address to the Southern Christian Leadership Conference in 1967, and in the sermon that he gave on April 3, 1968, the night before he was assassinated. Ackerman notes that King's paraphrase of Amos 5:24 is indelibly inscribed on the Civil Rights Memorial of Montgomery, designed by architect and artist Maya Lin.[89]

Ackerman highlights a few curious elements of King's use of Amos 5: 24 in order to address injustices in America. For instance, Ackerman points out that King's translation of "ever-flowing" (נחל איתן, *naḥal 'êtān*) as "mighty stream" is not found in most English translations. Ackerman thinks King must have adapted his presentation from the 1611 King James Bible version. Another curiosity is King's versatility in the use of different versions of the Scripture. For instance, he uses the term "justice" (משפט, *mišpāṭ*) in alternate sermons and speeches in place of the "judgment" attested in the King James Version.[90]

Ackerman argues that King's choice of the words "justice" (משפט, *mišpāṭ*) and "mighty stream" (נחל איתן, *naḥal 'êtān*) were intentional for

88. Ackerman, "Amos 5:18–24," 190–93.

89. Ibid., 191.

90. Other sermons and works of King's noted in Ackerman ("Amos 5:18–24," 190) include his "Paul's Letter to American Christians" (1956), various addresses in 1957, and his book *Stride toward Freedom* (1958).

his ministry to his contemporary American society. By avoiding the King James Version's language of "judgment," King unwaveringly upheld his politico-theological commitment to nonviolence. King did not want the oppressors of his African-American friends to be condemned, but to repent. He did not seek violence, but peace. King did not seek to defeat or humiliate his opponents, but to touch hearts and change minds.[91] In other words, like Amos, Martin Luther King Jr. sought redemption and reconciliation at the top of the mountain of despair, a position that has been underscored throughout this study of his prophecy.

By opting to use the imagery of a "mighty stream" instead of the "ever-flowing" or "everlasting" stream, King underlines not only the urgency and power of justice, but exposes where injustices had been swept away as if by a mighty stream. Ackerman believes this made much sense to African Americans, particularly those in King's native south (Mississippi, Alabama, Georgia, South Carolina, and Louisiana), who were familiar with the year-round "ever-flowing" or "slow-moving" stream. Amos' teaching certainly aligned with that of King, including his condemnation of economic and racial injustices, religious hypocrisy, and exploitation of the poor by the rich.[92] Christians in America (and elsewhere) today must also recognize that Martin Luther King Jr., like the Prophet Amos, was not afraid to preach the gospel and engage the harsh realities of life (Amos 4:4–13; 5:4–6, 14–15, 18–20, 21–24). Additionally he, like Amos, reworked the standard idioms of his culture in order to address unethical worship and combat the injustices of his time.

Summary of Chapter Six

Given these premises, it is fair to say that Amos 5 has relevance for the economic, religious, and socio-political situations of Africa (Nigeria) and the United States. Amos 5 is useful for worship, during sermons, and for human and civil rights activities, as illustrated in the sermons and addresses of Martin Luther King Jr. It resonates with the themes of Pope Francis' writings and could inform the ideal agenda of the United Nations. The prophet Amos should be a role model to the civil and ecclesiastical leaders who are called to be the prophetic champions and consciences of our times.

91. Ackerman, "Amos 5:18–24," 191.

92. Ibid., 192.

Perhaps there is no better way to conclude this section than to also appeal to the tradition of Psalm 15, as adapted in the *Christian Prayer: The Liturgy of Hours,* in the United States:[93]

> Lord, who shall be admitted to your tent
> And dwell on your holy mountain?
> He who walks without fault;
> He who acts with justice
> And speaks the truth from his heart;
> He who does not slander with his tongue;
> He who does no wrong to his brother
> Who cast no slur on his neighbor,
> Who holds the godless in disdain,
> But honors those who fear the Lord
> He who keeps his pledge . . . such a man will stand firm forever.

93. *Christian Prayer,* 724–25.

Summary and Conclusion

THE PRECEDING PAGES HAVE offered a thorough review of Amos of Tekoa, one of Israel's fountainhead prophets. Amos lived in a paradoxical time: on the one hand, great material prosperity; on the other, social and religious corruption. He prophesied in the middle of the eighth century BCE and challenged the socio-economic, religious and political ills of his time, including hypocrisy in religion, bribery, corruption, and exploitation of the poor. Of all of Israel's prophets, Amos seems to be the most pessimistic in his views and yet he is hopeful. Without doubt, he seems to be the most admired and researched among the prophets perhaps because his prophecy is socially outstanding and religiously elegant. The present study has added to scholarship on Amos in its attempt to evaluate Amos' theology of worship (Amos 5) and its relevance for contemporary society, particularly of Africa and America.

Chapter 5 formed the exegetical nucleus of this study. It provided a deeply engaged, extensive and robust theological exegesis of the text in a manner unprecedented in the history of the study of Amos 5. Leading to the exegesis were four chapters, beginning with an examination of the general background of Amos (chap. 1), followed by a textual critical analysis of the text (chap. 2), a discussion of its place among the Minor Prophets (chap. 3), and then analysis of its specific literary structure, which also enabled us to examine Amos 5 within the overall context of the entire book of Amos (chap. 4).

As delightful and even as morally compelling as Amos 5 can be to students, theologians, preachers, human rights activists, and exegetes, past studies on this subject have been broadly carried out within the general purview of the history of Israel' religion. In some of these broader studies, theological consciousness was not placed on Amos 5 as the Word of God.

Focus was often placed on the prophetic cult critique in the Hebrew Bible/ OT, and not specifically on the central and important theme of proper worship in Amos 5. The limited conclusions of these broad approaches, theologically speaking, did not take up the powerful prophecy of Amos or adequately apply its message and meaning to the specific spiritual, pastoral, economic, and socio-political needs of contemporary church and society, particularly in Africa (Nigeria) and in the United States of America.

As noted in the introductory section of this study, in different parts of Africa, and especially in Nigeria, there are various religious, social, political, and economic challenges that would benefit from the soothing effects of the message of Amos 5. The proliferation of religions (in particular African Traditional Religion [ATR], Islam, and Christianity) in Africa (Nigeria) today, is one of them. This development is accompanied by unethical practices in some worship centers. There have been recorded cases of abuses, such as the distribution of expensive material gifts and cash by public office holders to religious groups, without accountability, while at the same time civil servants in their areas of governance have not been duly compensated for months and even in some cases years. In the case of ATR, there are also some strong cultural inclinations to observe certain aspects of worship that contradict the tenets of Christian faiths, including the justice and righteousness emphasized in the theology of Amos, and more broadly, in Christianity.

The socio-political situation of many African countries, Nigeria in particular, is similar to that of Amos' time. Amos lived during a period of political equilibrium and economic prosperity that engendered conditions for religious hypocrisy and economic and political injustice against the poor. The rich constructed for themselves more homes (3:15), purchased more furnishings and other material comforts (3:12; 4:1; 6:6) while neglecting the poor. The less-privileged even became more less-privileged: they were exploited, trampled upon, and even exchanged, Amos tells us, for a pair of sandals (2:6–7; 5:10–12). They experienced extortion in the marketplaces and were denied justice in law courts by dictatorial and corrupt officials, kings, priests and the upper classes who made rules for themselves (8:5). African nations today can surely see themselves in these dark and festering problems that the prophet Amos fought so hard to address.

Besides these socio-political challenges, which all too often culminate in bad leadership across the continent of Africa, and particularly Nigeria, there are noticeable consequences of marketplace corruption in the public realm that have also led to generally unjust economic structures. The continent's currencies, the Nigerian *Naira* in particular has been mostly devalued compared to the dollar and euro. This is in addition to many other social and moral challenges, such as child trafficking, abuse of religions, violence, and tribal conflicts.

North America, and the United States in particular, today also faces socio-political, economic, and religious problems that beg for insight from the message of Amos 5. Society is marked by palpable and acute individualism, selfishness, isolationism, and syncretism. Electronic devices have weakened or even replace interpersonal communication and dialogue. Faith traditions have been usurped by the political ideologies of the Republicans and the Democrats.

In other words, in the United States, the integrity of worship and ethics has all too frequently been compromised by a false sense of socio-political security and a faith in exceptionalism, similar to what Amos experienced in his time. Besides mixing faith and national ideologies, the spiritual life of the culture of entertainment in secular society is increasingly engulfing the spirit of prayer and worship in the United States. Carroll R. thus notes that life in America, though driven by entertainment, electronics, and technology, is broken in so many ways, by personal trauma from the abuse of guns and drugs, ignorance of other people's cultures and world geography, family dysfunction, and isolationism. The church, he suggests, must not neglect its primary mission, which includes addressing issues of poverty, hunger, racism, and war as well as personal brokenness both at home and abroad.

Economically, the United States is blessed as one of the wealthiest of nations. Yet in the midst of this blessing, a shocking number of people lack access to housing, food, health, and education, as did the poor during the time of Amos. In the United States, the recent economic crash also revealed widespread predatory lending practices have led many students and families into insurmountable debt. There are also those in corporate life who utilize slave and cheap labor in developing countries from the shores of America who are also regular worshipers in American churches. Loopholes in the U.S tax system have sometimes placed the burdens of paying more taxes on the shoulders of the poor rather than on the rich, a phenomenon that was also common during the time of Amos. This study also cited cases of a paucity of market outlets in poor urban areas in the United States, which often make poor residents victims of predatory pricing. We have also noted that the poor in America, especially African American males, know that it can be difficult to find justice without disputes or controversy in the U.S. court system. A typical case in hand is the 2015 Ferguson report from the U.S. Department of Justice and the investigations into the rampant killings of people of color in Baltimore and across the United States.

Given these contemporary cultural problems in Africa and in the United State, this study has utilized different literary-historical and theological approaches with the hope of finding solutions in the prophecy of Amos which so deftly renders the problems. These approaches were complemented heavily by the hermeneutic of faith, with emphasis on the text, context, exegesis, and theology. The preceding pages of this work examined in detail the related themes in Amos 5 of lamentation (vv. 1–3), hope for the remnant, the exhortation to seek the Lord in justice and righteousness (vv. 4–6, 14–17, 24), and the Day of the Lord (vv. 18–20). This study also expressed how these themes function in relation to the entire ethics of worship in Amos (vv. 21–27).

What also distinguished the foregoing discussion from previous studies is that it has been situated within the overall context of the book of Amos and delineated its relationship with the Minor Prophets. Reading the Minor Prophets, of which Amos is a part, as a composite whole is a trend among scholars of Israel's prophets. Recent scholars have noticed not only some editorial activities common among the Twelve, but also familiar literary techniques and features such as catchwords, motifs, allusions, framing devices, quotations, repetitive phrases, *inclusio,* and major themes like the Day of the Lord that bind the eleven Minor Prophets to Amos as a composite unity. This is in addition to the importance of the socio-cultural and religious settings of Amos, his political worldview, idioms, genre, profession before prophecy, and his literary skills, which have been emphasized throughout this work.

Amos, as repeatedly noted, preached in a time of political equilibrium, relative peace with economic prosperity in Israel. Yet this prosperity bred economic injustice, religious hypocrisy, and exploitation of the poor. The rich appropriated multiple homes, which they furnished for themselves with ivory (3:15).[1] They purchased ostentatiously expensive furniture (6:4) and galvanized material goods for personal comfort (3:12; 4:1; 6:6).[2] Conversely, Israel's poor were made poorer, enslaved, trampled upon, exchanged for a pair of sandals, overtaxed (2:6, 7), judged unjustly in the

---

1. Ellis, "Amos Economics," 464–65.
2. Motyer, *Message of Amos,* 15.

courts (5:10, 12), and shamelessly extorted in marketplaces (8:5). Amos unequivocally condemned the socio-political and economic injustices of his time with some of the most pointed rhetoric in the OT; he also prophetically threatened the utter devastation of the nations.[3]

Chapters two, three, and four of this study were dedicated to the textual, literary, and formation criticism of the prophecy of Amos, which some scholars argue was delivered orally before being redacted and edited to its present canonical form. These criticisms invited us to appreciate how Amos' literary styles informed his critical rhetoric and function to integrate his theological themes (justice, righteousness, mercy, repentance, exhortation to worship the Lord alone, judgment/day of the Lord, hope, and salvation) in order to bring Israel back to God.

Nevertheless, be it his background and formation history, or rhetorical styles of communication (idioms, metaphors, parables, hymns, exhortations, lamentation, threats, indictments in prose, and poems), Amos used these devices and features to the advantage of his prophecy about the God of Israel and to critique worship practices in a nation characterized by economic prosperity but lacking a sense of justice. In other words, when Amos turned his prophetic gaze upon the religious communities of his time, he found a religion that was very religious and practiced what was traditional, but did so falsely and hypocritically. As stressed in chapter five, religious centers were apparently filled with festivals (v. 21), sacrifices (v. 22), songs, and music (v. 23). Worshipers, especially the elites, orchestrated Israel's external ritualism with a lack of ethical and inner conviction. For Amos, as presented in this study, this hypocrisy was contradictory to a God who is the sovereign of all creation (4:13; 5:8–9; 9:2–7). The elites of Amos' day did not demonstrate the worship of the one who intervenes in history (2:9–10; 5:25) and liberates and wishes to save Israel (4:6–11; 9:11–15). Amos' God demands that election theology be received with a sense responsibility (2:10; 3:1–2; 5:14–15). God opposes sinfulness and judges Israel (8:2; 9:1). He threatens judgment on his day (vv.18–20) and demands justice, righteousness, and accountability (5:7, 15, 24, 6:12). Amos' God deserves better. He rejects vain and empty sacrifices, and warns of placing misguided trust in pilgrimages (2:6–7; 4:4; 5:7–13; 7:7; 8:4–7).

In the religious assemblies of Amos' theology, God alone deserves true gestures of worship (festivals, sacrifices, songs, prayers, thanksgiving) and obedience. Since election comes with a responsibility, our worship today

3. Ellis, "Amos Economics," 463.

must not be characterized by hypocritical offerings, empty rituals, and idle songs (המון שרים). In Amos' view, the Lord of Hosts not only hates (שנאתי) but rejects (מאסתי) such empty songs, as reflected in the declarations "I hate and I refuse your festival gathering" (v.21a) and "Take away from me the noise of your song,"(v.23a). The strong verbs of warning ("hate/refuse/reject") Amos uses in these statements demonstrate his rhetorical power as well as his courage as a prophet. His command "let justice roll along like water and righteousness like ever flowing stream" highlights the importance of justice (משפט) and righteousness (צדקה) for any healthy society. While justice tends to be strict, righteousness connotes compassion, charity, peace, kindness, and generosity. Both have the common element of discerning good and evil.[4] Practicing righteousness, as Birch argued, "is one of the ways in which we might seek to fulfill our obligation to righteousness in the relationships of neighbor, community and nation."[5]

Amos' invitation to seek the Lord (vv.4–6, 14–15), which is emphasized throughout this study, has wider and unlimited implications for judgment (vv.18–20) and hope (9:11–15). There is always an invitation to repentance in every disaster, just as there is always a dimension of God's affection where compassion prevails over justice, and mercy is a perpetual possibility.[6] Amos, through his repeated exhortation "seek the Lord," reminded Israel that they were not turning to the Lord himself, but rather to empty forms of songs and ritual worship. His exhortations also open a window of hope for life and salvation, which is rare in Amos' prophecy. As pointed out earlier, Amos does so in conformity with the Lord's graciousness, kindness, charity, peace, steadfast love, and mercy, which the Lord has shown in the history of his relationship with Israel. Besides justice and righteousness, these are the virtues that must characterize Israel's worship.

Although applying Amos 5 to contemporary society (Africa and America) is quite challenging, doing so was the focus of chapter six. Here, we stressed the relevance and exegetical and theological fruits of Amos 5 for contemporary society. To this point Schreiter, Bevans, Brueggemann, Okure, Ukpong and many others affirmed that "universal reflection often neglects to take care of issues that were the most pressing in many local circumstances," such as "the burden of poverty and oppression, the struggle to create a new identity after the colonial past, or the question of how to meet

---

4. Heschel, *Prophets*, 256.

5. Birch, *Hosea, Joel and Amos*, 216.

6. Heschel, *Prophets*, 43.

the challenge of modernization, and the commodification of the economy in a traditional culture and village life."[7]

All this was done by recognizing that the Old Testament, of which Amos is a part, is the unfading and timeless Word of God. Like other biblical texts, Amos 5 is "capable of entering into, and finding expression in various cultures and languages."[8] The prophet Amos, as maintained throughout this work, remains a creative genius whose fidelity to the ancient covenant and concern for contemporary issues combined to reflect the manner in which both past and present must be creatively linked in order to ascertain the present relevance of divine revelation, its place on a continuum. Therefore, its contemporaneous message must somehow be connected with the realities of today's church and society. Amos' messages of judgment and hope for the remnant, who truly worship God, mediates several socio-political, economic, ethical, and religious challenges, which were particularly discussed in chapter six.

The poverty, corruption, and abuse of the poor seen in Amos' time is still prevalent in Africa today. Religiously, apart from *Boko Haram* extremists and their abduction of Chibok schoolgirls in northern Nigeria, adulteration and abuse of liturgical music, proliferation of churches and worship centers, and hypocrisies of worship similar to those of Amos' generation abound in African shrines. Some who frequent these African worship centers are often the same ones who practice exploitation, defraud the poor, embezzle public funds, and deny benefits and fundamental human rights to their workers, particularly the civil servants.

The socio-economic and political injustices common in Amos' time, such as the over-taxing of the poor and the creation of gaps between the "have'" and the "have-nots," are still prevalent in the United States. As in Amos' time, many in the United States today have trouble accessing housing, water, food, and health care; at the same time, the cost of sending their children to college is high, a barrier to the education that is the way out of poverty. Modern American society can thus relate to Amos' economics in the following ways: (1) in the prevalent and unfair lending practices of our time; (2) in the widespread predatory lending practices that recently led so many citizens into insurmountable debt; (3) in the loopholes in the U.S. tax system as well as the dysfunctional politics that sometimes leave the poor more vulnerable; (4) in the selfishness, consumerism, materialism,

7. Schreiter, *New Catholicity*, 1–2.

8. *Verbum Domini*, no. 1.

and culpable indifference to the plights of others, which parallels the pride found similarly among the elites of Amos' generation of worshipers; and (5) in the modern false sense of nationalism without morality, which reflects the false sense of "election theology/ideology" of Amos' time.

Amos' prophecy of true worship also offers American churches and society food for thought. Worship must be willing to question reigning ideologies (Amos 7:9–17; 9:1), and it must be able to engage in the harsh realities of life (4:4–13; 5:4–6). To this point, Mary Healy recommends that "preachers must display a profound unity between what they preach and what they live."[9] Again, worship in the United States must nurture a commitment to justice of all forms (Amos 5:18–27; 8:3–6).

Worship must be related to the full and equitable flow of justice and righteousness, as demonstrated through Martin Luther King Jr.'s appropriation of Amos 5 during the civil rights era and many decades later by Pope Francis.[10] There is also a need for high integrity of worship, especially in American culture with its devotion to entertainment. Amos challenges us not to mistake entertainment for worship, but to constantly keep God at the center of our worship life.

In each of these contexts (both African and American, Nigerian, United States), reading, studying, teaching, preaching, and living Amos 5 in the language of the people (e.g., local idioms, riddles, proverbs, and culture) can be very effective. Finally, as Healy rightly observed, "it is difficult to exaggerate the importance of good preaching in the life of the Church" since "Faith comes from what is heard, and what is heard comes by the preaching of Christ" (Rom. 10:17).[11] Preachers and teachers of Amos must stress exegesis, faith, and theology. They must courageously preach, teach, and live lives that show that authentic human relationships must be characterized by justice and righteousness, as these authentic human relationships lead to seeking and discovering an authentic human-divine relationship. Amos 5 demonstrates that our worship must be wholly ethical and with a sense of justice this worship must be carried into marketplaces and plazas and be courageously expressed in our everyday lives.

9. Healy, "Biblical Preaching," 122.

10. For Francis' views in defense of the poor, justice, and righteousness, see Francis (*Evangelii Gaudium*, nos. 2, 53–109); Francis ("No Longer Slaves"); Francis ("Overcoming Indifference and Win Peace," nos. 1–7).

11 Healy, "Biblical Preaching," 109.

Bibliography

Agboluaje, Timothy. "The Ministry of Amos in Israel and Its Socio-Religious Implication for the Nigerian Society." *OJT* 11 (2006) 1–10.

Achebe, Chinua. *The Trouble with Nigeria.* London: Heinemann, 1984.

Ackerman, Susan. "Between Text and Sermon: Amos 5:18–24." *Int* 57 (2003) 190–93.

Agibi, Felicia, "Still Searching: The Quest for Justice in Nigeria." *America The National Catholic Review,* May 2, 2016.

Alberts, Rainer. *A History of Israelite Religion in the Old Testament Period Volume I: From the Beginnings to the End of the Monarchy.* Translated by John Bowden. OTL. Louisville: Westminster John Knox, 1994.

———. *A History of Israelite Religion in the Old Testament Period Volume II: From the Exile to the Maccabees.* Louisville:Westminster John Knox, 1994.

Allen, Ronald, and Gordon Borror. *Worship: Rediscovering the Missing Jewel.* Portland, OR: Multnomah, 1982.

Alonso Schökel, Luis. *A Manual of Hebrew Poetics.* Subsidia Biblica 11. Rome: Editrice Pontificio Istituto Biblico, 2000.

Andersen, Francis I., and David Noel Freedman. *Amos: A New Translation with Introduction and Commentary.* AB 24a. New York: Doubleday, 1989.

Anderson, Bernhard W. *The Eighth Century Prophets: Amos, Hosea, Isaiah, Micah; The Old Testament Witnesses for Preaching.* Proclamation Commentaries. 1978. Reprinted, Eugene, OR: Wipf & Stock, 2003.

Barré, Michael L. "Amos." In *NJBC,* edited by Raymond E. Brown, Joseph A. Fitzmyer, and Roland E. Murphy, 209–16. Englewood Cliffs, NJ: Prentice Hall, 1990.

Barstad, Hans M. *The Religious Polemics of Amos: Studies in the Preaching of Am 2, 7B–8; 4, 1–13; 5, 1–27; 6, 4–7; 8, 14.* VTSup 34. Leiden: Brill, 1984.

Bechard, D. P. *The Scripture Documents: An Anthology of Official Catholic Teachings.* Collegeville, MN: Liturgical, 2002.

Ben Zvi, Ehud. "Is the Twelve Hypothesis Likely from an Ancient Readers' Perspective?" In *Two Sides of a Coin: Juxtaposing Views on Interpreting the Book of the Twelve / The Prophetic Books,* edited by Ehud Ben Zvi and James D. Nogalski, 47–96. Analecta Gorgiana 201. Piscataway, NJ: Gorgias, 2009.

———. "Twelve Prophetic Books or 'The Twelve': A Few Preliminary Considerations." In *Forming Prophetic Literature: Essays on Isaiah and the Twelve in Honor of John D. W. Watts,* edited by James W. Watts and Paul R. House, 125–57. JSOTSup 235. Sheffield: Sheffield Academic, 1996.

————. *A Historical-Critical Study of the Book of Zephaniah.* BZAW 198. Berlin: de Gruyter, 1991.

Benedict XVI, Pope. *Post-Synodal Apostolic Exhortation, Verbum Domini.* Vatican City: Libreria Editrice Vaticana, 2010.

Bentzen, A. "The Ritual Background of Amos 1:2—2:16." *OTS* 8 (1950) 85–99.

Begg, Christopher. "Course on Deuteronominc History." Washington, DC: Catholic University of America, 2007.

Berg, Werner. *Die Sogenannten Hymnenfragmente im Amosbuch.* Europäische Hochschulschriften, Reihe XXIII, Theologie 45. Bern: Lang, 1974.

Berlin, Adele. "Parallelism." In *ABD* 5:155–62.

————. "On Reading Biblical Poetry: The Role of Metaphor." In *Congress Volume Cambridge 1995*, edited by J. A. Emerton, 25–36. VTSup 66. Leden: Brill, 1997.

Berquist, Jon L. "Dangerous Waters of Justice and Righteousness: Amos 5:18–27." *BTB* 23 (1993) 54–63.

Berridge, J. M. "Zur Intention de Botschaft des Amos: Exegetished Überlegungen zu Am 5." *TLZ* 32 (1976) 321–40.

Bevans, Stephen. B. *Models of Contextual Theology.* Rev. ed. Faith and Cultures Series. Maryknoll, NY: Orbis , 2002.

Bhabha, H. K. *The Location of Culture.* London: Routledge, 1994.

Bibb, Bryan D. "The Prophetic Critique of Ritual in Old Testament Theology." In *The Priests in the Prophets: The Portrayal of Priests, Prophets and Other Religious Specialties in Latter Prophets*, edited by Lester L. Grabbe and Alice Ogden Bellis, 31–43. JSOTSup 408. London: T. & T. Clark, 2004.

Binz, Stephen J. *Introduction to the Bible: A Catholic Guide to Studying Scripture.* Collegeville, MN: Liturgical, 1986.

Birch, Bruce C. *Hosea, Joel and Amos.* Westminster Bible Companion. Louisville: Westminster John Knox, 1997.

Bligh, J. "Jesus in Samaria." *HeyJ* 3 (1962) 329–46.

Bosshard-Nepustil, Erich. "Beobachtungen zum Zwölfprophetenbuch." *BN* 40 (1987) 30–62.

Botterweck, G. J., and B. Kedar-Kopfstein. "ḥaḡ." In *TWAT* 2 (1977) 730–44.

Branick, Vincent P. *Understanding the Prophets and Their Books.* New York: Paulist, 2012.

Brettler, Marc Zvi, et al., *The Bible and the Believer: How to Read the Bible Critically and Religiously.* Oxford: Oxford University Press, 2012.

Brown, Raymond. *The Message of Nehemiah: God's Servant in a Time of Change.* Bible Speaks Today. Downers Grove, IL: InterVarsity, 1998.

Brown, Raymond E., and Sandra M. Schneiders. "Hermeneutics." In *NJBC*, edited by Joseph A. Fitzmyer and Roland E. Murphy, 1146–65. Englewood Cliffs, NJ: Prentice-Hall, 1990.

Brown, Francis, et al., *BDB.* Peabody, MA: Hendrickson, 2004.

Brueggemann, Walter. "Amos IV 4–13 and Israel's Covenant Worship." *VT* 15 (1965) 1–15.

————. *The Prophetic Imagination.* 2nd ed. Minneapolis: Fortress, 2001.

———— . *Worship in Ancient Israel: An Essential Guide.* Nashville: Abingdon, 2005.

Bruns, G. L. *Hermeneutics Ancient & Modern.* New Haven: Yale University Press, 1992.

Budde, Karl. "Eine folgenschwere Redaktion des Zwölfprophetenbuchs." *ZAW* 39 (1921) 218–29.

Burghardt, Walter J. *Let Justice Roll Down Like Waters: Biblical Justice Homilies throughout the Year.* New York: Paulist, 1998.

———. "Mercy, Not Sacrifice?" In *Speak the Word with Boldness: Homilies for Risen Christians,* 100–103. New York: Paulist, 1994.

Buss, Martin J. "The Meaning of 'Cult' and Interpretation of the Old Testament." *JBR* 32 (1964) 317–25.

Cahill, P. J. "Narrative Art in John IV." *RSB* 2 (1982) 41–55.

Carl, Scott, ed. *Verbum Domini and the Complementarity of Exegesis and Theology.* Catholic Theological Formation. Grand Rapids: Eerdmans, 2015.

Carroll R, M. Daniel. *Amos—The Prophet and His Oracles: Research on the Book of Amos.* Louisville: Westminster John Knox, 2002.

———. "Can the Prophets Shed Light on Our Worship Wars? How Amos Evaluates Religious Ritual." *Stone-Campbell Journal* 8 (2005) 215–27.

Carniti, C. "L'espressione 'il giorno di JHWH." *BeO* 12 (1970) 11–25.

Carvalho, Corrine L. "Why Read the Prophets through the Lens of Our World?" In *Pastoral Essays in Honor of Lawrence Boadt, CSP: Reading the Old Testament,* edited by Carrinne L. Carvelho, 135–47. New York: Paulist , 2013.

Castelot, J. J. "Religious Institutions of Israel." In *NJBC,* edited by Raymond E. Brown et al., 710–11. New Jersey: Prentice-Hall, 1990.

Catechism of the Catholic Church. Vatican City: Libreria Editrice Vaticana, 1994.

Cathcart, Kevin J. "Day of Yahweh." In *ABD* 2:84–85.

Černy, Ladislav. *The Day of Yahweh and Some Relevant Problems.* Práce z vědeckých ústavů 53. Prague: Karlovy University, 1948.

Chester, Andrew. *Future Hope and Reality.* Vol. 1, *Eschatology and Transformation in the Hebrew Bible.* WUNT 293. Tübingen: Mohr/Siebeck, 2012.

Childs, Brevard S. *Introduction to the Old Testament as Scripture.* Philadelphia: Fortress, 1979.

———. "Die theologische Bedeutung der Endform eines Textes." *TQ* 167 (1987) 242–51.

Chisholm, Robert B. "Theology of the Minor Prophets." *In Biblical Theology of the Old Testament,* edited by Roy B. Zuck, 399–420. Chicago: Moody, 1991.

Clifford, Richard J. "The Use of Hôy in the Prophets." *CBQ* 28 (1966) 458–64.

Coggins, R. J. "The Minor Prophets—One Book or Twelve?" In *Crossing the Boundaries: Essays in Biblical Interpretation in Honour of Michael D. Goulder,* edited by S. E. Porter, P. Joyce, and D. E. Orton, 57–68. Biblical Interpretation Series 8. Leiden: Brill, 1994.

Cohen, S. "The Political Background of the Words of Amos." *HUCA* 36 (1965) 153–60.

Coogan, Michael D. *The Old Testament: A Historical and Literary Introduction to the Hebrew Scriptures.* New York: Oxford University Press, 2006.

Cook, Joan E. *Hear, O Heavens and Listen O Earth: An Introduction to the Prophets.* Collegeville, MN: Liturgical, 2006.

Coote, Robert B. *Amos among the Prophets: Composition and Theology.* 1981. Reprinted, Eugene, OR: Wipf & Stock, 2005.

Countryman, L. William. *Interpreting the Truth: Changing the Paradigm of Biblical Studies.* Harrisburg, PA: Trinity, 2003.

Craghan, J. F. "The Prophet Amos in Recent Research." *BTB* 2 (1972) 242–61.

Craigie, Peter C. "Amos the *noqed* in the Light of Ugaritic." *SR* 11 (1982) 29–32.

Crenshaw, James L. *Hymnic Affirmations of Divine Justice: The Doxologies of Amos and Related Texts in the Old Testament.* SBLDS 24. Missoula, MT: Scholars, 1975.

Cripps, Richard S., ed., *A Critical and Exegetical Commentary on the Book of Amos.* London: SPCK, 1955.

Cross, Frank M. "The Divine Warrior in Israel's Early Cult." In *Biblical Motifs: Origins and Transformation*, edited by Alexander Altman, 11–30. Cambridge, MA: Harvard University Press, 1966.

———. *Canaanite Myth and Hebrew Epic: Essays in the History of the Religion of Israel.* Cambridge, MA: Harvard University Press, 1973.

Cuffey, Kenneth H. "Remnant, Redactor, and Biblical Theologian: A Comparative Study of Coherence in Micah and The Twelve." In *Reading and Hearing the Book of the Twelve,* edited by James D. Nogalski and Marvin A. Sweeney, 185–208. SBLSymS 15. Atlanta: SBL, 2000.

Dawn, Marva. *Reaching Out Without Dumbing Down: A Theology of Worship for this Urgent Time.* Grand Rapids: Eerdmans, 1995.

De Andrado, Paba Nidhani. "Ḥesed and Sacrifice: The Prophetic Critique in Hosea." *CBQ* 78 (2016) 47–67.

De Vaux, Ronald. *Ancient Israel: Its Life and Institutions.* Translated by John McHugh. Grand Rapids: Eerdmans, 1997.

Deji, Ayegboyin. "Corruption, an Obstacle to National Rebirth: The Religious Perspective." *Orita: Ibadan Journal of Religious Studies* 33 (2001) 99–122.

DeVries, Simon J. *Yesterday, Today and Tomorrow: Time and History in the Old Testament.* Grand Rapids: Eerdmans, 1975.

De Waard, Jan."The Chiastic Structure of Amos V 1–17." *VT* 27 (1977)170–77.

Doorly, William J. *Prophet of Justice: Understanding the Book of Amos.* New York: Paulist, 1989.

Ebo, D. J. I. "Another Look at Amos' Visions." *ATJ* 18 (1989) 17–27.

———. "'O That Jacob Would Survive': A Study on Hope in the Book of Amos." PhD diss., University of Nigeria, Nsukka, 1985.

———. "Re-Ordering of Amos' Visions." In *Perspective in Religious Studies,* edited by E. Dada Adelowo, 2:61–73. Ibadan, Nigeria: HEBN, 2014.

Edisana Nwed Abasi Ibom. Apapa, Nigeria: Bible Society of Nigeria, 1985.

Eichrodt, Walter. "The Holy One in Your Midst': The Theology of Hosea." *Int* 15 (1961) 259–73.

Ellis, Robert R. "Amos Economics." *RevExp* 107 (2010) 463–512.

Everson, Joseph. "The Day of Yahweh." *JBL* 93 (1974) 329–37.

Farr, Georges. "The Language of Amos, Popular or Cultic?" *VT* 16 (1966) 312–24.

Feinberg, Charles L. *The Minor Prophets.* Chicago: Moody, 1990.

Ficker, R. "šîr." *THAT* 2 (1976) 895–98.

Finley, Thomas J. *Joel, Amos, Obadiah.* Wycliffe Exegetical Commentary. Chicago: Moody, 1999.

Fitzmyer, Joseph A. *The Biblical Commission's Document The Interpretation of the Bible in the Church, Text and Commentary.* Subsidia Biblica 18. Rome: Biblical, 1995.

Flaming, Austin, and Victoria M. Turano. *Preparing for Liturgy: A Theology and Spirituality.* Chicago: Liturgy Training, 1997.

Fohrer, Georg. *Einleitung in das Alte Testament.* Heidelberg: Quelle & Meyer, 1977.

Folarin, George Olufemi, and Samson O. Olanisebe. "Threat of Judgement in Amos and Its Lessons for Nigeria." *European Scientific Journal* 10 (2014) 243–261.

Francis, Pope. *Apostolic Exhortation, The Joy of the Gospel, Evangelii Gaudium.* Vatican City: Libreria Editrice Vatican, 2013.

————. *Message of His Holiness, "No Longer Slaves, But Brothers and Sisters," for the World Day of Peace, 1 January, 2015*. Vatican City: Libreria Editrice Vaticana, December 2014.

————. *"Overcome Indifference and Win Peace," Message of His Holiness Pope Francis For the XLIX World Day of Peace, 1 January 2016*. Vatican City: Libreria Editrice Vaticana, 8 December, 2015.

Francisco, Clyde T. "Teaching Amos in the Churches." *RevExp* 63 (1966) 413–19.

Fuller, Russell. "The Form and Formation of the Book of the Twelve: The Evidence from the Judean Desert." In *Forming Prophetic Literature: Essays on Isaiah and the Twelve in Honor of John D. W. Watts*, edited by James. W. Watts and Paul R. House, 86–101. JSOTSup 235. Sheffield: Sheffield Academic, 1996.

Garret, Duane A. "The Structure of Amos as a Testimony to Its Integrity." *JETS* 27 (1984) 275–76.

Gerstenberger, Erhard. "The Woe-Oracle of the Prophets." *JBL* 81 (1962) 249–63.

————. *Theologies in the Old Testament*. Translated by John Bowden. Minneapolis: Fortress, 2002.

Gevirtz, Stanley. "A New Look at an Old Crux: Amos 5:26." *JBL* 87 (1968) 267–76.

Gottlied, Hans. "Amos und Jerusalem." *VT* 17 (1967) 430–63.

Gressmann, Hugo. *Der Ursprung der jüdisch-israelitischen Eschatologie*. Göttingen: Vadenhoeck & Ruprecht, 1905.

Gusmer, Charles. W. "Is It Worship? Evaluating the Sunday Eucharist." *Living Worship* 14 (1978) 5–11.

Guyette, Fred. "Amos the Prophet: A Meditation on the Richness of 'Justice.'" *JBQ* 36 (2008) 15–21.

Hadjiev, Tchavdar. "'Kill All Who Are in Front': Another Suggestion about Amos ix 1." *VT* 57 (2007) 386–89.

Hammershaimb, Erling. *The Book of Amos: A Commentary*. New York: Schocken, 1970.

Hahn, Scott W. *Covenant and Communion: The Biblical Theology of Pope Benedict XVI*. Grand Rapids: Brazos, 2009.

Hardon, John A. *The Catholic Lifetime Reading Plan*. Royal Oak, MI: Grotto, 1989.

Harrelson, Walter. *From Fertility Cult to Worship*. Garden City, NY: Doubleday, 1969.

Harrington, Daniel. *Interpreting the Old Testament*. Collegeville, MN: Liturgical, 1981.

Harrison, R. K. *Joel and Amos: A Commentary on the Books of the Prophets Joel and Amos*. Philadelphia: Fortress, 1997.

————. *Introduction to the Old Testament: With a Comprehensive Review of Old Testament Studies and a Special Supplement on the Apocrypha*. Grand Rapids: Eerdmans, 1979.

Hasel, Gerhard F. *The Remnant: The History and Theology of the Remnant Idea from Genesis to Isaiah*. Berrien Springs, MI: Andrews University Press, 1990.

————. *Understanding the Book of Amos: Basic Issues in Current Interpretations*. Grand Rapids: Baker, 1991.

Hayes, John H. *Amos, His Times and Preaching: The Eighth-Century Prophet*. Nashville: Abingdon, 1988.

Hays, J. D. "Racial Issues in the Prophets." In *From Every People and Nation: A Biblical Theology of Races*, 105–39. NSBT 14. Downers Grove, IL: InterVarsity, 2003.

————. "The Ethnic Make-up of the Old Testament World." In *From Every People and Nation: A Biblical Theology of Race*, 25–45. NSBT 14. Downers Grove, IL: InterVarsity, 2003.

Healy, Mary. "Verbum Domini and the Renewal of Biblical Preaching." In *Verbum Domini and the Complementarity of Exegesis and Theology,* edited by Scott Carl, 109–12. Catholic Theological Formation. Grand Rapids: Eerdmans, 2015.

Hentschke, Richard E. *Die Stellung der Vorexilischen Schriftpropheten zum Kultus.* BZAW 75. Berlin: 1957.

Hertberg, H. W. "Die prophetische Kritik am Kult." *ThLZ* 75 (1950) 219–26.

———. "No Religion Is an Island." *USQR* 21 (1965–66) 121–34.

Heschel, Abraham Joshua. *The Prophets.* New York: HarperCollins, 2001.

Hiers, Richard H. "Day of the Lord." In *ABD* 2:82.

Hill, Andrew E. *Enter His Courts with Praise! Old Testament Worship for the New Testament Church.* Grand Rapids: Baker, 1993.

Hoffmann, Yair. "Did Amos Regard Himself as a *Nābî*'?" *VT* 27 (1977) 209–12.

———. "The Day of the Lord as a Concept and a Term in the Prophetic Literature." *ZAW* 93 (1981) 37–50.

Holladay, William L. *A Concise Hebrew and Aramaic Lexicon of the Old Testament.* Grand Rapids: Eerdmans, 1988.

Holter, Knut. *Old Testament Research for Africa: A Critical Analysis and Annotated Bibliography of African Old Testament Dissertations, 1967–2000.* BTA 3. Bern: Lang, 2002.

———. *Yahweh in Africa: Essays on Africa and the Old Testament.* BTA 1. Bern: Lang, 2001.

Honeycutt, Roy L. "Amos and Contemporary Issues." *RevExp* 63 (1966) 441–57.

House, Paul R. *The Unity of the Twelve.* JSOTSup 97. Sheffield: Sheffield Academic, 1990.

Howington, Nolan P. "Toward an Ethical Understanding of Amos." *RevExp* 63 (1966) 405–12.

Hunter, Vanliar A. *Seek the Lord: A Study of the Meaning and Function of the Exhortation in Amos, Hosea, Isaiah, Micah and Zephaniah.* Baltimore: St. Mary's Seminary and University, 1982.

Hyatt, J. Philip. "The Translation and Meaning of Amos 5:23–24." *ZAW* 68 (1956) 17–24.

Idowu, E. B. *African Traditional Religion: Problem of Definition.* London: SCM, 1977.

Iroegbu, Chinwe Adolphus. *"Let Justice Roll Down Like Waters": An Exegetical and Pragmatic Study of Amos' Critique of Social Justice and Its Cruciality in the Contemporary Nigerian Context.* Studienreihe Theologische Forschungsergebnisse Band 79. Hamburg: Kovač, 2007.

Irsigler, H. *Gottesgericht und Jhwhtag: Die Komposition Zef 1, 1–2, 3 untersucht auf der Grundlage der Literarkritik des Zefanjabuches.* ATSAT 3. St. Ottilien, Germany: EOS, 1977.

Irwin, Brian. "Amos 4:1 and the Cows of Bashan on Mount Samaria: A Reappraisal." *CBQ* 74 (2012) 231–46.

Ishai-Rosenboim, Daniella. "Is יום הי (the Day of the Lord) a Term in Biblical Language?" *Bib* 87 (2006)395–401.

Jenni, E. "anf Sn' to hate." *TLOT* 3:1277–79.

Jeremias, Jörg. *The Book of Amos: A Commentary.* OTL. Louisville: Westminster John Knox, 1998.

John Paul II. *Post-Synodal Apostolic Exhortation Ecclesia in Africa.* Yaoundé, Cameroon, Sept 14, 1995.

———. *Post-Synodal Apostolic Exhortatiion Ecclesia in America.* Vatican City: Libreria Editrice Vaticana, 1999.

Jones, Barry Alan. *The Formation of the Twelve: A Study of Text and Canon*. SBLDS 149. Atlanta: Scholars, 1995.

Kaiser, Otto. *Introduction to the Old Testament: A Presentation of Its Result and Problems*. Translated by John Sturdy. Minneapolis: Augsburg, 1975.

Kaiser, Walter C., Jr. *Toward an Old Testament Theology*. Grand Rapids: Zondervan, 1991.

Kapelrud, Arvid S. "Cult and Prophetic Words." *ST* 4 (1951) 5–12.

———. "God as Destroyer in the Preaching of Amos and in the Ancient Near East." *JBL* 71 (1952) 33–38.

Kapelrud, Arvid S. "The Role of the Cult in Old Israel." In *The Bible in Modern Scholarship*, edited by J. Philip Hyatt, 44–56. New York: Abingdon, 1965.

———. *Central Ideas in Amos*. Oslo: Oslo University Press, 1961.

Kelle, Brad E. "Political Critique: Church Praxis from the Framework of the Book of Amos." *Wesleyan Theological Journal* 41 (2006) 72–95.

Kellermann, Ulrich. "Der Amoschluss als Stimme deuteronomistischert Heilschoffnung." *EvTh* 29 (1969) 169–83.

King, Philip J. *Amos, Hosea, Micah: An Archaeological Commentary*. Philadelphia: Westminster John Knox, 1988.

Klawans Jonathan. *Purity, Sacrifice, and the Temple; Symbolism and Supersessionism in the Study of Ancient Judaism*. New York: Oxford University Press, 2006.

Klein, Ralph W. "The Day of the Lord." *Concordia Theological Monthly* 39 (1968) 517–25.

Klingbeil, Gerald A., and Martin G. Klingbeil. "The Prophetic Voice of Amos as a Paradigm for Christians in the Public Square." *TyBul* 58 (2007) 161–82.

Knight, Douglas A., and Amy-Jill Levine. *The Meaning of the Bible: What the Jewish Scriptures and Christian Old Testament Can Teach Us*. New York: HarperCollins, 2001.

Knight, Douglas A. *Methods of Biblical Interpretation*. Nashville: Abingdon, 2004.

Ko, Grace. "The Ordering of the Twelve as Israel's Historiography." In *Prophets, Prophecy, and Ancient Israelite Historiography,* edited by Mark J. Boda and Lissa M. Wray Beal, 315–32. Winona Lake, IN: Eisenbrauns, 2013.

Kock, Klaus. *Amos: Untersucht mit den Methoden einer strukturalen Fromageschichte*. 3 vols. Kevelaer: Butzon & Bercker, 1976.

Koch, Klaus. *The Prophets: The Assyrian Period, Volume 1*. Philadelphia: Fortress, 1983.

Komonchak, Joseph A., et al., *The New Dictionary of Theology*. Bangalore: Theological, 1996.

Kraus, Joachim-Hans. *Worship in Israel: A Cultic History of the Old Testament*. Oxford: Blackwell, 1966.

———. "Hôj als prophetische Leichenklage über das eigene Volk im 8 jahrdundert." *ZAW* 85 (1973) 15–46.

———. *Theology of the Psalms*. Translated by Keith Crim. Minneapolis: Augsburg, 1986.

Kugel, James L. *The Idea of Biblical Poetry: Parallelism and Its History*. Baltimore: John Hopkins University Press, 1981.

Lafferty, Veronica Theresa. *The Prophetic Critique of the Priority of the Cult: A Study of Amos 5:21–24 and Isaiah 1:10–17*. Eugene, OR: Pickwick, 2012.

———. "The Prophetic Critique of the Priority of the Cult: A Study of Amos 5:21–24 and Isaiah 1:10–17." PhD diss., Catholic University of America, 2010.

Lambdin, Thomas O. *Introduction to Biblical Hebrew*. Upper Saddle River, NJ: Prentice-Hall, 1971.

Leclerc, Thomas L. *Introduction to the Prophets: Their Stories, Sayings, and Scrolls*. New York: Paulist, 2007.

Levin, Christoph. "Amos und Jeroboam 1." *VT* 45 (1995) 307–17.

Limburg, James. "Sevenfold Structures in the Book of Amos." *JBL* 106 (1987) 217–22.

————. *Hosea–Micah*. Interpretation: A Bible Commentary for Teaching and Preaching. Louisville: Westminster John Knox, 1988.

Lindblom, Johannes. *Prophecy in Ancient Israel*. Philadelphia: Fortress, 1962.

Lineamenta Synod for Africa, The Church in Africa and her Evangelizing Mission towards the Year 2000 "You shall be my Witnesses" (Acts 1:8). Rome: Editrice Vaticana, 1990.

Long, Kenneth J. *The Trouble with America: Flawed Government, Failed Society*. New York: Lexington.

Magesa, Laurenti. *African Religion in the Dialogue Debate: From Intolerance to Coexistence*. Interreligious Studies 3. Berlin: Lit, 2010.

Markert, Ludwig. *Struktur und Bezeichnung des Scheltworts: e. gattungskrit. Studie anhand d. Amosbuches*. BZAW 140. Berlin: de Gruyter, 1977.

Martin-Achard, R., and S. Paul Re'emi. *Amos & Lamentations: God's People in Crisis*. ITC. Edinburgh: Handsel, 1984.

Martin-Achard, Robert. *Amos: L'homme, le message, l'influence*. Geneva: De L'Université de Genève, 1984.

Marti, Karl. *Das Dodekapropheton*. KHC 13. Tübingen: Mohr/Siebeck, 1904.

Mays, James Luther. "Words about the Words of Amos." *Interpretation* 13 (1959) 259–72.

————. *Amos: A Commentary*. OTL. Philadelphia: Westminster John Knox, 1969.

Mbiti, John S. *African Religions & Philosophy*. New York: Praeger, 1969.

McComiskey, Thomas E. "The Hymnic Elements of the Prophecy of Amos: A Study of Form-Critical Methodology." *JETS* 30 (1987) 139–57.

————. "Hosea." In *An Exegetical & Expository Commentary: The Minor Prophets*, 1–237. Grand Rapids: Baker, 1992.

McCullough, W. S. "Some Suggestions about Amos." *JBL* 72 (1953) 247–54.

McKenzie, John L. *Dictionary of the Bible*. New York: Touchstone, 1995.

McKenzie, Steven L., and Stephen R. Haynes, eds. *An Introduction to Biblical Criticisms and Their Application: To Each Its Own Meaning*. Rev. ed. Louisville: Westminster John Knox, 1999.

Melugin, Roy F. "Amos in Recent Research." *CR* 6 (1998) 65–101.

Michael, O. "μισεω." *TDNT* 4:683–94.

Mitchell, H. G. "The Idea of God in Amos." *Journal of the Exegetical Society* 7 (1887) 33–35.

Miller Patrick D. "The Divine Council and the Prophetic Call to War." *VT* 18 (1968) 100–107.

————. "The Sovereignty of God." In *The Hermeneutical Quest: Essays in Honor of James Luther Mays*, edited by Donald G. Miller, 129–44. Allison Park, PA: Pickwick, 1986.

————. *They Cried to the Lord: The Form and Theology of Biblical Prayer*. Minneapolis: Fortress, 1994.

————. *The Religion of Ancient Israel*. Library of Ancient Israel. Louisville: Westminster John Knox, 2000.

Moore, Michael S. "Yahweh's Day." *ResQ* 29 (1987) 193–208.

Moore, R. Kelvin. "The Book of Amos: Amos; An Introduction." *Theological Educator* 52 (1995) 27–36.

Morgan, G. Campbell. *The Minor Prophets: The Men and Their Messages*. Westwood, NJ: Revell, 1960.

Motyer, J. A. *The Message of Amos: The Day of the Lion*. The Bible Speaks Today. Downers Grove, IL: InterVarsity, 1974.

Mowinckel, Sigmund. *He That Cometh*. Translated by G. W. Anderson. New York: Abingdon, 1954.

Müller, Ernst W., and Dietrich H. Preuss. *Die Vorstellung vom Rest im Alten Testament*. Neukirchen-Vlyn: Neukirchener, 1973.

Murtonen, A. "The Prophet Amos—A Hepatoscoper?" *VT* 1 (1951) 293–96.

Nel, W. A. G. "Amos 9:11–15—An Unconditional Prophecy of Salvation during the Period of the Exile." *OTE* 2 (1984) 81–97.

Neubauer, Karl W. "Erwägungen zu Amos 5, 4–15." *ZAW* 78 (1966) 292–316.

Niehaus, Jeffrey. "Amos." In *The Minor Prophets: An Exegetical & Expository Commentary*, edited by Thomas Edward McComiskey, 315–494. Grand Rapids: Baker, 1992.

Noble, Paul R. "The Literary Structures of Amos: A Thematic Analysis." *JBL* 114 (1995) 209–26.

Nogalski, James. "The Day (s) of YHWH in the Book of the Twelve." In *SBLSP 1999: One Hundred and Thirty-Fifth Annual Meeting: November 20–23, 1999*, 617–42. SBL Seminar Paper 38. Atlanta: Scholars, 1999.

——— "Intertextuality in the Twelve." In *Forming Prophetic Literature: Essays on Isaiah and the Twelve in Honor of John D. W. Watts*, edited by James. W. Watts and Paul R. House, 102–24. JSOTSup 235. Sheffield: Sheffield Academic, 1996.

———. "Joel as 'Literary Anchor' for the Book of the Twelve." In *Reading and Hearing the Book of the Twelve*, edited by James D. Nogalski and Marvin A. Sweeney, 91–124. SBLSymS 15. Atlanta: SBL, 2000.

———. *Literary Precursors to the Book of the Twelve*. BZAW 217. Berlin: de Gruyter, 1993.

———. *Reading and Hearing the Book of the Twelve*. SBLSymS 15. Atlanta: SBL, 2000.

———. *Redactional Processes in the Book of the Twelve*. BZAW 218. Berlin: de Gruyter, 1993.

Nogalski, James D., and Marvin A. Sweeney. "Preface." In *Reading and Hearing the Book of the Twelve*, vii–ix. SBLSymS 15. Atlanta: SBL, 2000.

Nwanunobi, C. O. *African Social Institutions*. Nsuka, Nigeria: University of Nigeria Press, 1992.

Odozor, Paulinus I. "Africa and the Challenge of Foreign Religious, Ethical Ideologies, Viruses, and Pathologies." In *Reconciliation, Justice and Peace: The Second African Synod*, edited by Agbonkhianmeghe E. Orobator, 214–25. Maryknoll, NY: Orbis, 2011.

Offiong, Immaculata. "Liturgical Hymns." In *Reconciliation and Renewal of Services in the Church: Lineamenta for the First Synod Catholic Diocese of Ikot Ekpene*, 94–104. Uyo, Nigeria: Trinity, 2002.

Okoye, James Chukwuma. *Scripture in the Church: The Synod on the Word of God*. Collegeville, MN: Liturgical, 2011.

Okure, Teresa. *The Johannine Approach to Mission: A Contextual Study of John 4:1–24*. WUNT 2/31. Tübingen: Mohr/Siebeck, 1988.

Onwubiko, Oliver. A. *Theory and Practice of Inculturation, Christian Mission & Culture in Africa*. Vol. 2. Enugu, Nigeria: Snaap, 1992.

Park, Aaron W. *The Book of Amos as Composed and Read in Antiquity*. SBL 37. New York: Lang, 2001.

Paul VI, Pope. *Dogmatic Constitution on Divine Revelation, Dei Verbum.* Vatican City: Libreria Editrice Vatican. 1965.

Paul, Shalom M. *Amos: A Commentary on the Book of Amos.* Hermeneia. Minneapolis: Fortress, 1991.

Petersen, David. L. "A Book of the Twelve?" In *Reading and Hearing the Book of the Twelve,* edited by James D. Nogalski and Marvin A. Sweeney, 3–10. SBLSymS 15. Atlanta: SBL, 2000.

———. "The Book of the Twelve—The Minor Prophets: Hosea, Joel, Amos, Obadiah, Jonah, Micah, Nahum, Habakkuk, Zephaniah, Haggai, Zechariah, Malachi." In *The Hebrew Bible Today: An Introduction to Critical Issues,* edited by Steven L. McKenzie and M. Patrick Graham, 95–126. Louisville: Westminster John Knox, 1998.

Peterson, David. *Engaging with God: A Biblical Theology of Worship.* Downers Grove, IL: InterVarsity, 1992.

Pferfer, Gerhard. "Das Ja des Amos." *VT* 39 (1989) 497–503.

Pigott, Susan M. "Amos: An Annotated Bibliography." *SWJT* 38 (1995) 29–35.

Pinto, Alphonso L. "Sacred Music and Loving God: *Cantare Amantis Est.*" http://www.inhisname.com.article.php.

Plato. *The Republic.* Translated by Benjamin Jowett. New York: Arimount, 1967.

Plein, W-J. *Vorformen de Shriftexegese innerhalb des Alten Testaments.* BZAW 119. Berlin: de Gruyter, 1971.

Pratico, Gary D., and Miles V. Van Pelt. *Basics of Biblical Hebrew Grammar.* 2nd ed. Grand Rapids: Zondervan, 2007.

Preez, Jannie du. "'Let Justice Roll on Like . . .' Some Explanatory Notes on Amos 5:24." *Journal of Theology for South Africa* 109 (2001) 95–98.

Premnath, D. N. *Eighth Century Prophets: A Social Analysis.* St. Louis: Chalice, 2003.

Rad, Gerhard von. *Der Heilege Kreig im alten Israel.* Zurich: Evangelische, 1951.

———. *Old Testament Theology.* 2 vols. OTL Louisville: Westminster John Knox, 2001.

———. "The Origin of the Concept of the Day of Yahweh." *JSS* 4 (1959) 97–108.

Ratzinger Joseph (Pope Benedict XVI). *Behold the Pierced One: An Approach to a Spiritual Christology.* Translated by Graham Harrison. San Francisco: Ignatius, 1986.

Rector, Larry J. "Israel's Rejected Worship: An Exegesis of Amos 5." *ResQ* 21 (1978) 161–75.

Redditt, Paul L. "Recent Research on the Book as One Book." *CR* 9 (2002) 47–80.

———. "The Book of Joel and Peripheral Prophecy." *CBQ* 48 (1986) 225–40.

———. "Zechariah 9–14, Malachi, and the Redaction of the Book of the Twelve." In *Forming Prophetic Literature: Essay on Isaiah and the Twelve in Honor of John D. W. Watts,* edited by James. W. Watts and Paul R. House, 245–68. JSOTSup 235. Sheffield: Sheffield Academic, 1996.

Redditt, Paul L., and Aaron Schart, eds. *Thematic Threads in the Book of the Twelve.* BZAW 325. Berlin: de Gruyter, 2003.

Rendtorff, Rolf. "Alas for the Day! The 'Day of the Lord' in the Book of the Twelve." In *God in the Fray: A Tribute to Walter Brueggemann,* edited by Tod Linafelt and Timothy K. Beal, 192–93. Minneapolis: Fortress, 1998.

———. *Das Alte Testament. Einführung.* Neukirchen-Vluyn: Neukirchener, 1983.

———. "How to Read the Book of the Twelve as a Theological Unity." In *Reading and Hearing the Book of the Twelve,* edited by James D. Nogalski and Marvin A. Sweeney, 75–87. SBLSymS 15. Atlanta: SBL, 2000.

Robert, J. J. M. "Recent Trends in the Study of Amos." *ResQ* 13 (1970) 1–16.

Robinson, H. Wheeler. *Inspiration and Revelation in the Old Testament*. Oxford: Oxford University Press, 1946.

Roget's 21st Century Thesaurus in Dictionary Form. New York: Philip Group, 1999.

Rösel, Hartmut N. "Kleine Studien zur entwicklung des Amosbuches." *VT* 43 (1993) 88–101.

Rosenbaum, Stanley N. *Amos of Israel: A New Interpretation*. Macon, GA: Mercer University Press, 1990.

Rowley, H. H. *The Old Testament and Modern Study: A Generation of Discovery and Research; Essays by Members of the Society for Old Testament Study*. Oxford: Clarendon, 1952.

———. "Ritual and the Hebrew Prophets." *JSS* 1 (1956) 338–60.

———. *Worship In Ancient Israel: Its Forms and Meaning*. London: SPCK, 1967.

Rudolph, Wilhelm. *Joel-Amos-Obadja-Jona*. Kommentar zum Alten Testament 13/2. Gütersloh: Mohn, 1971.

Ruiz, Jean-Pierre. *Readings From the Edges: The Bible & People on the Move*. Maryknoll, NY: Orbis, 2011.

Schart, Aaron. "Reconstructing the Redaction History of the Twelve Prophets: Problems and Models." In *Reading and Hearing the Book of the Twelve*, edited by James. D. Nogalski and Marvin A. Sweeney, 38–48. SBLSymS 15. Atlanta: SBL, 2000.

———. *Die Entstehung des Zwölfprophetenbuches: Neubearbeitungen von Amos in Rahmen schriftenübergreifender Redaktionsprozesse*. BZAW 260. Berlin: de Gruyter, 1998.

Schmidt, Nathaniel. "On the Text and Interpretatiion of Amos 5:25–27." *JBL* 13 (1894) 1–15.

Schmidt, Werner H. "Die deuteronomistische Redaktion des Amosbuches: Zu den theologischen Unterschieden zwishen dem Prophetenwort un seinem Sammler." *ZAW* 77 (1965) 168–93.

———. *Alttestamentilicher Galube und seine Umwelt: Zur Geschichte des alttestamentlichen Gottesverständnisses*. Neukirchener Studienbücher 6. Neukirchen-Vluyn: Neukirchener, 1968.

Schneiders, Sandra M. *The Revelatory Text: Interpreting the New Testament as Sacred Scripture*. Collegeville, MN: Liturgical, 1999.

Schreiter, Robert J. *The New Catholicity: Theology between the Global and the Local*. Maryknoll, NY: Orbis, 1997.

Second Special Assembly for Africa. *The Church in Africa in Service to Reconciliation, Justice and Peace: "You Are the Salt of the Earth; You Are the Light of the World . . . (Matt 5:13–14),"* Instrumentum Laboris. Vatican City: Libreria Editrice, 2009.

Segovia, Fernando. F., and Mary. A. Tolbert, eds. *Decolonizing Biblical Studies: A View from the Margin*. Maryknoll, NY: Orbis, 2000.

———. *Reading from This Place*. Vol. 1, *Social Location and Biblical Interpretation in the United States*. Minneapolis: Fortress, 1995.

Sekine, M. "Das Problem der Kultpolemik bei den Propheten." *EvTh* 28 (1968) 605–9.

Sider, Ron. *The Scandal of the Evangelical Social Conscience: Why Are Christians Living Just Like the Rest of the World?* Grand Rapids: Baker, 2005.

Simundson, Daniel J. *Hosea, Joel, Amos, Obadiah, Jonah, Micah*. Abingdon Old Testament Commentaries. Nashville: Abingdon, 2005.

Ska, Jean-Louis. *Introduction to Reading the Pentateuch*. Winona Lake, IN: Eisenbrauns, 2006.

Smart, J. D. "Amos." In *IDB* 1. Nashville: Abingdon, 1962.

Smelik, K. A. D. "The Meaning of Amos V 18–20." *VT* 36 (1986) 246–47.

Smith, Gary V. *Amos: A Commentary*. Grand Rapids: Zondervan, 1989.

Smith. John M. P. "The Day of Yahweh." *AJT* 4 (1901) 505–33.

Sobhidanandan, Balakirshnan. "The Day of the Lord in the Book of Joel: A Day of Judgement." PhD diss., Rome: Pontifical University of St. Thomas Aquinas, 2007.

Soédé, Nathanael Yaovi. "The Enduring Scourge of Poverty and Evangelization in Africa." In *Reconciliation, Justice and Peace: The Second African Synod*, edited by Agbonkhianmeghe E. Orobator, 181–90. Maryknoll, NY: Orbis, 2011.

Soggin, J. Alberto. *The Prophet Amos: A Translation and Commentary*. Translated by John Bowden. London: SCM, 1987.

Soulen, Richard N., and R. Kendall Soulen. *Handbook of Biblical Criticism*. 3rd ed. Louisville: Westminster John Knox, 2001.

Stamm, Johann Jakob. "Der Name des Propheten Amos und sein sprachlicher Hintergrund." In *Prophecy: Essays Presented to Georg Fohrer on His Sixty-Fifth Birthday, 6 September 1980*, edited by J. A. Emerson, 137–42. BZAW 150. Berlin: de Gruyter, 1980.

Steiner, Richard C. *Stockmen from Tekoa, Sycamores from Sheba: A Study of Amos' Occupation*. CBQMS 36. Washington, DC: Catholic Biblical Association of America, 2003.

Steijdom, P. D. F. "What Tekoa Did to Amos." *OTS* 9 (1966) 273–93.

Stintespring, William. "Hosea, Prophet of Doom." *Crozer Quarterly* 27 (1950) 220–27.

Story, Cullen I. "Amos: Prophet of Praise." *VT* 30 (1980) 67–80.

Stuart, Douglas K. *Hosea–Jonah*. Word Biblical Commentary 31. Dallas: Word, 1992.

Stumph, C. *Philosophy, History and Problem*. New York: Mcgraw-Hill, 1971.

Sweeney, Marvin A. "Amos." In *The Twelve Prophets*, edited by David W. Cooter, 1:191–272. Berit Olam: Studies in Hebrew Narrative and Poetry. Collegeville, MN: Liturgical, 2000.

———. *The Book of the Twelve Prophets*. 2 vols. Berit Olam. Collegeville: Liturgical, 2000.

———. "Sequence and Interpretation in the Book of the Twelve." In *Reading and Hearing the Book of the Twelve*, edited by James. D. Nogalski and Marvin A. Sweeney, 49–50. SBLSymS 15. Atlanta: SBL, 2000.

———. "Zephaniah: A Paradigm for the Study of the Prophetic Books." *CR* 7 (1999) 119–45.

Terrien, Samuel. "Amos and Wisdom." In *Israel's Prophetic Heritage*, edited by Bernhard W. Anderson and Walter Harrelson, 108–15. New York: Haper & Bros., 1962.

Torrey, Charles C. "On the Text of Amos v.26; vi, 1, 2; vii.2." *JBL* 13 (1894) 61–63.

Uche,Chimobi. "Poverty in Nigeria: Some Dimension and Contributing Factors." *Global Majority E-Journal* 1 (2010) 1–47.

Udoekpo, Michael Ufok. *The Concept of Unen (Justice) in Annang Political Philosophy*. BPh Essay, Nigeria, Claretian Institute of Philosophy, 1991.

———. *Corruption in Nigerian Culture: The Liberating Mission of the Church*. Enugu, Nigeria: Snaap, 1994.

———. "Theology of Liberation, vis-à-vis, Moral, Socio-Economic-cum Political Opression in Nigeria." BTh thesis, Enugu, Bigard Memorial Seminary, 1995.

———. *The Limits of A Divided Nation*. Enugu: Nigeria: Snaap, 1999.

———."Liturgy as the Primary Role of the Priests." In *Reconciliation and Renewal of Services in the Church*, 83–94. Lineamenta for the First Synod Catholic Diocese of Ikot Ekpene. Uyo, Nigeria: Trinity, 2002.

———. *Re-thinking the Day of YHWH and Restoration of Fortunes in the Prophet Zephaniah: An Exegetical and Theological Study of 1:14–18; 3:14–20.* ATID 2. Bern: Lang, 2010.

———. "The Theological Function of 'Seek the Lord' (*bāqqaš 'ădōnāy*) in Zephaniah 2:1–3, for Contemporary Society." *International Journal of African Catholicism* 6 (2015) 77–91.

Ukpong, Justin. "Inculturation Hermenueutics: An African Approach to Biblical Interpretation." In *The Bible in World Context: An Experiment in Contextual Hermeneutics,* edited by Walter Dietrich and Ulrich Luz, 17–32. Grand Rapids: Eerdmans, 2002.

U.S. Catholic Bishops. *Christian Prayer: The Liturgy of the Hours*: New York: Catholic Book, 1976.

Vatican II. "The Constitution on the Sacred Liturgy, Sacrasanctum Concilium, 4 December 1963." In *the Basic Sixteen Documents, Vatican Council II: Constituitons Decrees Declariations,* edited by Austin Flannery, 117–61. Dublin: Dominican, 1996.

Van der Wal, Adri. "The Structure of Amos." *JSOT* 26 (1983) 107–13.

Volz, Paul. "Die radikale Ablehnung der Kultreligion durch die alttestamentlichen Propheten." *ZST* 14 (1937) 63–65.

Vollmer, Jochen. *Geschichtliche Rückblicke und Motive in der prophetie des Amos, Hosea, und Jesaja.* BZAW 123. Berlin: de Gruyter, 1971.

Wagner, Siegfried. "Überlegungen zur Frage nach den Beziehungen des Propheten Amos zum Südreich." *TLZ* 96 (1971) 653–70.

———. "בקש, *biqqēsh*; בקשה; *baqqāshāh*." In *TDOT* 2: 229–41.

———. "דרש, *dārash*; מדרש' *midhrāsh*." In *TDOT* 3: 293–307.

Wallis, Jim. *God's Politics: Why the Right Gets it Wrong and the Left Doesn't Get It.* New York: HaperSanFrancisco, 2005.

Wanke, G. "*ōy* and *hōy.*" *ZAW* 78 (1966) 215–18.

Ward, James M. "The Message of the Prophet Hosea." *Int* 23 (1969) 387–407.

———. *Amos and Isaiah.* Nashville: Abingdon, 1969.

Watts, James D. W. "An Old Hymn Preserved in the Book of Amos." *JNES* 15 (1956) 33–99.

Wcela, Emil A. *The Prophets: God's Spokesmen through the Years.* God's Word Today III: A New Study Guide to the Bible. New York: Pueblo, 1980.

Weimer, Peter. "Der Schluss des Amos-Buches: Ein Beitrag zur Redaktionsgeschichte des Amos-Buches." *BN* 16 (1981) 60–100.

———. "Obadja: Eine redaktionskritische Analyse." *BN* 27 (1985) 35–99.

Weiser, Artur. *Die Profetie des Amos.* BZAW 53. Berlin: Töpelmann, 1929.

Weiss, Meir. "The Origin of the 'Day of the Lord'–Reconsidered." *HUCA* 37 (1966) 29–62.

———. "Concerning Amos' Repudiation of the Cult." In *Pomegranates and Golden Bells: Studies in Biblical, Jewish, and Near Eastern Ritual, Law and Literature in Honor of Jacob Milgrom,* edited by David. P. Wright, David N. Freedman, and Avi Hurvitz, 199–214. Winona Lake, IN: Eisenbrauns, 1995.

Wellhausen, Juilius. *Israelitisheche und Jüdische Geschichte.* 2nd ed. Berlin: Reimer, 1895.

———. *Prologemena to the Hisotry of Ancient Israel.* Reprint of "Israel" from the *Encyclopedia Britannica.* 1957. Reprinted, Eugene, OR: Wipf & Stock, 2003.

Wells, David. *God in the Wasteland: The Realty of Truth in a World of Fading Dreams.* Leicester, UK: InterVarsity, 1994.

Wenham, Gordon J. *The Book of Leviticus.* NICOT. Grand Rapids: Eerdmans, 1979.

————."The Akedah: Paradigm of Sacrifice." In *Pomegranates and Golden Bells: Studies in Biblical, Jewish, and Near Eastern Ritual, Law and Literature in Honor of Jacob Milgrom*, edited by David. P. Wright, David N. Freedman, and Avi Hurvitz, 93–102. Winona Lake, IN: Eisenbrauns, 1995.

Westermann, Claus. *Basic Forms of Prophetic Speech*. Translated by H. C. White. Philadelphia: Westminster, 1967.

Westermeyer, Paul. "A Church Musician's Journey with Amos." *Word & Word* 28 (2008) 150–58.

Wikipedia Free Encyclopedia. "Chibok Schoolgirls Kidnapping." 14 April, 2016.

Willoughby, Bruce G. "Amos, Book of." In *ABD* 1:202–12.

Wolfe, Roland Emerson. "The Editing of the Book of the Twelve." *ZAW* 53 (1935) 90–129.

Wolff, Hans Walter. "Guilt and Salvation: A Study of the Prophecy of Hosea." *Int* 15 (1961) 274–85.

————. *Amos' geistige Heimat*. Wissenschaftliche Monographien zum Alten und Neuen Testament 18. Neukirchen-Vluyn: Neukirchener, 1964.

————. *Amos the Prophet: The Man and His Background*. Translated by Foster R. McCurley. Philadelphia: Fortress, 1973.

————. *Joel and Amos: A Commentary on the Books of the Prophets Joel and Amos*. Hermeneia. Philadelphia: Fortress, 1977.

Wright, Ernst. *The Old Testament and Theology*. New York: Harper & Row, 1969.

Würthwein, Ernst. "Amos 5: 21–27." *ThLZ* 72 (1947) 143–52.

————. "Kultpolemik oder Kultbescheid: Beobachtungen zu dem Thema 'Prophetie un Kult.'" Tradition und Situation; Studien zur alttestamentlichen prophetie; Artur Weiser zum 70 Geburstag. Göttingen: Vandenhoeck & Ruprecht (1963) 115–37.

————. *The Text of the Old Testament*. 2nd ed. Grand Rapids: Eerdmans, 1995.

————. *Wort und Existenz: Studien zum Alten Testament*. Göttingen: Vandenhoeck & Ruprecht, 1970.

Younger, K. Lawson. "The Deportations of the Israelites." *JBL* 117 (1998) 201–27.

Zvi, Ehud Ben. "Twelve Prophetic Books or 'Twelve': A Few Preliminary Considerations." In *Forming Prophetic Literature: Essays on Isaiah and the Twelve in Honor of John D. W. Watts*, edited by James W. Watts and Paul R. House, 125–56. JSOTsup 235, Sheffield: Sheffield Academic, 1996.

Author Index

Subject Index

Abasi, 126
Abasi Ibom, 121, 126n57
Abraham, xxvi, 7–8, 78, 81–82
Africa, xi, xx, xxii–xxiv, xxvii, xxxi, 75,
    98, 113–14, 117–27, 130, 135,
    137–38, 140, 142–43
Africa today, xxii
African American, 135
African American males, xxvi, 128, 139
African
    countries, xxiii, 117, 119, 138
    languages, 126
    musician, 125
    people, xxxi, 124
    nations, xxiv, 138
    religious communities, xviii
    shrines, 143
    theologians, xviii, xxii, 124, 132
African Traditional Religion, xxiii, 121,
    125, 138
Akkadian
    deity, 41
    language, 6n28, 35
Allah, 121
Amaziah, 3–4, 128
American
    churches, xxv, 139, 144
    culture, 132, 144
    society, 135, 143
Americans, xxxi, 127, 135
Amos of Tekoa, 13, 137
Amos' critique, xxix, 83, 85, 101, 106, 125
Ancient text, xxx, 1, 20, 88
Ancient Near Eastern culture, 54

Ancient Near Eastern texts, 55, 88
Announcements, 17, 73
Announcing judgment, 73
Appropriating, xxi–xxii, xxx
Aristotle, 105
Artistic structure, 18
Authentic worship, xxi, xxiv, 112, 126,
    132

Babylonian, xxiii, 8, 52, 112
Background, xxx–xxxi, 9, 10n49, 20, 43,
    60, 137, 141
Beersheba, 8, 12n64, 27–28, 53, 75,
    81–83, 94, 119–20,
Bethel, 3–5, 8, 12, 21, 27–29, 53, 63, 68,
    70–71, 75, 80–83, 119–20, 128,
    131
Biblia Hebraica, 2n6, 25
Biblical
    exegesis, xxii, xxxin57, 42
    interpretation, xxix
    literature, 108
    studies, xxx, 114
    theology, xxvii, 78, 105
Biographical narrative, 19
Birthplace, 3–5
Bloodless sacrifice, 100
Boko Haram, xxiii, 117, 143
Book of visions, 18
Books of woes, 17
Bride of YHWH, 77

Canaanites, 8
Canonical, xxix, xxxi, 44, 48–49, 65, 141

Scripture Index

Amos (continued)